THE LANGUAGE GYM

ITALIAN SENTENCE BUILDERS

A lexicogrammar approach
Beginner to Pre-Intermediate

THIRD EDITION

Imprint: Independently Published

Edited by Stefano Pianigiani & Gabriele Ragnini

About the authors

Gianfranco Conti taught for 25 years at schools in Italy, the UK and in Kuala Lumpur, Malaysia. He has also been a university lecturer, holds a Master's degree in Applied Linguistics and a PhD in metacognitive strategies as applied to second language writing. He is now an author, a popular independent educational consultant and professional development provider. He has written around 2,000 resources for the TES website, which have awarded him the Best Resources Contributor in 2015. He has co-authored the best-selling and influential book for world languages teachers, "The Language Teacher Toolkit" and "Breaking the sound barrier: Teaching learners how to listen", in which he puts forth his Listening As Modelling methodology. Gianfranco writes an influential blog on second language acquisition called The Language Gym, co-founded the interactive website language-gym.com and the Facebook professional group Global Innovative Language Teachers (GILT). Last but not least, Gianfranco has created the instructional approach known as E.P.I. (Extensive Processing Instruction).

Dylan Viñales has taught for 15 years, in schools in Bath, Beijing and Kuala Lumpur in state, independent and international settings. He lives in Kuala Lumpur. He is fluent in five languages, and gets by in several more. Dylan is, besides a teacher, a professional development provider, specialising in E.P.I., metacognition, teaching languages through music (especially ukulele) and cognitive science. In the last five years, together with Dr Conti, he has driven the implementation of E.P.I. in one of the top international schools in the world: Garden International School. This has allowed him to test, on a daily basis, the sequences and activities included in this book with excellent results (his students have won language competitions both locally and internationally). He has designed an original Spanish curriculum, bespoke instructional materials, based on Reading and Listening as Modelling (RAM and LAM). Dylan co-founded the fastest growing professional development group for modern languages teachers on Facebook, Global Innovative Languages Teachers, which includes over 12,000 teachers from all corners of the globe. He authors an influential blog on modern language pedagogy in which he supports the teaching of languages through E.P.I. Dylan is the lead author of Spanish content on the Language Gym website and oversees the technological development of the site.

Simona Gravina has taught for 15 years, in schools in Italy and the UK, both in state and independent settings. She lives in Glasgow, Scotland. She is fluent in three languages and gets by in a few more. Simona is, besides a teacher, a mum, a bookworm, a passionate traveller and a fitness enthusiast. In the last couple of years she has been testing and implementing E.P.I. in one of the top Independent schools in Scotland, St Aloysius'College, where she is currently Modern Languages Curriculum Leader in the Junior School.

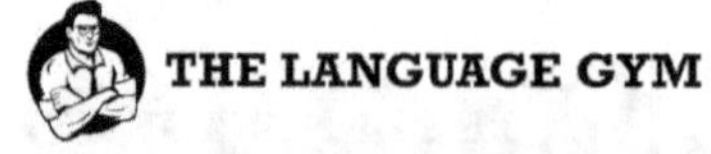

DEDICATION

For my daughter Giulia
-Simona

For Skyla
-Stefano

For Catrina
-Gianfranco

For Ariella & Leonard
-Dylan

Acknowledgements

Translating a book is a time-consuming yet rewarding endeavour. Simona would like to thank her family for all the support but most importantly her daughter, Giulia, for all her encouragement and for being a caring and wonderful daughter.

Secondly, a huge thanks to our first editor, Stefano Pianigiani, from Rome. Stefano is a real pleasure to work with; good humoured, and extremely passionate and dedicated. His contributions have gone far beyond proofreading for accuracy, into advising on formatting and best selection of language content. Stefano holds an MA in Education. He is a committed teacher based in Leeds, UK, and has been a real asset to our team.

Thirdly, our gratitude to our second editor, Gabriele Ragnini, who has been instrumental of the creation of this Third Edition volume. Gabriele is an Italian freelance journalist who graduated in 2022 from the University of Leeds, achieving a BA in Journalism. Gabriele regularly writes for several newspapers such as Corriere del Mezzogiorno, L'Edicola del Sud and the popular sports website gianlucadimarzio.com. Gabriele is a talented and meticulous linguist with a sharp eye for detail and has worked tirelessly over the course of a whole year to make countless language, formatting and other usability tweaks to bring us this greatly improved version of the classic original.

In addition, our gratitude to the MFL Twitterati for their ongoing support of E.P.I. and the Sentence Builders book series. In particular, a heartfelt thanks to our team of guest proofreaders: Christian Moretti, Cristina Mari, Giovanni Calandro, Stefano Pianigiani, Alberta Capasso, Angela Benedetti, Maria Grazia Giglione, Sophie Neil & Regina Vara Corella. Their contributions have ranged from picking up accuracy errors to making comments with regard to choice of lexis, exercise formatting and more. It is thanks to their time, patience, professionalism and detailed feedback that we have been able to produce such a refined and highly accurate product.

Lastly, thanks to Dr Mario Conti for his efforts and insight during the final rounds of proofreading. His contributions to making this book as accurate as possible and his comments surrounding usage of language have been of great help.

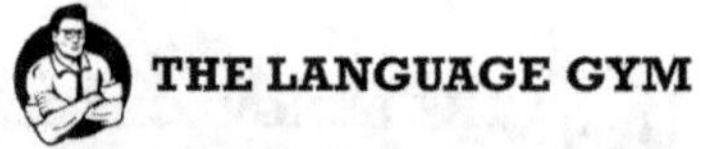

Introduction

Hello and welcome to the first 'text' book designed to be an accompaniment to an Italian, Extensive Processing Instruction course. The book has come about out of necessity, because such a resource did not previously exist.

How to use this book if you have bought into our E.P.I. approach

This book was originally designed as a resource to use in conjunction with our E.P.I. approach and teaching strategies. Our course favours flooding comprehensible input, organising content by communicative functions and related constructions, and a big focus on reading and listening as modelling. The aim of this book is to empower the beginner-to-pre-intermediate learner with linguistic tools - high-frequency structures and vocabulary - useful for real-life communication. Since, in a typical E.P.I. unit of work, aural and oral work play a huge role, this book should not be viewed as the ultimate E.P.I. coursebook, but rather as a **useful resource** to **complement** your Listening-As-Modelling and Speaking activities.

Sentence Builders – Online Versions

Please note that all these sentence builders are available on the ***SentenceBuilders.com** website, together with an extensive range of self-marking homework or class assignments, designed to practice listening, reading and writing in keeping with the EPI approach.

The sentence builders will be available in editable versions on the **Language-Gym.com** website, available to download, editable and in landscape design optimised for displaying in the classroom, via the ***Locker Room** section.

**Please note that SentenceBuilders.com and the Language Gym are only accessible via a paid subscription. Access to the Locker Room requires a site licence.*

How to use this book if you don't know or have NOT bought into our approach

Alternatively, you may use this book to dip in and out of as a source of printable material for your lessons. Whilst our curriculum is driven by communicative functions rather than topics, we have deliberately embedded the target constructions in topics which are popular with teachers and commonly found in published coursebooks.

If you would like to learn about E.P.I. you could read one of the authors' blogs. The definitive guide is Dr Conti's "Patterns First – How I Teach Lexicogrammar" which can be found on his blog (www.gianfrancoconti.com).

There are also blogs on Dylan's wordpress site (mrvinalesmfl.wordpress.com) such as "Using sentence builders to reduce (everyone's) workload and create more fluent linguists" which can be read to get teaching ideas and to learn how to structure a course, through all the stages of E.P.I.

The book "Breaking the Sound Barrier: Teaching Learners how to Listen" by Gianfranco Conti and Steve Smith, provides a detailed description of the approach and of the listening and speaking activities you can use in synergy with the present book.

The basic structure of the book

The book contains 19 macro-units which concern themselves with a specific communicative function, such as 'Describing people's appearance and personality', 'Comparing and contrasting people', 'Saying what you like and dislike' or 'Saying what you and others do in your free time'. You can find a note of each communicative function in the Table of Contents. Each unit includes:

- a sentence builder modelling the target constructions;
- a set of vocabulary building activities which reinforce the material in the sentence builder;
- a set of narrow reading texts exploited through a range of tasks focusing on both the meaning and structural levels of the text;

- a set of translation tasks aimed at consolidation through retrieval practice;
- a set of writing tasks targeting essential writing micro-skills such as spelling, functional and positional processing, editing and communication of meaning.

Each sentence builder at the beginning of a unit contains one or more constructions which have been selected with real-life communication in mind. Each unit is built around that construction <u>but not solely on it</u>. Based on the principle that each E.P.I instructional sequence must move from modelling to production in a seamless and organic way, each unit expands on the material in each sentence builder by embedding it in texts and graded tasks which contain both familiar and unfamiliar (but comprehensible and learnable) vocabulary and structures. Through lots of careful recycling and thorough and extensive processing of the input, by the end of each unit the student has many opportunities to encounter and process the new vocabulary and patterns with material from the previous units.

Alongside the macro-units you will find:

- grammar units: one or two pages of activities occurring at regular intervals. They explicitly focus on key grammar structures which enhance the generative power of the constructions in the sentence builders. At this level they mainly concern themselves with full conjugations of key verbs, with agreement and preposition usage. Note that these units recycle the same verbs many times over by revisiting at regular intervals but in different linguistic contexts;
- question-skills units: one or two pages on understanding and creating questions. These micro-units too occur at regular intervals in the book, so as to recycle the same question patterns in different linguistic contexts;
- revision quickies: these are retrieval practice tasks aimed at keeping the previously learnt vocabulary alive. These too occur at regular intervals;
- self-tests: these occur at the end of the book. They are divided into two sections, one for less confident and one for more confident learners.

The point of all the above micro-units is to implement lots of systematic recycling and interleaving, two techniques that allow for stronger retention and transfer of learning.

Important *caveats*

1) This is a '**no frills**' book. This means that there are a limited number of illustrations (only on unit title pages). This is because we want every single little thing in this book to be useful. Consequently, we have packed a substantive amount of content at the detriment of its outlook. In particular, we have given serious thought to both **recycling** and **interleaving**, in order to allow for key constructions, words and grammar items to be revisited regularly so as to enhance exponentially their retention.

2) **All content** in this booklet matches the content on the **Language Gym** website. For best results, we recommend a mixture of communicative, retrieval practice games, combined with Language Gym games and workouts, and then this booklet as the follow-up, either in class or for homework.

3) This booklet is suitable for **beginner** to **pre-intermediate** learners. This equates to a **CEFR A1-A2** level, or a beginner **Y6-Y8** class. You do not need to start at the beginning, although you may want to dip in to certain units for revision/recycling. You do not need to follow the booklet in order, although many of you will, and if you do, you will benefit from the specific recycling/interleaving strategies. Either way, all topics are repeated frequently throughout the book.

We do hope that you and your students will find this book useful and enjoyable.

Gianfranco, Dylan and Simona

TABLE OF CONTENTS

UNIT 1
Saying how I feel and talking about my age

In this unit you will learn:

- How you feel
- How to say your name and age
- How to say someone else's name and age
- How to count from 1 to 15
- A range of common Italian names
- The words for brother and sister

Ho un anno

Ho dieci anni

Ho sei anni

Ho quindici anni

UNIT 1a
Saying how you feel
'Come stai? - Perché?'
How you do feel? - Why?

					MASCH.	FEMM.
Ciao *Hi*		**bene** *well*			**arrabbiato** *angry*	**arrabbiata**
Salve *Hello*	**Sto** *I am*	**molto bene** *very well*	**perché** *because*	**sono** *I am*	**contento** *happy*	**contenta**
Buongiorno *Good morning*	**Mi sento** *I feel*	**così così** *so so*			**emozionato** *excited*	**emozionata**
Buonasera *Good evening*		**male** *bad*			**felice** *happy*	**felice**
		molto male *very bad*			**in gran forma** *in great form*	**in gran forma**
					nervoso *nervous*	**nervosa**
					preoccupato *worried*	**preoccupata**
					stanco *tired*	**stanca**
					stressato *stressed*	**stressata**
					tranquillo/ calmo *calm*	**tranquilla/ calma**
					triste *sad*	**triste**

Author's note: *Bear in mind that adjectives end in –**o** for masculine and –**a** for feminine. The ones ending in –**e** do not change.*

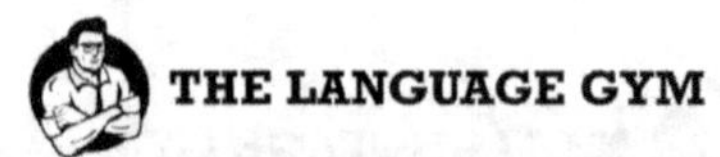

Unit 1a. Saying how you feel: VOCABULARY BUILDING

1. Match up

1. sono contento	a. I feel so so
2. perché	b. I am nervous
3. sono stanco	c. I feel unwell/ I feel bad
4. sono triste	
5. sono felice	d. I am happy
6. sono stressato	e. I feel well
7. sono nervoso	f. I am stressed
8. mi sento bene	g. I am sad
9. mi sento male	h. hello
10. mi sento così così	i. I am happy
11. buongiorno	j. because
12. salve	k. I am tired
	l. good morning

3. Choose *"Mi sento"* or *"sono"*

Mi sento/sono	Adjective
	contento
	bene
	felice
	male
	preoccupata
	così così

2. Complete with the missing word

a. Salve _____ bene perché __________ felice.
[Hi, I feel good because I am happy]

b. Buonasera, mi sento __________ perché sono ________. [Good evening, I feel bad because I am tired]

c. Ciao, mi sento________ bene ________ sono in gran forma. [Hi, I feel very good because I am feeling great]

molto	male	stanco
perché	sono	sto

4. Complete the table

Masculine	Feminine
contento	
	felice
stressato	
	tranquilla
emozionato	
	stanca
arrabbiato	
	triste
nervoso	

5. Translate into Italian

1. Good morning, I feel good because I am happy
2. Hi, I feel very bad because I am tired (feminine)
3. Good evening, I feel very good because I am joyful (masculine)
4. Hello, I feel very well because I am calm (feminine)
5. Good morning, I feel very bad because I am worried (masculine)
6. Hello, I feel so so because I am nervous (masculine)
7. Good evening, I feel very well because I am excited (masculine)
8. Good morning, I feel well because because I am feeling joyful.

UNIT 1b
Talking about my age
'Come ti chiami? - Quanti anni hai?'
What is your name? - How old are you?

Io *I*	mi chiamo *am called*	Alessio		ho *I have**	un 1	anno *year*
		Antonio				
		Anna			due 2	anni *years*
		Barbara			tre 3	
		Davide			quattro 4	
		Dylan			cinque 5	
		Emanuela	e *and*		sei 6	
		Filippo			sette 7	
Mio fratello *My brother*		Gabriele		ha *he/she has**	otto 8	
		Gianfranco			nove 9	
		Giulia			dieci 10	
		Katia			undici 11	
Mia sorella *My sister*	si chiama *is called*	Mario			dodici 12	
		Paolo			tredici 13	
		Simona			quattordici 14	
		Stefano			quindici 15	

Author's notes:

*1) The number **"uno"** becomes **"un"** when it goes before a noun. E.g. " Ho un fratello".*

2) In Italian, we use the verb "to have" for age. So, we say "ho dieci anni" to say how old we are, evern though it means, literally "I have ten years". There are a few Latin languages (e.g. Spanish/French) that also do this :D

3) In Italian, you do not say 'my name is', you say: I am called.

Unit 1b. Talking about my age: VOCABULARY BUILDING

1. Match up

1. un anno	*a. seven years*
2. due anni	*b. four years*
3. tre anni	*c. five years*
4. quattro anni	*d. six years*
5. cinque anni	*e. eleven years*
6. sei anni	*f. ten years*
7. sette anni	*g. twelve years*
8. otto anni	*h. nine years*
9. nove anni	*i. two years*
10. dieci anni	*j. eight years*
11. undici anni	*k. one year*
12. dodici anni	*l. three years*

2. Complete with the missing word

a. Ho __________ anni. *[I am twelve years old]*

b. Mio fratello ____ chiama Davide.
[My brother is called Davide]

c. Mi ____________ Roberto. *[My name is Roberto]*

d. Mio fratello _ due anni. *[My brother is two years old]*

e. Mia sorella ha _____ anni. *[My sister is four years old]*

f. _____ chiamo Anna. *[My name is Anna]*

quattro	ha	si
mi	dodici	chiamo

3. Translate into English

a. Ho tre anni

b. Ho cinque anni

c. Ho undici anni

d. Ha quindici anni

e. Ha tredici anni

f. Ha sette anni

g. Mio fratello

h. Mia sorella

i. Si chiama

4. Broken words

a. H___ *[I have]*

b. Mi chia____ *[my name is]*

c. Mia sor______ *[my sister]*

d. Quin______ *[fifteen]*

e. Sed______ *[sixteen]*

f. Und_____ *[eleven]*

g. No_____ *[nine]*

h. Quatto________ *[fourteen]*

i. Do________ *[twelve]*

5. Rank the people below from oldest to youngest as shown in the example

Michele ha quindici anni	1
Giorgia ha tredici anni	
Luca ha due anni	
Piero ha quattro anni	
Alex ha un anno	
Roberta ha cinque anni	
Benedetta ha nove anni	
Dorotea ha tre anni	

6. For each pair of people write who is the oldest, as shown in the example

A	B	OLDER
Ho undici anni	Ho tredici anni	B
Ho tre anni	Ho sei anni	
Ho undici anni	Ho dodici anni	
Ho quindici anni	Ho tredici anni	
Ho quattordici anni	Ho undici anni	
Ho otto anni	Ho nove anni	
Ho undici anni	Ho sette anni	

Unit 1b. Talking about my age: READING

Ciao, mi chiamo Leo e ho dodici anni. Sto molto bene perché sono felice. Ho un fratello che si chiama Stefano. Stefano ha quattordici anni.

Buongiorno, mi chiamo Dita e ho dieci anni. Ho una sorella che si chiama Flutura e un fratello che si chiama Bledar. Flutura ha cinque anni. Bledar ha nove anni.

Mi chiamo Tian e ho tredici anni. Sto male, perché sono arrabbiato. Ho un fratello che si chiama Cheng. Cheng ha quindici anni.

Salve, mi chiamo Marine. Mi sento bene perché sono tranquilla. Sono francese e ho dieci anni. Ho una sorella che si chiama Fabienne. Fabienne ha undici anni. Ho **anche** *[also]* un fratello che si chiama Pierre. Pierre ha otto anni.

Mi chiamo Kaori e ho sette anni. Ho una sorella che si chiama Yoko. Yoko ha tredici anni. Ho anche un fratello che si chiama Hiroto. Hiroto ha dieci anni.

Ciao, mi chiamo Moritz e ho quattordici anni. Ho due fratelli. Mio fratello maggiore si chiama Patrick e mio fratello minore si chiama Philip. Patrick ha sedici anni e Philip ha quindici anni.

1. Find the Italian for the following items in Leo's text

a. I have a brother

b. My name is

c. I feel very well

d. I am happy

e. Who is called Stefano

f. I am twelve

g. He is fourteen

2. Answer the following questions about Dita

a. What is the name of Dita's sister?

b. How old is Dita?

c. How many siblings does she have?

d. What's her brother called?

e. What age is he?

3. Complete the table below

	Age	How many siblings	Ages of siblings
Tian			
Leo			
Dita			

4. Moritz, Kaori or Marine?

a. Who has a 15- year-old brother?

b. Who has an 11-year-old sister?

c. Who is 11?

d. Who has an older brother aged 16?

e. Who is calm?

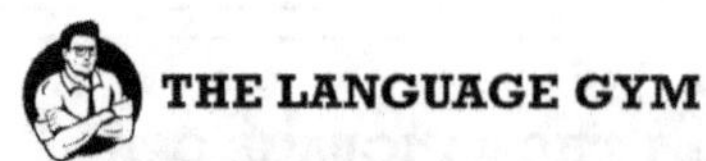

Unit 1b. Talking about my age: TRANSLATION

1. Faulty translation: spot and correct (in the English) any translation mistakes you find below

a. Mi chiamo Patrizia: *Her name is Patrizia*

b. Ho due sorelle: *I have two brothers*

c. Mia sorella si chiama Marta: *My mother is called Marta*

d. Mio fratello ha cinque anni: *My sister is 5*

e. Ho quindici anni: *I am five*

f. Mio fratello ha otto anni: *My brother is seven*

g. Non ho fratelli: *I don't have a sister*

h. Ho diciotto anni: *I am 17*

i. Ho dodici anni: *I am 13*

j. Mi chiamo Gianni: *My name is Gianni*

2. From Italian to English

a. Mio fratello si chiama Dario.

b. Ho quindici anni.

c. Mio fratello ha sei anni.

d. Mia sorella si chiama Marina.

e. Ho sette anni.

f. Sto bene

g. Mia sorella ha quattordici anni.

h. Ho un fratello e una sorella.

i. Marta ha dodici anni.

j. Annamaria ha nove anni.

3. English to Italian translation

a. Hello, my name is Guido. I am six.

b. My brother is fifteen years old.

c. I am twelve. I am happy.

d. My sister is called Emanuela.

e. My name is Gianfranco. I am joyful.

f. I have a brother and a sister.

g. My name is Filippo and I am fourteen.

h. My name is Gianfranco and I am eleven.

i. My name is Rossana. I am ten. I have a brother and a sister.

j. My sister is called Alberta. She is twelve.

k. I do not have a brother. I am sad.

Unit 1b. Talking about my age: WRITING

1. Complete the words

a. M___ ch__________ Roberto.

b. Ho quattor_______ a______.

c. H___ un f___________o.

d. M____ f___________o si chi________ Giulio.

e. Mi _______mo Patrizio.

f. Mio ______tello s___ _______ma Marco.

g. ___o tr______ci anni.

h. Mia so__________a si ch________ Katia.

2. Write out the number in Italian

nine = n______________________

seven = s____________________

twelve = d___________________

five = c_____________________

fourteen = q_________________

sixteen = s__________________

thirteen = t_________________

four = q_____________________

3. Spot and correct the mistakes

a. Mi ciamo Paolo.

b. Ho tredici anno.

c. Mio fratelo ha cinqe anni.

d. Mio fratello se chiama Gianmaria.

e. Me chiamo Patrizio.

f. Mi sorela si chiama Alessandra.

4. Complete with a suitable word

a. Mia sorella si ____________ Laura.

b. ______ fratello ha quindici anni.

c. Mi __________ Mario.

d. Ho un ____________ che si chiama Filippo.

e. Ho una ____________ che si chiama Annamaria.

f. Mio fratello ______ quattordici anni.

5. Guided writing – write 4 short paragraphs in the first person singular ['I'] each describing the people below

	Age	Feeling	Reason	Brother's name and age	Sister's name and age
Johann	12	well	joyful	Franz 9	Martha 8
Flutura	15	very well	excited	Bledar 13	Luljeta 5
Michael	11	bad	sad	Thomas 7	Gerda 12
Kyoko	10	very bad	angry	Ken 6	Rena 1

6. Describe this person in the third person:

Name: Giovanni

Age: 12

Brother: Marco, 13 years old

Sister: Serena, 15 years old

UNIT 2
Saying when my birthday is, where I am from and what languages I speak.

In this unit you will learn to say:

- When your birthday is
- Numbers from 15 to 31
- Months
- I am, he/she is
- Names of Italian speaking locations
- Where you live
- What is your nationality
- What languages you speak

UNIT 2
Saying when my birthday is
'Quando é il tuo compleanno?'
When is your birthday?

Mi chiamo Leonardo *My name is Leonardo*	**ho x anni** *I am x years old*	**e** **il mio compleanno è il/*l'** *and my birthday is the*	1 - uno/primo 2 - due 3 - tre 4 - quattro 5 - cinque 6 - sei 7 - sette 8 - otto 9 - nove 10 - dieci 11 - undici 12 - dodici 13 - tredici 14 - quattordici 15 - quindici 16 - sedici 17 - diciassette 18 - diciotto 19 - diciannove 20 - venti 21 - ventuno 22 - ventidue 23 - ventitré 24 - ventiquattro 25 - venticinque 26 - ventisei 27 - ventisette 28 - ventotto 29 - ventinove 30 - trenta 31 - trentuno	**gennaio** *January* **febbraio** *February* **marzo** *March* **aprile** *April* **maggio** *May* **giugno** *June* **luglio** *July* **agosto** *August* **settembre** *September* **ottobre** *October* **novembre** *November* **dicembre** *December*
La mia amica si chiama Caterina *My friend is called Caterina* **Il mio amico si chiama Francesco** *My friend is called Francesco*	**ha x anni** *he/she is x years old*	**e** **il suo compleanno è il/*l'** *and his/her birthday is the*		

*Author's note: **il** and **l'** means 'the'. **Il tre aprile** translates 'the 3ʳᵈ of April'. Beware that before **uno/otto/undici** you will need **l'** instead. Example: **l'otto marzo**. Can you guess why?*

Unit 2a. Saying when my birthday is: VOCABULARY BUILDING

1. Complete with the missing word

a. Mi __________ Gabriella [*My name is Gabriella*]

b. La mia _______ si chiama Eva [*My friend is called Eva*]

c. Il ____ amico si chiama Luca [*My friend is called Luca*]

d. Il mio _________________ è il [*My birthday is on the*]

e. Il ___________ maggio [*The 5th of May*]

f. L' ___________ novembre [*The 8th of November*]

g. Il quattro _______________ [*The 4th of July*]

h. Il _____ compleanno è il... [*His/her birthday is on...*]

2. Match up

1. aprile		a. May	
2. novembre		b. My birthday	
3. dicembre		c. My friend (f)	
4. maggio		d. April	
5. gennaio		e. November	
6. febbraio		f. S/he is called	
7. il mio compleanno		g. December	
8. il mio amico		h. I am called	
9. la mia amica		i. February	
10. mi chiamo		j. January	
11. si chiama		k. My friend(m)	

3. Translate into English

a. Il quattordici gennaio =

b. L'otto maggio =

c. Il sette febbraio =

d. Il venti marzo =

e. Il diciannove agosto =

f. Il venticinque luglio =

g. Il ventiquattro settembre =

h. Il quindici aprile =

4. Add the missing letter

a. com_leanno   c. ma_zo   e. a_rile   g. ge_naio   i. lu_lio   k. d_cembre

b. feb_raio   d. mag_io   f. giug_o   h. ag_sto   j. novem_re   l. se_tembre

5. Broken words

a. I_ t______ g____________ [*the 3rd of Jan*]

b. I__ c_________ l__________ [*the 5th of July*]

c. I__ n________ a____________ [*the 9th of Aug*]

d. I__ d________ m__________ [*the 12th of March*]

e. I__ s___________ a________ [*the 16th of April*]

f. I_ d__________ d___________ [*the 19th of Dec*]

g. I__ v________ o____________ [*the 20th of Oct*]

h. I__ v___________ m_______ [*the 27th of May*]

i. I_ t_________ s____________ [*the 30th of Sept*]

6. Complete with a suitable word

a. Mi ______________ Simona.

b. Il mio ____________ è il due marzo.

c. Ho nove _________.

d. Il mio _________ si chiama Gianni.

e. Gianni __________ dieci anni.

f. Il suo _____________ è il tre giugno.

g. Il mio____________ è il primo aprile.

h. La mia amica ____ chiama Claire.

i. Il ____ compleanno è il sei maggio.

j. Oggi è l'otto _______________.

k. ______ chiamo Leonardo Rossi.

Unit 2a. Saying when my birthday is: READING

Mi chiamo Alberto. Ho dodici anni e il mio compleanno è il quindici settembre. La mia amica si chiama Gabriella e ha quattordici anni. Il suo compleanno è il ventotto maggio. Nel mio tempo libero suono sempre la chitarra con Gabriella! Il mio amico si chiama Carlo. Lui ha quindici anni ed è studente. Il suo compleanno è il ventuno giugno. Carlo ha un fratello maggiore. Il suo compleanno è l'otto gennaio.

Mi chiamo Mohamed. Ho ventidue anni e il mio compleanno è il dieci settembre. La mia amica si chiama Fatima e ha vent'anni. Il suo compleanno è il ventotto maggio. Nel mio tempo libero guardo sempre la televisione.

Mi chiamo Martina. Ho sette anni e il mio compleanno è il cinque dicembre. Ho due fratelli, Giulio ed Enrico. Giulio ha undici anni ed è molto bravo. Il suo compleanno è il trenta settembre. Enrico invece è cattivo. Ha tredici anni e il suo compleanno è il sette agosto.

Mi chiamo Gianluca. Ho otto anni e il mio compleanno è il nove agosto. Mia sorella minore ha quattro anni. È molto simpatica. Il suo compleanno è il nove agosto. Lo stesso giorno! Il mio amico si chiama Renzo e ha dieci anni. Il suo compleanno è il venticinque ottobre.

1. Find the Italian for the following items in Alberto's text

a. I am called:

b. I am 12 years old:

c. the eight of January:

d. my birthday is:

e. the 15th of:

f. her birthday is on:

g. in my free time:

h. my friend (m):

i. is called:

j. he is 15:

k. the 21st of June:

l. has an older brother:

3. Answer the following questions about Martina's text

a. How old is she?

____

b. When is her birthday?

____

c. How many brothers does she have?

____

d. Which brother is good?

____

e. How old in Enrico?

____

f. When is his birthday?

____

2. Complete with the missing words

Mi chiamo Anna. _____ tredici _____. _____ un gatto in casa. Il mio _____________ è il ventinove dicembre Mio fratello ______ nove ______ e il suo compleanno è ___ dieci aprile.

4. Find Someone Who:

a. has a birthday in December

____

b. is 22 years old

____

c. shares a birthday with a sibling

____

d. likes to play the guitar with his friend

____

e. has a friend who is 15 years old

____

f. has a birthday in September

____

g. has a little sister

____

h. has one good and one bad sibling

____

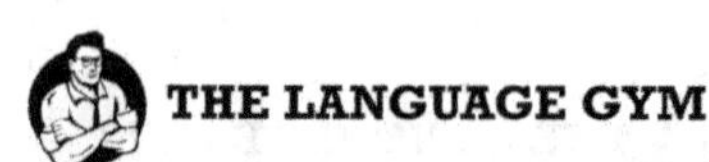

Unit 2a. Saying when my birthday is: WRITING

1. Complete with the missing letters

a. Mi chia_ _ Giorgio.

b. So_ _ d_ Torino.

c. I_ m_ _ complean_ _ è il die_ _ giu_ _o.

d. H_ quatt_ _ _ici an _ _.

e. La mi_ ami_a si c_iam_ Carla.

f. Il mi_ amico _i chiama Gianfranco.

g. Il mi_ am_co s_ c_iama Michele.

h. Michele h_ und_ _ _ a _ _i.

2. Spot and correct the mistakes

a. Il mia cumpleanno è il quattro gennaio.

b. Mi ciamo Giovanni.

c. Mi chiama Simona.

d. La mia amiga si chiamo Caterina.

e. Caterina ho undici anno.

f. Io ho cuattordici anni.

g. Il mio compleano e il primo de marzo.

h. Ho cuindici anni.

3. Answer the questions in Italian

a. *Come ti chiami? Mi chiamo _______________________.

b.*Quanti anni hai? Ho _______________ anni.

c. *Quando è il tuo compleanno? Il mio compleanno è il

___________ _________________ .

d. Quanti anni ha tuo fratello/sorella? Mio fratello ha ____anni.

*Author's note: * Come means "what/how", *Quanti means "how many", *Quando means "when" ☺*

4. Write out the dates below in words as shown in the example

a. 15/05 = il quindici maggio

b. 10/06 =

c. 20/03 =

d. 19/02 =

e. 25/12 =

f. 01/01 =

g. 22/11 =

h. 14/10 =

5. Guided writing – write 4 short paragraphs in the 1st person singular ['I'] describing the people below

Name	Age	Birthday	Name of brother	Brother's birthday
Samuel	11	25/12	Nico	19/02
Francesca	14	21/07	Marco	21/04
Li	12	01/01	Wen	20/06
Andrea	16	02/11	Alfonso	12/10

6. Describe this person in the third person:

Name: Alessio

Age: 12

Birthday: 21/06

Brother: Leo, 16 years old

Birthday: 01/12

Unit 2a. Saying when my birthday is: TRANSLATION

1. Faulty translation: spot and correct (in the English) any translation mistakes you find below

a. Il mio compleanno è il ventotto aprile:
His birthday is on the 27th April

b. Mi chiamo Roberto: *His name is Roberto*

c. Ho ventitré anni: *I am 22 years old*

d. Il mio amico si chiama Paul:
My friend I am called Paul

e. Lui ha ventisei anni: *I have 26 years old*

f. Il suo compleanno è il quattro luglio:
My birthday and the 14th of July

2. From Italian to English

a. L'otto ottobre

b. Il mio compleanno è…

c. Il mio amico si chiama …

d. Il suo compleanno è …

e. L'undici gennaio

f. Il quattordici febbraio

g. Il venticinque dicembre

h. Il sette luglio

i. Il primo giugno

3. Phrase-level translation

a. my name is…

b. I am ten years old

c. my birthday is the…

d. the 1st of May

e. my friend is called Bella

f. she is twelve years old

g. her birthday is the…

h. the 23rd of August

i. the 29th April

Author's note: *go back to e.*
Did you make Bella a girl? "amica" Well done if you did! ☺

4. Sentence-level translation

a. My name is Luigi. I am 30 years old. My birthday is on the 11th March.

b. My brother is called Piero. He is 14 years old. His birthday is on the 18th August.

c. My friend is called Simone. He is 22 years old and his birthday is on the 14th January.

d. My friend is called Angela. She is 18 years old and her birthday is on the 25th July.

e. My friend is called William. He is 20 years old. His birthday is on the 24th September.

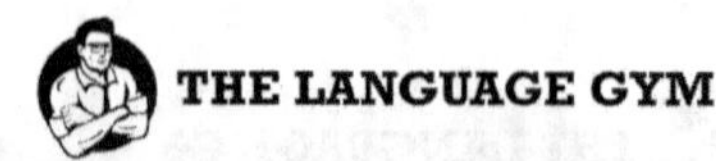

UNIT 2b
Saying what my nationality is and what languages I speak
'Di dove sono? - Quali lingue parlo?'
Where am I from? - What languages do I speak?

Sono *I am*	**australiano/a** *Australian*	**Parlo** *I speak*	**un po'** *a little*	**inglese** *English*	**e** *and*
	cinese *Chinese*		**abbastanza bene** *quite well*	**cinese** *Chinese*	
	francese *French*		**molto bene** *very well*	**francese** *French*	**anche** *also*
La mia amica Simona è *My friend Simona is*	**italiano/a** *Italian*	**Parla** *He/She speaks*	**perfettamente** *fluently*	**italiano** *Italian*	**inoltre** *moreover*
	inglese *English*			**inglese** *English*	**invece** *instead*
	polacco/a *Polish*			**polacco** *Polish*	**però/ma** *but*
Il mio amico Stefano è *My friend Stefano is*	**portoghese** *Portuguese*			**portoghese** *Portoguese*	
	rumeno/a *Romanian*			**rumeno** *Romanian*	
	scozzese *Scottish*			**spagnolo** *Spanish*	
	spagnolo/a *Spanish*			**tedesco** *German*	
	tedesco/a *German*				

Author's note: *When making the negative form we simply add **non** before the verb.*
*i.e. **parlo** = I speak; **non parlo** = I don't speak; **mia sorella parla** = my sister speaks; **mia sorella non parla** = my sister doesn't speak. N.B. Nationalities and languages have no capital letter in Italian.*

Unit 2b. Saying what languages I speak: READING

Mi chiamo Giovanna. Ho dodici anni e vivo a Napoli. Sono italiana. Parlo perfettamente italiano e abbastanza bene polacco, peró non parlo bene inglese.
La mia amica Simona è francese e ha quindici anni. Parla molto bene italiano e tedesco. Parla perfettamente francese ma non parla cinese.

Mi chiamo Florin. Ho undici anni e sono rumeno. Parlo perfettamente il rumeno. Parlo anche molto bene italiano e un po' bulgaro, ma non parlo tedesco. La mia amica Katrina parla perfettamente inglese perché sua mamma è inglese. Inoltre parla francese, però non parla bene italiano.

Mi chiamo Mario. Ho nove anni e sono polacco. Parlo perfettamente polacco e molto bene italiano, peró non parlo bene inglese
Il mio amico Salvatore vive in Bulgaria peró é italiano. Ha dodici anni e parla perfettamente inglese e bulgaro, inoltre parla molto bene italiano, ma non parla francese.

1. Find the Italian for the following items in Mario's text

a. I am Polish

b. I speak Polish fluently

c. He speaks English fluently

d. He lives in Bulgaria

e. He speaks very well Italian

f. but I don't speak English well

2. Find Someone Who: answer the questions below about all 3 texts

a. Who speaks Italian fluently?

____

b. Who speaks English fluently and why?

____

c. Who would like to speak German?

____

d. Who doesn't speak Italian well?

____

e. Who speaks Romanian?

____

f. Who doesn't speak English well?

____

WRITING

1. Broken words

a. P_________ p______________ i_________ e f__________. P______ n______ p______ c _________

[I speak English and French fluently. But I don't speak Chinese]

b. l__ m___ a_________ p__________ b______ p__________ p_____ n____ p________ r_________.

[My friend (girl) speaks well Polish, but she doesn't speak Romanian]

c. S_____ i__________ e p_______ m_______ b______ i__________m ___ n____ p______ p__________.

[I am Italian and I speak very well English but I don't speak Portuguese]

d. P_________ p_____________ s__________ e p___________ m___ n____ p_________ m________
b__________ i__________.

[I speak perfectly Spanish and Portuguese but I don't speak very well Italian]

e. I__ m__ a_______ Simone é t___________ e n______ p______ i__________, p______ p__________
t_______________ e i_________.

[My friend Simone is German and he doesn't speak Italian, but he speaks perfectly German and English]

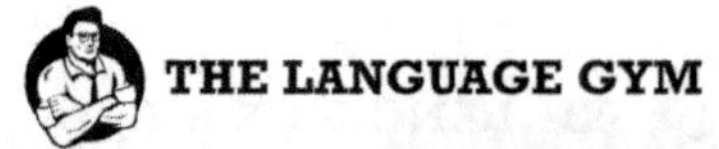

UNIT 2c
'Dove vivi? - Ti piace?'
Where do you live? - Do you like it?

Vivo a *I live in*	**Bari** **Bologna** **Milano** **Roma** **Siena** **Torino** **Venezia**	**Adoro** *I love* **Adora** *He/she loves* **Mi piace** *I like* **Gli/le piace** *He/she likes*	**la mia città** *my city* **la sua città** *his/her city*		**abbastanza** *quite* **molto** *very* **piuttosto** *rather*	**bella** *pretty* **brutta** *ugly* **grande** *big* **noiosa** *boring* **piccola** *small* **rumorosa** *noisy* **tranquilla** *calm* **turistica** *touristic*
Mia sorella vive a *My sister lives in*	**Casperia** **Garda** **Montalcino** **Jesolo** **Ostuni** **Senigallia** **Viareggio**	**Non mi piace** *I don't like* **Non gli/le piace** *He/she doesn't like* **Odio** *I hate* **Odia** *He/she hates*	**il mio paese** *my town* **il suo paese** *his/her town*	**perché è** *because it is*	**troppo** *too much* **un po'** *a little*	**bello** *pretty* **brutto** *ugly* **grande** *big* **noioso** *boring* **piccolo** *small* **rumoroso** *noisy* **tranquillo** *calm* **turistico** *touristic*

Unit 2c. Where you live: Translating

Paragraph 1	Tick a box each time you spot the correct translation in the text			Translate the paragraph into English
Ciao, mi chiamo Roberto. Sono italiano e ho undici anni. Parlo bene inglese e perfettamente italiano. Vivo a Bologna. Mi piace la mia città perché è molto grande e turistica. Mia sorella ha ventuno anni e vive a Venezia.	I live in Bologna	I like my city	My sister	______________
	and she lives in Venezia	and touristic	and Italian fluently	______________
	Hi, my name is Roberto	because it is very big	I speak English well	______________
	I am Italian	and I am 11	is 21	______________
Paragraph 2				
Salve, mi chiamo Maria, sono polacca e ho dodici anni. Parlo bene italiano e perfettamente il polacco. Vivo a Ostuni. Adoro il mio paese perché è bello e abbastanza piccolo. Mio fratello ha ventidue anni e vive a Roma.	Hello, my name is Maria	and he lives in Rome	I speak Italian well	______________
	and Polish fluently	because it is pretty	I live in Ostuni	______________
	and quite small	I love my town	I am Polish	______________
	and I am 12	My brother	is 22	______________
Paragraph 3				
Buonasera, mi chiamo Francisco. Sono spagnolo e ho quattordici anni. Parlo un po' italiano e molto bene spagnolo. Vivo a Roma. Non mi piace la mia città perché è troppo grande e rumorosa. Mio fratello vive a Catania e ha trenta anni.	I am Spanish	and I am 14	I live in Rome	______________
	Good evening, my name is Francisco	I speak Italian a little	and Spanish very well	______________
	I don't like my city	My brother	because it is too big	______________
	lives in Catania	and noisy	and he is 30	______________

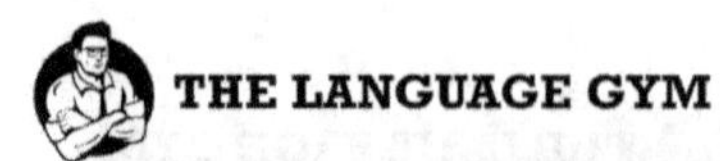 THE LANGUAGE GYM

UNIT 3
Describing hair and eyes

In this unit you will learn:

- To describe what a person's hair and eyes are like
- To describe details about their faces (e.g. beard and glasses)
- Colours
- I wear / s/he wears

You will also revisit:
- Common Italian names
- The verb "Avere" in the first and third person singular
- Numbers from 1 to 15

UNIT 3
Describing hair and eyes
'Di che colore sono i tuoi occhi e i tuoi capelli?'
What colour are your eyes and hair?

(Io) Mi chiamo *My name is/ I am called / I call myself...* **(Lui/Lei) Si chiama** *He/she is called*	Antonio Carlo Diego Emilia Francesca Gianfranco Giulia Isabella Marta Roberto	**e** *and*	**ho** *I have* **ha** *he/she has*	**sei anni** *6 years* **sette anni** *7 years* **otto anni** *8 years* **nove anni** *9 years* **dieci anni** *10 years* **undici anni** *11 years* **dodici anni** *12 years* **tredici anni** *13 years* **quattordici anni** *14 years* **quindici anni** *15 years*
Ho *i̲ capelli̲ *I have...hair* **Ha i̲ capelli̲** *He/she has...hair*	**biondi̲** *blond* **castani̲** *brown* **colorati̲** *coloured* **neri̲** *black* **rossi̲** *red* **scuri̲** *dark brown*	**e**	**a spazzola** *spiky* **corti** *short* **di media lunghezza** *medium length* **lisci** *straight* **lunghi** *long* **ondulati** *wavy* **rasati** *very short/crew-cut* **ricci** *curly*	
Ho gli occhi *I have... eyes* **Ha gli occhi** *He/she has... eyes*	**azzurri** *blue* **marroni** *brown* **neri** *black* **verdi** *green*	**e**	**(non) porto** *I (don't) wear* **(non) porta** *he/she (doesn't) wear* **(non) ho** *I (don't) have* **(non) ha** *he/she (doesn't) have*	**gli occhiali** *glasses* **i baffi** *a moustache* **la barba** *a beard*

Author's note: *the word for 'hair'- **i capelli** in Italian is a masculine <u>plural</u> noun. When describing hair you should follow this order: colour/length/style: **Ho i capelli castani, lunghi e lisci** ☺. As a result, all adjectives referring to capelli have to be plural and masculine*

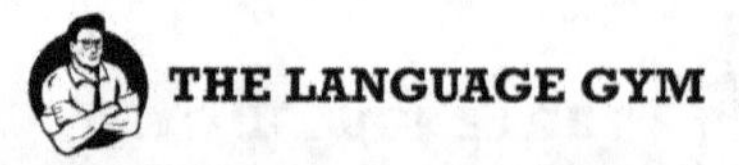

Unit 3. Describing hair and eyes: VOCABULARY BUILDING

1. Complete with the missing word

a. Ho i capelli c___________ *[I have brown hair]*

b. Ho i capelli b_________ *[I have blond hair]*

c. Porto gli o________________ *[I wear glasses]*

d. Ho gli occhi a___________ *[I have blue eyes]*

e. Non porto gli o____________ *[I don't wear glasses]*

f. Ho i capelli di me______ lunghe________
[I have mid-length hair]

g. Ho i capelli n_________ *[I have black-coloured hair]*

h. Ho i capelli r_________ *[I have red hair]*

2. Match up

1. i capelli castani	a. brown hair
2. i capelli neri	b. black eyes
3. i capelli biondi	c. moustache
4. gli occhi neri	d. green eyes
5. gli occhiali	e. black hair
6. i baffi	f. short hair
7. gli occhi azzurri	g. long hair
8. gli occhi verdi	h. red hair
9. i capelli corti	i. blond hair
10. i capelli lunghi	j. glasses
11. i capelli rossi	k. blue eyes

3. Translate into English

a. i capelli ricci =

b. gli occhi azzurri =

c. porto gli occhiali =

d. i capelli biondi =

e. gli occhi verdi =

f. i capelli rossi =

g. gli occhi neri =

h. i capelli scuri =

4. Add the missing letter

a. Lu__ghi　　c. ca__elli　　e. azzur__i　　g. ric__i　　i. s__uri　　　　k. o__chi

b. occ__iali　　d. baf__i　　f. v__rdi　　h. __isci　　j. di media lun__hezza　　l. por__o

5. Broken words

a. H__ i c____________ r________　　*[I have curly hair]*

b. P______ g___ o____________　　*[I wear glasses]*

c. __o i c___________ c_______　　*[I have short hair]*

d. N___ h__ i b________　　*[I don't have a moustache]*

e. __o g___ o______ m____________　　*[I have brown eyes]*

f. __o __a b__________　　*[I have a beard]*

g. H__ o______ a_______　　*[I am eight years old]*

h. M__ c________ M________　　*[My name is Maria]*

i. __o n______ a_______　　*[I am nine years old]*

6. Complete with a suitable word

a. Ho dieci __________ .

b. ________ la barba.

c. Mi _________ Antonio Bianchi.

d. Porto gli __________________.

e. Ho i ___________ lisci e corti.

f. Ho __ baffi.

g. Ho _____ occhi marroni.

h. Ho _____ capelli neri.

i. Non _____ i baffi.

j. _____ i capelli lunghi e ondulati.

k. _____ chiamo Luca Ferrari.

l. Ho ____________ anni.

Unit 3. Describing hair and eyes: READING

Mi chiamo Marta. Ho dodici anni e vivo a Napoli, il capoluogo della Campania. Ho i capelli neri, lisci e corti e gli occhi azzurri. Porto gli occhiali. Il mio compleanno è il dieci settembre. Mia sorella ha i capelli lisci. Lei ha dieci anni e parla un po' tedesco.

Mi chiamo Alice. Ho quindici anni e vivo a Bellinzona, in Svizzera. Parlo italiano e francese. Ho i capelli rossi, ondulati e lunghi e gli occhi azzurri. Non porto gli occhiali. Il mio compleanno è il sedici dicembre.

Mi chiamo Naima. Ho nove anni e sono indiana. Vivo a Torino, il capoluogo del Piemonte. Ho i capelli castani, ondulati e di media lunghezza e gli occhi marroni. Non porto gli occhiali. Il mio compleanno è il cinque dicembre. Mio fratello si chiama Yamir. Ha quindici anni. Ha i capelli scuri, lunghi e lisci e gli occhi neri. Lui porta gli occhiali. Il suo compleanno è il tredici novembre. È molto muscoloso.

Mi chiamo Federico. Ho otto anni e vivo a Perugia, il capoluogo dell'Umbria. Ho i capelli castani, corti e ricci e gli occhi verdi. Porto gli occhiali. Il mio compleanno è il nove maggio. A casa ho tre animali: un cavallo, un cane e un gatto. Mio fratello si chiama Sergio. Ha quattordici anni. Ha i capelli biondi, lunghi e lisci e gli occhi verdi come me. Porta anche gli occhiali come mio padre. Il suo compleanno è il due giugno. È molto intelligente e parla il cinese.

Mi chiamo Giuseppe. Ho dieci anni e vivo a Bari, il capoluogo della Puglia. Ho i capelli biondi, lisci e corti e gli occhi verdi. Porto gli occhiali. Il mio compleanno è l'otto aprile. Parlo molto bene spagnolo ma non parlo inglese.

1. Find the Italian for the following items in Marta's text

a. I am called:

b. in Naples:

c. I wear glasses:

d. My birthday is:

e. the tenth of:

f. I have:

g. straight:

h. speaks German:

i. the eyes:

2. Answer the following questions about Alice's text

a. How old is she?

____

b. Where is Bellinzona?

____

c. What colour is her hair?

____

d. What is her hair like?

____

e. What languages does she speak?

____

f. What colour are her eyes?

____

g. When is her birthday?

3. Complete with the missing words

Mi chiamo Roxana. _______ dieci anni e sono rumena. Vivo _______ Palermo, il capoluogo _______ Sicilia. Ho i _________ biondi, lisci e scalati e gli _______ verdi. _________ gli occhiali.
Il mio compleanno ___ il ventisette maggio.

4. Find someone who: answer the questions below about all 5 texts

a. Who has a brother called Sergio?

____

b. Who is eight years old?

____

c. Who celebrates their birthday on 9 May?

____

d. How many people wear glasses?

____

e. Who has dark brown hair and black-coloured eyes?

____

f. Who can speak a bit of Chinese?

____

g. Whose birthday is in April?

____

h. Who has brown, wavy hair and brown eyes?

____

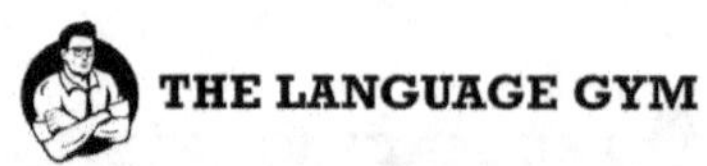

Unit 3. Describing hair and eyes: TRANSLATION

1. Faulty translation: spot and correct (in the English) any translation mistakes you find below

a. Ho i capelli biondi: *I have black eyes*

b. Ho gli occhi azzurri: *He has brown eyes*

c. Ho la barba: *He has a beard*

d. Si chiama Pedro: *I am called Pedro*

e. Ha i capelli a spazzola: *I have long hair*

f. Ho i capelli rasati: *I have coloured hair*

g. Vivo a Roma: *He is from Rome*

2. From Italian to English

a. Ho i capelli biondi.

b. Ho gli occhi azzurri.

c. Ho i capelli lisci.

d. Porta gli occhiali.

e. Ho i baffi e la barba.

f. Porto gli occhiali da sole.

g. Non ho la barba.

h. Ho i capelli a spazzola.

i. Ho i capelli ondulati.

3. Phrase-level translation

a. 'The' blond hair ___________________________

b. I am called___________________________

c. I have___________________________

d. 'The' blue eyes___________________________

e. 'The' straight hair___________________________

f. He has___________________________

g. Ten years___________________________

h. I have black eyes___________________________

i. I have nine years___________________________

j. 'The' brown eyes___________________________

k. 'The' black hair___________________________

4. Sentence-level translation

a. My name is Mark. I am ten years old. I have black and curly hair and blue eyes.

b. I am twelve years old. I have green eyes and blond, straight hair.

c. I am called Jessica. I live in Milan. I have long blond hair and brown eyes.

d. My name is Pietro. I live in Rome. I have black hair, short and spiky.

e. I am fifteen-years-old. I have black, curly long hair and green eyes.

f. I am thirteen years old. I have red, straight long hair and brown eyes.

Unit 3. Describing hair and eyes: WRITING

1. Split sentences

Ho i capelli	occhi verdi
Ho la	barba
Ho gli	biondi
Ho i	e ricci
Ho i capelli biondi	capelli neri
Mi chiamo	anni
Ho dieci	Marta

2. Rewrite the sentences in the correct order

a. capelli i ho ricci

b. ho la non barba

c. chiamo mi Riccardo

d. capelli ho rossi i

e. si fratello chiama Paolo mio

f. verdi occhi ho gli

3. Spot and correct the grammar and spelling errors

a. Ho i capelli nero

b. Mio fratello mi chiamo Antonio

c. Ho capelli ricci

d. Si chiamo Nadia

e. o cuatordici anni

f. Ho il capello lisci

g. Ho l'occhi verde

h. o la barba

i. Porto li ochiali

j. Ho no baffi

4. Anagrams

a. pellica = capelli

b. rbaba=

c. ohicc=

d. nina=

e. zuzarri=

f. dinbio=

g. rine=

h. cicri=

i. siros=

5. Guided writing – write 3 short paragraphs in the first person singular ['I'] describing the people below

Name	Age	Hair	Eyes	Glasses	Beard	Moustache
Peter	12	brown curly long	green	wears	does not have	has
Carla	11	blond straight short	blue	does not wear	does not have	does not have
Igor	10	red wavy medium length	black	wears	has	does not have

6. Describe this person in the third person:

Name: Cristian

Age: 15

Hair: black, curly, very short

Eyes: brown

Glasses: no

Beard: yes

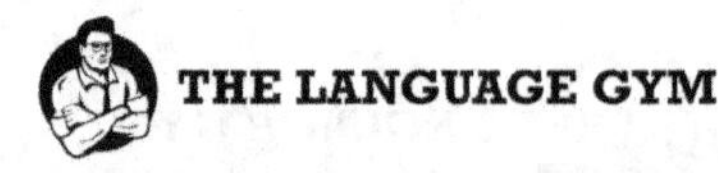

UNIT 4
Saying where I live and am from

**In this unit you will learn
to talk about:**

- Where you live and are from
- If you live in an apartment or a house
- What your accommodation looks like
- Where it is located
- The names of cities and countries
  where Italian is spoken
- Describe the weather
- The verb 'I am'

You will also revisit:
- Introducing yourself
- Telling age and birthday

UNIT 4

Saying where I live and I am from

'Dove vivi?' *Where do you live?*

Mi chiamo Paolo e... *My name is Paolo and...*	**vivo in** *I live in*	**un appartamento** *a flat* **un palazzo/ un edificio** *a building*	**antico** *old* **bello** *pretty* **brutto** *ugly* **confortevole** *comfortable* **grande** *big* **piccolo** *small* **moderno** *modern*	**in centro** *in the centre* **in campagna** *in the countryside* **in montagna** *in the mountains*
		una casa *a house* **una villa** *a villa*	**antica** *old* **bella** *pretty* **brutta** *ugly* **confortevole** *comfortable* **grande** *big* **piccola** *small* **moderna** *modern*	**in periferia** *on the outskirts* **sulla costa** *on the coast*
	sono di *I am from*	**Bari** **Bologna** **Cagliari** **Firenze** **Genova** **Lugano** **Milano** **Palermo** **Roma** **Torino**	**una città** *a city*	**in Puglia** **in Emilia-Romagna** **in Sardegna** **in Toscana** **in Liguria** **in Svizzera** **in Lombardia** **in Sicilia** **nel Lazio** **in Piemonte**	**nel nord dell'Italia** *in the north of Italy* **nel centro dell'Italia** *in the centre of Italy* **nel sud dell'Italia** *in the south of Italy*

Author's note: *Italy surrounds two independent states: the Republic of San Marino and the Vatican City. In both states the official language is Italian. The language is also spoken in Croatia, Slovenia and Malta.* ☺

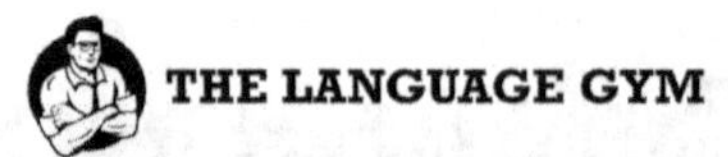

Unit 4. Saying where I live and am from: VOCABULARY BUILDING

1. Complete with the missing word

a. Vivo in _________ casa bella *[I live in a pretty house]*

b. Mi piace il mio _____________________ *[I like my flat]*

c. Sono ___ Firenze *[I am from Florence]*

d. _______ in una villa *[I live in a villa]*

e. Un appartamento in un ____________ moderno
[A flat in a modern building]

f. Sono di Roma, la____________ d'Italia
[I'm from Rome, the capital of Italy]

g. Vivo in una casa molto ______________ in campagna
[I live in a very old house in the countryside]

h. Vivo in ___________________ *[I live on the outskirts]*

2. Match up

1. il centro	a. big
2. bello	b. small
3. grande	c. old
4. palazzo	d. pretty
5. antico	e. the centre
6. la periferia	f. the coast
7. la costa	g. I am from
8. Italia	h. the outskirts
9. sono di	i. ugly
10. brutto	j. I live in
11. piccolo	k. comfortable
12. vivo in	l. building
13. confortevole	m. Italy

3. Translate into English

a. Sono di Venezia =

b. Vivo in una casa =

c. Il mio appartamento è piccolo =

d. Sono di Siena, in Toscana =

e. in un palazzo moderno =

f. Sono di Cosenza, nel sud dell'Italia =

g. Vivo in una villa a Positano sulla costa =

h. Sono di Torino, nel nord dell'Italia =

4. Add the missing letter

a. Rom_   c. Mil_no   e. Ital_a   g. Ven_zia   i. F_renze

b. Bar_   d. Sviz_era   f. Cos_nza   h. To_ino   j. Tosc_na

5. Broken words

a. S____ d___ L__________, i___ S ______________
= *[I am from Lugano, in Switzerland]*

b. V___ i___ u____ c_______ v_________
= *[I live in an old house]*

c. S___ d___ R_________, l___ c__________ d' I___________
= *[I am from Rome, the capital of Italy]*

d. V_____ i__ u___ c______ s_____ c________ d__ Calabria
= *[I live in a house on the coast of Calabria]*

e. V____ i___ u___ v_____ p________ i__
c________________ = *[I live in a small villa in the countryside]*

6. Complete with a suitable word

a. Sono _____ Bologna.

b. Vivo _____ centro.

c. In un ________________ antico.

d. Vivo in una casa in _____________.

e. Roma è la capitale dell' _________.

f. Vivo in un appartamento _________.

g. Sono di ____________________.

h. Una __________sulla costa.

i. Città di San ________, a San Marino.

j. Vivo a Positano sulla __________.

Unit 4. "Geography test": Using your own knowledge (and a bit of help from Google/your teacher) match the numbers to the city or region

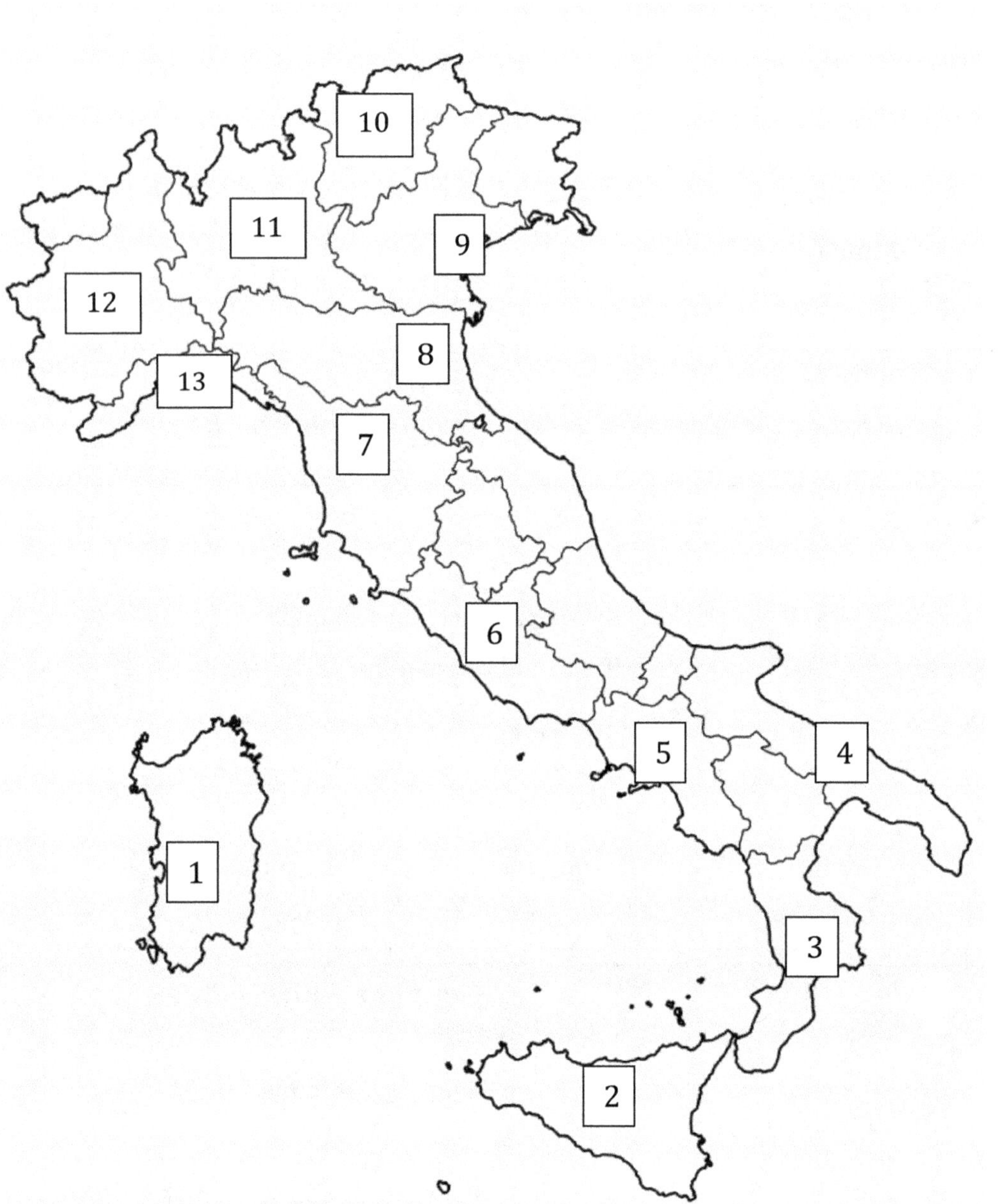

Italy	
Num	**City or Region**
	Bologna
	Bolzano
	Calabria
	Firenze
	Genova
	Milano
	Napoli
	Puglia
	Roma
	Sardegna
	Sicilia
	Torino
	Venezia

Unit 4. Saying where I live and am from: READING

Mi chiamo Gianluigi. Ho ventidue anni e il mio compleanno è il nove agosto. Vivo a Borgo Maggiore, in San Marino. Vivo in una casa piccola in centro città.

Ho due fratelli, Edoardo e Dario. Mi piace molto Edoardo ma Dario non mi piace perché è stupidino.

Il mio amico Francesco vive a Siena, in Toscana. Lui vive in un appartamento in un palazzo abbastanza antico, in centro.

Mi chiamo Matilda. Ho quindici anni e vivo a Cagliari, in Sardegna. Nella mia famiglia siamo quattro persone: i miei genitori, mio fratello Giorgio ed io. Il mio compleanno è l'undici settembre, anche quello di Giorgio. Siamo gemelli! Mio zio vive a Malta.

Mi chiamo Stefania. Ho nove anni e vivo a Rimini, sulla costa adriatica in Italia. Vivo con la mia famiglia: i miei genitori, mia sorella maggiore Sara ed io. Il mio compleanno è il nove maggio e il compleanno di Sara è il trenta marzo. Lei ha undici anni. La mia casa è piuttosto grande e confortevole e si trova sulla costa. Mi piace troppo!

Mi chiamo Bella. Ho ventuno anni e vivo a Monte Carlo con la mia amica Marina. Abitiamo in un appartamento piccolo e moderno in periferia. Il mio compleanno è il due giugno e il compleanno di Marina è il dodici giugno.

Ho un cane che si chiama Buck. È molto grande e buono. Il suo compleanno è il primo aprile. Buck ha tre anni. Ho **anche** *[also]* un ragno, buono **ma** *[but]* brutto, che si chiama Aracno. Anche il compleanno del mio ragno è il primo aprile. **Quindi** *[therefore]* faccio una festa per i due animali lo stesso giorno. È **più** *[more]* pratico.

1. Find the Italian for the following in Bella's text

a. my name is

b. I am 21 years old

c. I live in…

d. a small flat

e. on the outskirts

f. the 2nd of June

g. I have a dog

h. he is very big

i. his birthday is on the 1st April

j. he is 3 years old

k. I also have a spider

2. Complete the statements below based on Gianluigi's text

a. I am _______ years old

b. My birthday is on the _____ of _____________

c. I live in a _______ house in the _________ of the city

d. I have two _____________

e. I like Edoardo but Dario is _____________

f. My friend Francesco _________ in Siena

g. He lives in a _______ in a quite old _____________

3. Answer the questions on the four texts above

a. How old is Matilda?

b. When is Matilda and Giorgio's birthday? What do you think a '**gemelli**' means?

c. Who only likes one of his siblings?

d. Who has two pets that share a birthday?

e. Why is it convenient that they share a birthday?

f. Who has a friend that lives in a different city?

g. Who lives with their really good friend?

h. Who lives in Monte Carlo?

i. Whose birthday is on the 12th of June?

4. Correct any of the statements below [about Stefania's text] which are incorrect

a. Stefania vive a Napoli, nel sud Italia.

b. Nella famiglia di Stefania ci sono *[there are]* quattro persone.

c. Il suo compleanno è a marzo.

d. Il compleanno di Sara è il tre marzo.

e. Stefania vive in una casa piuttosto grande ma brutta sulla costa.

f. Le piace molto la sua casa.

Unit 4. Saying where I live and am from: TRANSLATION/WRITING

1. Translate into English

a. vivo in

b. una casa

c. un appartamento

d. confortevole

e. molto grande

f. in un palazzo

g. antico

h. moderno

i. in centro

j. in periferia

k. sulla costa

l. sono di

m. in Italia

n. in Svizzera

o. vivo a Glasgow

2. Gapped sentences

a. Vivo a Bari in una _______ antica *[I live in Bari in an old villa]*

b. Una casa in __________________ *[A house in the countryside]*

c. Vivo in un __________________ piccolo *[I live in a small flat]*

d. Una _______ in _______________ *[A house on the outskirts]*

e. _______ ___ Roma, la capitale d' ________, ma vivo a Malta.
[I am from Rome, the capital of Italy, but I live in Malta]

3. Complete the sentences with a suitable word

a. Sono ______ Borgo Maggiore, nella Repubblica di San Marino.

b. _______ di Firenze,il capoluogo della Toscana.

c. Sono argentino, vivo nella __________ del Vaticano.

d. Vivo in un ________________ grande in __________________.

e. Vivo a Bologna, in una casa nuova e __________________ .

f. Vivo in un appartamento________________ in centro.

g. Vivo a Grisignana, in Croazia, in _______ casa moderna.

4. Phrase-level translation [En to It]

a. I live in ______________________________

b. I am from ______________________________

c. A house ______________________________

d. A flat ______________________________

e. Ugly (m) ______________________________

f. Small (m) ______________________________

g. In an old building

____

h. In the centre ______________________________

i. On the outskirts ______________________________

j. On the coast ______________________________

k. In Tuscany ______________________________

5. Sentence-level translation [En to It]

a. I am from Pisa, in Tuscany in Italy. I live in a big and pretty house on the outskirts.

____

____

b. I am from Amalfi, in the south of Italy. I live in a small and comfortable apartment near the coast.

____

____

c. I am from Bellinzona, in Switzerland. I live in a big flat in a new building in the centre.

____

____

d. I am from Venice, in the north of Italy. I live in a flat in a building on the outskirts. I like my flat.

____

____

Unit 4. Saying where I live and am from: WRITING

1. Complete with the missing letters

a. Mi chia_ _ Angela

b. Vi_ _ in una ca_ _ m_d _ rn_

c. V_v_ in un ap_artam_nto grand_

d. _ _vo a Pisa, in una _ _sa i_ cent_ _

e. So_ _ di Mil_ no in Lom_ ard_a

f. Io _ono d_ Rom_, la cap_tale d'Ital_a

g. V_ _ o in una v_l_a grand_ in per_ feri_

h. _ono di Firen_ e in T_ scan_

2. Spot and correct the mistakes

a. Sono de Cosenza en Calabria.

b. Sono en Bari a Puglia.

c. Vivo in una casa piccolo a Malta.

d. Vivo in una appartamento grando.

e. Vivo a un palazzo nuovo.

f. Vivo en Rome con la mia familia.

g. Sono de Siena en Tuscana.

h. Vivo in una vila in campana.

3. Answer the questions in Italian

a. Come ti chiami? M____

b. Quanti anni hai? H______________________________________

c. *Di dove sei? Sono di _____________________________________

d. *Dove vivi? Vivo a _______________________________________

e. Vivi in una casa o in un appartamento? Vivo in _____________

*Author's note:
Di dove sei? = 'Where are you from?'
Dove vivi ?= 'Where do you live?'
Vivo a Edimburgo/Roma = I live in Edinburgh/Rome

4. Anagrams (regions of Italy and countries)

a. neVeto = *Veneto*

b. scanaTo =

c. gliaPu =

d. laCabria =

e. monPiete =

f. diaLombar =

g. noVacati =

h. razzeSvi =

i. noMariSan =

j. gnadeSar =

5. Guided writing – write 4 short paragraphs in the 1st person singular ['I'] describing the people below

Name	Age	Birthday	City	Country or region
Samuel	12	20/06	Roma	Lazio (Italia)
Alex	14	14/10	Lugano	Svizzera
Andrea	11	14/01	Monte Carlo	Monaco
Charles	13	17/01	Taormina	Sicilia (Italia)
Nina	15	19/10	Amalfi	Campania (Italia)

6. Describe this person in the third person:

Name: Alessio

Age: 16

Birthday: 15th May

Country of origin: Glasgow, Scotland [Scozia]

Country of residence: Lucca, Italy [Italia]

UNIT 4b
Describing the weather
'Che tempo fa in Italia?'
What is the weather like in Italy?

A volte *Sometimes* **Di solito** *Usually* **Mai** *Never* **Normalmente** *Normally* **Ogni tanto** *Every now and then* **Raramente** *Rarely* **Sempre** *Always* **Spesso** *Often* **Tutti i giorni** *Every day*	**in estate** *in the summer* **in autunno** *in the autumn* **in inverno** *in the winter* **in primavera** *in the spring*	**in Italia** **in Puglia** **in Trentino** **in Veneto** **in Sardegna** **in Calabria** **in Toscana** **in Liguria** **in Lombardia** **in Sicilia** **in Piemonte** **in Veneto** **in montagna** *in the mountains* **al mare** *at the seaside*	**fa** *it's*	**caldo** *warm* **freddo** *cold* **bel tempo** *good weather* **brutto tempo** *bad weather* **fresco** *cool*
			***c'è** *it's*	**sole** *sunny* **nebbia** *foggy* **vento** *windy* **tempesta** *stormy*
			nevica *it snows* **piove** *it rains* **pioviggina** *it drizzles*	

Author's note: *** c'è** literally means "there is". *C'è sole- there is sun/c'è nebbia- there is fog*

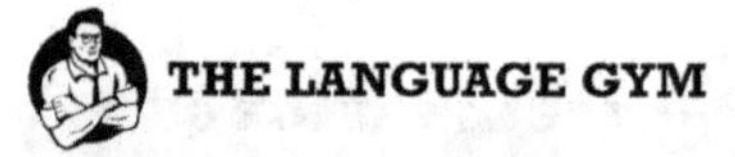

Unit 4b. Saying where I live and the weather: READING

Mi chiamo Massimo. Vivo a Roma in una casa piccola in centro.
In inverno spesso piove. Però in estate vado a Cecina, in Toscana con la mia famiglia. Ho una casa piuttosto grande e tutti i giorni fa bel tempo. Vado sempre al mare perché fa troppo caldo e mi piace.

Mi chiamo Mario. Ho diciotto anni e vivo a Milano con la mia amica Roberta. Abitiamo in un appartamento moderno in periferia. Il mio compleanno è il tre aprile. In Lombardia, in inverno c'è nebbia. In primavera pioviggina tutti i giorni e non mi piace. In estate o vado in montagna con la mia famiglia, o vado al mare con i miei amici. Preferisco la montagna perché fa fresco e in estate fa sempre bel tempo.

Mi chiamo Daniela. Ho tredici anni e vivo a Trento, in Trentino, con mia sorella, in una casa molto grande in montagna. In inverno fa freddo e nevica sempre. Mi piace la primavera perché fa fresco e piove raramente.

Mi chiamo Alessandro. Ho dieci anni e vivo a Catania in Sicilia. La mia casa è piccola ma confortevole e si trova sulla costa. Mi piace molto!

Tutti i giorni vado al mare perché fa sempre bel tempo e piove raramente. Non mi piace in estate perché fa troppo caldo.

1. Find the Italian for the following in Massimo's text

a. a small house

b. I live in

c. I go to

d. with my family

e. in city centre

f. it's good weather

g. every day

h. always

i. it's too warm

j. to the seaside

2. Complete the statements below based on Daniela's text

a. I am _______ years old

b. I live in ________, in ________ with my ____________

c. My house is __________

d. In winter it's __________

e. I like __________ because it's __________

f. It rarely ____________

g. My _______ ___ Daniela

3. Answer the questions about Mario

a. How old is Mario?

b. Who does he lives with?

c. Where does he live?

d. When is his birthday?

e. What's the weather like in Lombardia in spring?

f. Does he like the weather in Lombardia?

g. Where does he go with his family during the summer?

h. Where does he go with his friends during the summer?

i. Which one does he prefer and why?

4. Correct any of the statements below [about Alessandro's text] which are incorrect

a. Alessandro vive a Catania in una casa grande.

b. In Sicilia nevica sempre.

c. In estate ogni tanto va al mare.

d. A Catania in estate fa troppo caldo.

e. Ogni tanto va al mare.

f. Gli piace l'estate perché fa caldo.

g. In Sicilia fa sempre bel tempo.

h. In Sicilia fa brutto tempo.

i. La sua casa si trova in centro.

UNIT 5
Talking about my family and relationships.
Counting to 100

Revision quickie – Numbers 1-100 / Dates / Birthdays

In this unit you will learn to talk about:
- How many people there are in your family and who they are
- If you get along with them
- Words for family members
- What their age is
- Numbers from 31 to 100

You will also revisit
- Numbers from 1 to 31
- Hair and eyes description

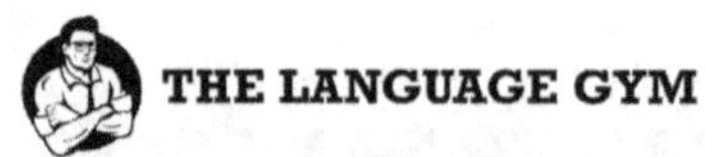

UNIT 5
Talking about my family
Quante persone ci sono nella tua famiglia? - Vai d'accordo con...?
How many people are there in your family? - Do you get on well with...?

	mio nonno Alfonso *my grandfather Alfonso*		**un** *1*	**anno**
Ci sono quattro persone nella mia famiglia *There are four people in my family...*	**mio padre Giuseppe** *my father Giuseppe*	**Lui ha**	**due** *2* **tre** *3* **quattro** *4* **cinque** *5* **sei** *6* **sette** *7* **otto** *8* **nove** *9* **dieci** *10* **venti** *20* **ventuno** *21* **ventidue** *22*	
	mio zio Luciano *my uncle Luciano*			
	mio fratello maggiore /minore *my older/younger brother*			
Nella mia famiglia siamo in quattro *We are a family of four...*	**mio cugino Marco** *my cousin Marco*			
	mia nonna Rosa *my grandmother*	**Lei ha**	**ventitré** *23* **trenta** *30* **trentuno** *31* **trentadue** *32* **trentatré** *33* **trentaquattro** *34* **trentacinque** *35* **trentasei** *36* **trentasette** *37* **trentotto** *38* **trentanove** *39* **quaranta** *40* **cinquanta** *50* **sessanta** *60* **settanta** *70* **ottanta** *80* **novanta** *90* **cento** *100*	**anni**
Vado d'accordo con... *I get on well with...*	**mia madre Lina** *my mother Lina*			
	mia zia Anna *my aunt Anna*			
Non vado d'accordo... *I do not get on well with...*	**mia sorella maggiore /minore** *my older/younger sister*			
	mia cugina Lara *my girl cousin Lara*			

Author's note: *the number 1,* **uno,** *becomes shortened to* **'un'** *before a noun. After 20 in Italian simply put numbers together, no space, no hyphen. i.e. 25* **venticinque.** *The final vowel of the tens number disappears when you add* **uno**(1) *or* **otto**(8); *i.e. 41* **quarantuno,** *48* **quarantotto.** *When you add the number* **tre** *(3) the final vowel becomes* **é**: *53* **cinquantatré**

Unit 5. Talking about my family + Counting to 100: VOCAB BUILDING

1. Complete with the missing word

a. Nella mia f___________ c'è   *[In my family there is]*

b. Ci sono __________ persone *[There are five people]*

c. Mio __________ Alfonso *[My grandfather Alfonso]*

d. Mio nonno ________ ottant'anni *[My grandfather is 80 years old]*

e. Mia ________ Lina   *[My mother Lina]*

f. Lei __________ cinquant'anni *[She is 50 years old]*

g. Vado d' ___________ con mio fratello *[I get on well with my bro]*

2. Match up

1. Sedici	*a.* 66	
2. Sessantasei	*b.* 48	
3. Ventuno	*c.* 13	
4. Dieci	*d.* 16	
5. Trentatré	*e.* 10	
6. Tredici	*f.* 21	
7. Quarantotto	*g.* 15	
8. Cinquantadue	*h.* 5	
9. Cinque	*i.* 33	
10. Quindici	*j.* 52	

3. Translate into English

a. Non vado d'accordo con =

b. Mia nonna Luigina =

c. Mio zio =

d. Ci sono quattro persone =

e. Nella mia famiglia=

f. Vado d'accordo con =

g. Mio padre =

h. Ha vent'anni =

4. Add the missing letter

a. fami _lia c. p _rsone e.frat _llo g. ma_re i. vado _'accordo k. tren_adue

b. z_o d. n_nno f. ma_giore h. cugi _o j. n_lla l. nov_nta

5. Broken words

a. C__ s______ s____ p__________ n____ m__ f___________
= *[there are 6 people in my family]*

b. M___ s_________ h__ d________ a_______
= *[My sister is 12 years old]*

c. N_____ m___ f__________ c'__ = *[In my family there is]*

d. M__ c________ s__ c________ = *[my male cousin is called]*

e. M__ p________ h____ q_______________ a______
= *[My father is 46 years old]*

f. N___ v____ d' a__________ c___ m__ f____________
m__________ = *[I do not get on well with my older brother]*

g. V___ d'a____________ c___ = *[I get on well with]*

6. Complete with a suitable word

a. Nella mia _________________

b. Ci__________ tre persone

c. Mia sorella ______________

d. Ha quattordici ____________

e. Mia __________ Gina ha trentacinque anni

f. _________ d'accordo con mio padre

g. _____ mia famiglia ci sono …

h. Non vado d'_________ con mia zia

i. Mio zio _____ quarantasei anni

j. Mio __________ ha trentanove anni

k. Vado d'accordo ______ mio nonno

Unit 5. Talking about my family + Counting to 100: VOCABULARY DRILLS

1. Match up

nella mia	there are
famiglia	in my
ci sono	with
sette	I get on well
persone	seven
vado d'accordo	family
con	people

2. Complete with the missing word

a. Ci _______ cinque persone [There are five people]

b. Mio ______ John ha sessanta anni [my uncle John is 60]

c. Vado ____________ con mia cugina [I get on well with my cousin]

d. ____ vado d'accordo ____ mia zia [I don't get on well with my aunt]

e. Mia zia Anna _____ quarantasette anni [My aunt Anna is 47]

f. Lui ha ________________ anni [He is 18]

g. Lei ________ ventinove anni [She is 29]

h. Mia _______ Luigina ha ottanta anni [my grandmother Luigina is 80]

3. Translate into English

a. Lui ha settantacinque anni.

b. Lei ha quaranta anni.

c. Mio padre ha cinquantatré anni.

d. Non vado d'accordo con mio nonno.

e. Vado d'accordo con mia sorella.

f. Mia sorella minore ha cinque anni.

g. Ci sono sei persone nella mia famiglia

h. Vai d'accordo con tua sorella?

4. Complete with the missing letters

a. Mio fratello m_ _giore [My older brother]

b. Nella mia fa_ _ _lia ci s_ _ _ tre persone
[In my family there are 3 people]

c. Mio cugino h_ dici_ _nove anni [My cousin is 19]

d. Vado molto d' acc_ _do con mio fratello
[I get on very well with my brother]

e. Mio z_ _ ha quaranta_ _ _ anni
[My uncle is 46 years old]

f. _ _ _ _ molto d'accordo con mi_ cugin_
[I get on very well with my female cousin]

g. Mio cug_ _ _ ha q_ _ndici anni
[My male cousin is 15 years old]

h. Vado abbastanza d'accordo con _ _ _ sorella
[I get on ok with my sister]

5. Translate into Italian:

a. In my family:______________________

b. There are: ______________________

c. My father: ______________________

d. Is 40 years old:______________________

e. I get on well with my brother:

____

6. Spot and correct the errors.

a. Nella mi familia ci sono tre persona

b. Mia nona Carla

c. Mio fratello a nove ani

d. Vado dacordo con mio cugino

e. Mia cugino ha otto anni

f. Mia sorrela maggior Benedetta

Unit 5. Talking about my family + Counting to 100: TRANSLATION

1. Match up

1. Venti	*a. 30*
2. Cinquanta	*b. 70*
3. Settanta	*c. 100*
4. Trenta	*d. 50*
5. Sessanta	*e. 20*
6. Novanta	*f. 80*
7. Ottanta	*g. 40*
8. Quaranta	*h. 60*
9. Cento	*i. 90*

2. Write out in Italian

a. 35 = trentacinque

b. 63 = s________________________

c. 89 = o________________________

d. 74 = s________________________

e. 98 = n________________________

f. 100 = c________________________

g. 82 = o________________________

h. 24 = v________________________

i. 17 = d________________________

3. Write out with the missing number

a. Io ho t________________ anni *[I am 32]*

b. Mio padre ha c________________________ anni
[My father is fifty-seven]

c. Mia madre ha q________________________ anni
[My mother is forty-eight]

d. Mio nonno ha c____________ anni
[My grandfather is one-hundred years old]

e. Noi abbiamo t____________ anni *[We are thirteen]*

f. Loro hanno n________________ anni *[They are ninety]*

g. I miei cugini hanno q________________________ anni
[My cousins are forty-four]

h. Lei ha s________________ anni? *[Is she seventy?]*

4. Correct the translation errors

a. My father is forty = mio padre ha quattordici anni

b. My mother is fifty = mia madre ha cinquantadue anni

c. We are forty-eight = noi abbiamo quarantadue anni

d. I am forty-two = ho quarantuno anni

e. They are thirty-four = loro hanno trentadue anni

5. Translate into Italian (please write out the numbers in letters)

a. In my family there are six people:____

b. My mother is called Sara and she is 43:________________________________

c. My father is called Mohamed and he is 48:________________________________

d. My older sister is called Fatima and she is 31:________________________________

e. My younger sister is called Carmen and she is 18:________________________________

f. I am called Ariana and I am 27: ________________________________

g. My grandfather is called Antonio and he is 87:________________________________

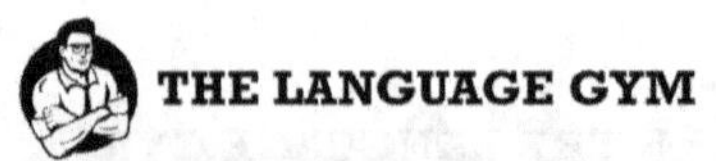

1. Spot and correct the spelling mistakes

a. querenta = *quaranta*

b. trentoono = _______________________

c. otantadue = _______________________

d. veintuno = _______________________

e. novente = _______________________

f. ciento = _______________________

g. septenta =_______________________

h. sedicci = _______________________

3. Rearrange the sentence below in the correct word order

a. mia Nella quattro famiglia persone sono ci
[In my family there are four people]

b. vado con mio d'accordo Non fratello
[I don't get on well with my brother]

c. padre, Mio si chiama che Piero anni cinquantadue ha
[My father, who is called Piero, is fifty-two]

d. padre mio ed io Nella famiglia mia madre, ci persone: sono tre mia
[In my family there are three people: my mother, my father and I]

e. si Mio che cugino, anni Ivan chiama ha trentasette
[My cousin, who is called Ivan, is thirty-seven]

f. nonno, anni Fernando che Mio si chiama ottantasette ha,
[My grandfather, who is called Fernando, is eighty-seven]

g. Vado con madre d'accordo mia. Lei anni cinquanta ha
[I get on well with my mother. She is 50]

2. Complete with the missing letters

a. Mia m__dre h__ quar__nta ann__

b. Mio pad__e h__ cin__uantuno a__ni

c. I miei nonni h__nno ott__nta an__i

d. M__a sore__la mino__e ha vent__ __nni

e. __ia no__na __a sett__ntasei a __ __ __

f. Mio fr__ tel__o ma__g__ore ha ven__i an__i

4. Complete

a. in my family: n_______ m____ f_______________

b. there are: c____ s_________

c. who is called: c______ s____ c______________

d. my mother: m____ m__________

e. my father: m_____ p___________

f. he is fifty: l____ h_____ c_______________ a________

g. I am sixty: i__ h___ s________________ a_________

h. she is forty: l____ h__ q___________ a________

5. Write a relationship sentence for each person as shown in the example

e.g. Il mio migliore amico si chiama Paolo e ha quindici anni. Vado molto d'accordo con lui.

Name	Relationship to me	Age	How I get on with them
e.g. Paolo	*best friend*	*15*	*very well*
Gianfranco	father	57	well
Lina	mother	45	not well
Rosa	aunt	60	*quite* well
Andrew	uncle	67	not well
Alfonso	grandfather	75	*very* well

Author's note: quite=abbastanza/ very=molto ☺
*Vado abbastanza d'accordo con mio zio

Revision Quickie 1:
Numbers 1-100, dates and birthdays, hair and eyes, family

1. Match up

a. 11	*1. quindici*
b. 12	*2. dodici*
c. 18	*3. sedici*
d. 14	*4. diciotto*
e. 17	*5. undici*
f. 16	*6. diciannove*
g. 15	*7. quattordici*
h. 13	*8. venti*
i. 19	*9. diciassette*
j. 20	*10. tredici*

2. Translate the dates into English

a. il trenta giugno

b. il primo luglio

c. il quindici settembre

d. il ventidue marzo

e. il trentuno dicembre

f. il cinque gennaio

g. il sedici aprile

h. il ventinove febbraio

i. il diciotto maggio

3. Complete with the missing words

a. Il mio compleanno _____ il quindici aprile.

b. Ho quattordici _________.

c. Mio fratello _______ i capelli ___________.

d. Di ________ sei?

e. Sono ______ Pisa.

e. Nella mia famiglia ___ _________ quattro persone.

f. _____ madre ha gli _______ marroni.

h. Vivo ____ Glasgow, in Scozia.

dove	è	di	ha	a
biondi	occhi	anni	ci sono	mia

4. Write out the solution in words as shown in the example

a. quaranta - trenta = *dieci*

b. trenta - dieci = _____________________

c. quaranta + trenta = _____________________

d. venti x due = _____________________

e. ottanta - venti = _____________________

f. novanta - cinquanta = _____________________

g. trenta x tre = _____________________

h. venti + cinquanta = _____________________

i. venti + trenta = _____________________

5. Complete the words

a. Mio no_ _ _ _   *[My grandfather]*

b. Mia cug_ _ _ _   *[My female cousin]*

c. G_ _ oc_ _ _ _   *[The eyes]*

d. Ver_ _   *[Green]*

e. La ba_ _ _ _   *[Beard]*

f. Gli o_ _ hi_ _ _ _   *[Glasses]*

g. Mia sor_ _ _ _ _   *[Sister]*

h. I_ h_   *[I have]*

6. Translate into English

a. Mia madre ha i capelli castani, corti e ricci

b. Ho gli occhi azzurri.

c. Mia zia ha quarantatré anni.

d. Mio nonno ha novantadue anni.

e. Mio padre porta gli occhiali.

f. Mio fratello ha i baffi e la barba.

g. Mio fratello minore ha i capelli rossi.

h. Mia sorella ha gli occhi blu e i capelli neri.

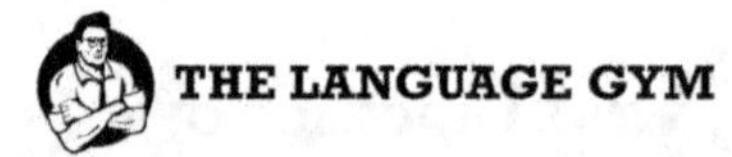

UNIT 6: (Part 1/2)
Describing myself and another family member (physical and personality)

In this unit you will learn:

- What your immediate family members are like
- Useful adjectives to describe them
- The third person of the verb 'Essere'(to be): 'è' (he/she is)
- All the persons of the verb 'Avere' in the present indicative

You will also revisit

- Numbers from 1 to 31
- Hair and eyes description

UNIT 6 (Part 1/2)
Intro to describing myself and another family member:
'Come sei fisicamente? – Che tipo di persona sei?'
What do you look like? - What kind of person are you?

MASCULINE			
Io *I*	**sono** *am*	**alto** *tall* **basso** *short* **bello** *handsome*	**antipatico** *unfriendly* **cattivo** *bad* **generoso** *generous* **noioso** *boring* **simpatico** *nice/friendly*
Lui *He* **Mio fratello maggiore** *My older brother* **Mio padre** *My father*	**è** *is*	**brutto** *ugly* **buono** *good* **grasso** *fat* **magro** *slim* **forte** *strong*	**sportivo** *sporty* **testardo** *stubborn* **timido** *shy* **divertente** *fun* **gentile** *kind* **socievole** *sociable*

FEMININE			
Io *I*	**sono** *am*	**alta** **bassa** **bella** **brutta** **buona** **grossa** **magra** **forte**	**antipatica** **cattiva** **generosa** **noiosa** **simpatica** **sportiva** **testarda** **timida** **divertente** **gentile** **socievole**
Lei *She* **Mia sorella minore** *My younger sister* **Mia madre** *My mother*	**è** *is*		

Unit 6. Vocabulary building

1. Match up

1. Sono simpatico	*a. I am friendly*
2. Sono antipatico	*b. I am generous*
3. Sono testardo	*c. I am unfriendly*
4. Sono timida	*d. I am short*
5. Sono generoso	*e. I am strong*
6. Sono forte	*f. I am shy*
7. Sono cattiva	*g. I am bad*
8. Sono basso	*h. I am tall*
9. Sono alto	*i. I am kind*
10. Sono gentile	*j. I am stubborn*

2. Complete

a. Mio fratello minore è s______________________
[My younger brother is sporty]

b. Mio padre è s______________________
[My father is sociable]

c. Mia sorella maggiore è ______________________
[My older sister is stubborn]

d. Mio fratello maggiore è d______________________
[My older brother is fun]

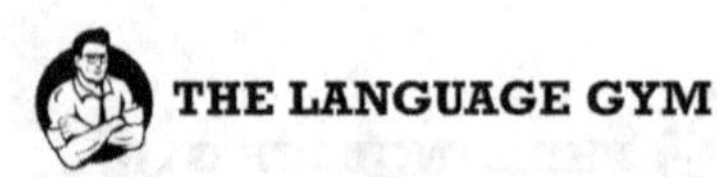

3. Categories – sort the adjectives below in the categories provided

a. forte; b. sportivo; c. simpatico; d. testardo; e. bello;
f. intelligente; g. paziente; h. cattivo; i. generoso;
j. alto; k. grosso; l. noioso; m. brutto; n. divertente

Il fisico	La personalità

4. Complete the words

a. Sono noi_ _ _ (m)

b. Sono bel_ _ (m)

c. Sono spor_ _ _ _ (f)

d. Sono test_ _ _ _ (m)

e. Sono gener_ _ _ (f)

f. Sono al_ _ (f)

g. Sono sim_ _ _ _ _ _ (f)

h. Sono gro_ _ _ (m)

5. Translate into English

a. Mia sorella maggiore è generosa

b. Mio fratello minore è buono

c. Mio cugino è noioso

d. Mia cugina è divertente

e. Sono alto e magro

f. Sono molto intelligente

g. Sono abbastanza sportiva

h. La mia amica Valentina è forte

6. Spot and correct the translation mistakes

a. **Sono forte**: He is strong

b. **Lei è grossa**: He is slim

c. **Sono molto bella**: I am very ugly

d. **Mi madre è alta**: My mother is short

e. **Mio fratello è basso**: My brother is tall

f. **Mia sorella è gentile**: My sister is boring

g. **Mio padre è buono**: My father is mean

7. Complete

a. M_a m_ _ _ e è g_ _ _ile

b. M_o f_ _ t_ _ _ _o è te_ _ _ _ _do

c. Mi_ p_ _ re è br_ _to ma simp_ _ ico

d. S_ _o f_ _ _ e e b_ _ _ _a

e. Lu_ è t_ _ _ a_ _ _ _

f. Le_ è ca_ _ _ _ v_ _

8. English to Italian translation

a. I am strong and funny (f)

b. My mother is very stubborn

c. My sister is short and slim

d. My brother is intelligent and sporty

e. I am friendly and generous (f)

f. My father is tall and fat

g. My brother is strong and funny

h. I am strong and tall (m)

i. I am slim and sporty (f)

j. My mother is intelligent and friendly

k. My sister is generous but stubborn

l. I am not shy, I am sociable (f)

Grammar Time 1: ESSERE - To be (Part 1)

		Masculine (singular)
io	**sono** *I am*	alt<u>o</u> antipatico
tu	**sei** *you are*	basso chiacchierone *chatty*
lui mio fratello mio padre	**è** *he is*	forte grosso magro paziente simpatico

		Masculine (plural)
noi mio padre ed io	**siamo** *we are*	alti antipatici bassi
voi	**siete** *you all are*	chiacchieroni forti
loro, essi i miei fratelli i miei genitori	**sono** *they are*	grossi magri pazienti simpatici

		Feminine (singular)
io	**sono** *I am*	alta antipatica
tu	**sei** *you are*	bassa magra
lei mia sorella mia madre	**è** *she is*	forte grossa chiacchierona paziente simpatica

		Feminine (plural)
noi mia madre ed io	**siamo** *we are*	alte antipatiche basse
voi	**siete** *you all are*	chiacchierone forti
loro, esse le mie sorelle le mie zie	**sono** *they are*	grosse magre pazienti simpatiche

Present indicative of *"Essere"* (to be) – Drills 1

1. Match up

1. Siamo	*a. I am*
2. Sono	*b. You are*
3. Sei	*c. He is*
4. È	*d. They are*
5. Siete	*e. We are*
6. Sono	*f. You all are*

2. Complete with the missing forms of *'Essere'*

a. (io) __________ molto chiacchierone   *[I am very talkative]*

b. Mia madre _______ divertente   *[My mother is funny]*

c. Le mie sorelle _________ pazienti   *[My sisters are patient]*

d. Noi ____________ molto pigri   *[We are very lazy]*

e. I miei genitori ________ severi   *[My parents are strict]*

f. Come ________ tu?   *[What are you like?]*

g. Tu _______ generoso e timido   *[You are generous and shy]*

h. Voi _______ molto forti!   *[You all are very strong!]*

3. Translate into English

a. Mio padre è simpatico.

b. Mia madre è chiacchierona.

c. I miei fratelli sono timidi.

d. Mia sorella minore non è molto alta.

e. Il mio migliore *[best]* amico è bello.

f. Mio nonno è molto gentile.

g. Mia sorella maggiore è molto buona.

h. Voi siete abbastanza sportivi.

4. Complete with the missing letters.

a. Noi siam_ molto simp_tici *[We are very friendly]*

b. Mia madre _ molto severa *[My mother is very strict]*

c. I miei genitori s_ _ _ molto pazient_
[My parents are very patient]

d. I miei cugini s_ _o un po' antipatici
[My cousins are a bit unfriendly]

e. Mia sorella __ un po' grossa *[My sister is a bit fat]*

f. Voi s _ _ _ _ molto chiacchieroni!
[You are very talkative]

g. S_ _ _ un po' timido *[I am a bit shy]*

h. I miei amici s_ _ _ molto gentili
[My friends are very kind]

i. Come s_ _ tu? *[What are you like?]*

5. Translate into Italian

a. You are: (tu) _ _ _

b. He is: (lui) _

c. You guys are: (voi) _ _ _ _ _

d. They are: (loro) _ _ _ _ _

e. We are: (noi) _ _ _ _ _

f. She is: (lei) _

6. Spot and correct the errors.

a. Mi madre e molto simpatica

b. I miei genitori siamo molto pazienti e gentile

c. Mia sorella sei antipatico

d. Mia sorella ed io sono alta

e. Come siamo tu?

Present indicative of "Essere" (to be) – Drills 2

7. Complete with the missing letters

a. Sia____o alti *[We are tall]*

b. Se__ basso *[You are short]*

c. Mia madre __ magra *[My mother is slim]*

d. I miei professori so____ molto buoni
[My teachers are very good]

e. S__i molto bella *[You are very pretty]*

f. Non s__no timido *[I am not shy]*

g. Mio fratello ed io s____mo molto diligenti
[My brother and I are very hard-working]

h. Lui ____ molto simpatico *[He is very nice]*

8. Complete with the missing forms of the verb ESSERE

a. Mia madre ______

b. I miei genitori ______

c. (io) ______

d. (loro) ______

e. Mia madre ed io ______

f. Mio nonno ______

g. Tu e le tue sorelle ________

h. Tu ________

i. Voi __________

9. Complete with the missing forms of ESSERE

a. (io) ________ di Londra.

b. Mia madre ______ molto alta e bella.

c. I miei amici________ molto simpatici.

d. Mio fratello ______ abbastanza sportivo.

e. (io) ________ un po' grosso.

f. (loro) ______ basse.

g. Mio fratello ed io ________ forti.

h. Mio cugino Andrea ______ italiano.

10. Translate into Italian. Make sure the <u>underlined words</u> have a feminine ending in Italian ('a')

a. My mother is <u>tall</u>

b. My father is short

c. My brother is not bad

d. My sister is <u>generous</u>

e. My grandfather is strict

f. My grandmother is patient

g. My mother is intelligent

11. English to Italian translation. Make sure that the <u>words underlined</u> end in the plural forms, as shown in the example below:

Ex. My mother and my sister are very **<u>tall</u>**: *Mia madre e mia sorella sono molto alte*

a. My sisters are **patient** and **nice**: ______________________________

b. My parents are very **friendly**: ______________________________

c. I (f) am talkative and lazy:______________________________

d. My brother and I are very **tall**: ______________________________

e. My mother and my sister are **beautiful**: ______________________________

f. My girlfriend and her (sua) sister are very **short**:______________________________

Grammar Time 2: AVERE – to have (Part 1)
(Present indicative)

Io	**ho** *I have*		**biondi** *blond*
Tu	**hai** *you have*		**castani** *brown*
Lui			**colorati** *coloured*
Lei			**neri** *black*
Mia sorella			**rossi** *red*
Mio fratello	**ha** *he/she has*		**scuri** *dark brown*
Mia madre		**i capelli** *the hair*	**corti** *short*
Mio padre			**di media lunghezza** *mid length*
			lunghi *long*
Noi			**a spazzola** *spiky*
Mio padre ed io	**abbiamo** *we have*		**lisci** *straight*
Mia madre ed io			**ondulati/mossi** *wavy*
Voi	**avete** *you all have*		**rasati** *very short/crew-cut*
			ricci *curly*
			scalati *layered*
Loro			**azzurri/blu** *blue*
I miei fratelli	**hanno** *they have*		**marroni** *brown*
I miei genitori		**gli occhi** *the eyes*	**neri** *black*
			verdi *green*
			grandi *big*
			piccoli *small*

Verb drills

1. Translate into English	**2. Spot and correct the mistakes**
a. Abbiamo i capelli neri.	a. Mia madre ha il capello biondo.
b. Lui ha i capelli biondi e ondulati.	b. I miei fratelli hanno i cappeli neri.
c. Tu hai i capelli a spazzola.	c. (Io) ha i capelli castani e lunghi.
d. Voi avete i capelli rossi e di media lunghezza.	d. Lui hanno i capelli cortis è lisci.
e. Loro hanno gli occhi verdi e grandi.	e. (Noi) abbiamo capelli rossi e rici.
f. Lei ha gli occhi azzurri e piccoli.	f. Tu avete i capelli biondi è scalati.
g. Noi abbiamo i capelli castani e gli occhi neri.	

3. Complete with the missing verb ending

a. (Io) H___ i capelli biondi.

b. Mia madre h__ gli occhi azzurri

c. Le mie sorelle han___ i capelli rossi

d. Mio padre h___ i capelli grigi

e. (Noi) abbi______ i capelli neri

f. Mio nonno h___ i capelli bianchi

g. Tu h_____ gli occhi marroni

h. Mio cugino ed io abbia___ i capelli rossi

i. (Voi) Av_____ i capelli lunghi?

j. Mio fratello ed io abb_______ i capelli corti.

k. La mia amica Alberta h__ gli occhi scuri.

l. (Voi) Av_____ i capelli mossi e corti.

m. (Io) H___ i capelli castani e mossi

n. (Tu) H___ i capelli neri come tua madre?

4. Complete with: *ha, abbiamo* or *hanno*

a. Mia madre ______ i capelli biondi e mossi

b. I miei genitori ________ gli occhi marroni

c. Mia sorella ed io ___________ i capelli rossi

d. I miei nonni _________ i capelli bianchi

e. I miei genitori ________ gli occhi verdi

f. Noi ____________ i capelli castani e lunghi

g. Mia sorella minore ed io __________ i capelli neri ed ondulati.

h. Mio cugino _____ i capelli di media lunghezza.

i. Le mie tre sorelle __________ i capelli lisci.

5. Translate into Italian

a. We have black hair

b. You all have long hair

c. You guys have blue eyes

d. She has green eyes

e. My father has brown curly hair

f. My sister has blond straight hair

g. My uncle has grey short hair

h. My grandfather has no hair

i. My father and I have blond hair

j. My uncle Paolo has green eyes

6. Guided writing – Write a text in <u>the first person singular</u> (*Io*) including the details below:

- ➢ You are 10 years old
- ➢ You have a brother and a sister
- ➢ Your brother is 15
- ➢ He has brown, straight, short hair and green eyes
- ➢ He is tall and handsome
- ➢ You have a sister
- ➢ She is 12
- ➢ She has black, curly, long hair and brown eyes
- ➢ Your parents are short, have dark hair and brown eyes

7. Write an 80 to 100 words text in Italian in which you describe four people you know very well, relatives, or friends. You must include their:

a. Name

b. Age

c. Hair (colour, length and type)

d. Eye colour

e. If they wear glasses or not

f. Their physical description

g. Their personality description

UNIT 6 (Part 2/2)
Describing my family and saying why I like/dislike them:
'Ti piace tuo/tua...? Perché?'
Do you like your...? Why?

Ci sono <u>**quattro**</u> **persone nella mia famiglia** *There are <u>four</u> people in my family...* **La mia famiglia è composta da...** *My family consists of...* **Nella mia famiglia** *siamo* **in quattro** *We are a family of four...*	**mio nonno Alfonso** *my grandfather Alfonso* **mio padre Giuseppe** *my father Giuseppe* **mio zio Luciano** *my uncle Luciano* **mio fratello maggiore/minore Davide** *my big/little brother Davide* **mio cugino Marco** *my cousin Marco*	**Mi piace mio ________ perché è** *I like my ________ because he is* **Mio padre è molto/abbastanza** *My dad is very/quite* **Mio padre è anche un po'** *My dad is also a bit*	**antipatico** *unfriendly* **bello** *handsome* **bravo** *good* **cattivo** *bad* **educato** *polite* **generoso** *generous* **noioso** *boring* **severo** *strict* **simpatico** *nice/friendly* **sportivo** *sporty* **divertente** *fun* **forte** *strong* **gentile** *kind*
Vado d'accordo con... *I get on well with...* **Non vado d'accordo...** *I do not get on well with*	**mia nonna Luigina** *my grandmother Luigina* **mia madre Lina** *my mother Lina* **mia zia, Anna** *my aunt Anna* **mia sorella maggiore /minore Emanuela** *my big/little sister Emanuela* **mia cugina Lara** *my girl cousin Lara*	**Mi piace mia ________ perché è** *I like my _____ because she is* **Mia madre è molto/abbastanza** *My mum is very/quite* **Mia madre è anche un po'** *My mum is also a bit*	**antipatica** **bella** **brava** **cattiva** **educata** **generosa** **noiosa** **severa** **simpatica** **sportiva** **divertente** **forte** **gentile**

Unit 6. Describing my family: VOCABULARY BUILDING

1. Complete with the missing word

a. Nella mia famiglia _________ in…[*We are… in my family*]

b. Ci sono__________ persone [*There are five people*]

c. Mia _________ Giulia __… [*My mother Giulia is…*]

d. Vado d' __________con mio… [*I get on well with my…*]

e. Non ______d'accordo con mio nonno
[*I don't get on well with my grandfather*]

f. Mio zio___ molto educato [*My uncle is very polite*]

g. Mia _____ è molto simpatica [*My aunt is very nice*]

2. Match up

1. forte	a. *intelligent*
2. simpatica	b. *kind*
3. intelligente	c. *good*
4. bravo	d. *fun*
5. chiacchierone	e. *boring*
6. divertente	f. *generous*
7. generoso	g. *friendly*
8. gentile	h. *polite*
9. educato	i. *talkative*
10. noioso	j. *pretty*
11. bella	k. *strong*

3. Translate into English

a. Mi piace mio zio =

b. …perché è generoso =

c. È molto sportivo =

d. Vado d'accordo con… =

e. Non mi piace mia zia…=

f. …perché è cattiva e severa =

g. Sono gentile =

h. Mio nonno è chiacchierone =

4. Add the missing letter

a. gent_le   c. _impatico   e. _ugino   g. d'ac_ordo   i. ci s_no   k. mi pi_ce

b. pers_ne   d. n_ioso   f. di_ertente   h. ant_patico   j. m_lto   l. per_hé

5. Broken words

a. N___ m__ fam______c_ s____ [*In my family there are*]

b. Q_________ p____________ [*Four people*]

c. M___ m_________ è m _______s____________________
[*My mother is very nice*]

d. V______ d'___________c____ [*I get on well with*]

e. M___ z_____ è m________ g________________
[*My uncle is very generous*]

f. L_ m_____ f__________ è c___________ da…
[*My family consists of…*]

g. M__ s_________ h___ i c___________ l___________
[*My sister has long hair*]

h. M___ p_______ è a_____________i________________
[*My father is quite clever*]

6. Complete with a suitable word

a. Ci sono quattro______________

b. _______ simpatica

c. ________ d'accordo

d. È molto _________________

e. Ha i ___________ biondi

f. _____ piace mia madre

g. Vado ___________ con mia nonna

h. …perché è _________ e buona

i. Ha gli ________blu e grandi

j. Mio cugino è _______ divertente

k. Mia _________ è intelligente

l. Mio nonno ha settanta _______

Unit 6. Describing my family: READING

Mi chiamo Alice. Ho nove anni e vivo a Glasgow, in Scozia. Siamo in cinque nelle mia famiglia: mio padre Mariusz, mia madre Giulia e le mie due sorelle, Olivia e Luna. Vado d'accordo con mia madre perché è paziente e gentile. **Invece** *[instead]* non vado d'accordo con Olivia perché è antipatica.

Mi chiamo Malika. Sono africana e vivo a Reggio Calabria, nel sud dell'Italia. Mi piace molto mio nonno perché è molto divertente . È intelligente ma timido.
Mio padre è abbastanza alto e grosso. Ha gli occhi marroni e i capelli rasati.

Mi chiamo Manolo. Ho quindici anni, sono argentino e vivo in Sicilia. Ho i capelli biondi a spazzola. Nella mia famiglia siamo in sei. Non vado d'accordo con mia sorella perché è testarda e antipatica. Vado d'accordo con i miei cugini perché sono molto simpatici.
Il mio cugino preferito si chiama Ian, è muscoloso e forte. È anche divertente ed educato. Ha i capelli scuri e corti e porta gli occhiali.

Sono Carlo Rossetti. Ho dieci anni e vivo a Milano, il capoluogo della Lombardia. Sono bello e intelligente. Nelle mia famiglia ci sono otto persone in totale. Mi piace mio zio Cesare e vado d'accordo **con lui** *[with him]* perché è simpatico e allegro. Invece, non mi piace mia zia perché è antipatica e severa!
Mia zia Maria ha i capelli biondi e ricci e gli occhi azzurri, **come me** *[like me]*. Il suo compleanno è il cinque maggio.

Mi chiamo Vasile. Ho dieci anni e vivo a Garda, in Italia. La mia famiglia è composta da cinque persone. Non vado d'accordo con mio padre perché è molto noioso e severo. Mi piace molto mia nonna perché è brava e generosa.

1. Find the Italian for the following items in Malika's text

a. I am called:

b. in the south:

c. my grandfather:

d. but:

e. very:

f. my father:

g. brown eyes:

h. very short hair:

2. Answer the following questions about Carlo's text

a. How old is he?
____

b. Where is he from?
____

c. Who does he get on well with?
____

d. Why does he like Cesare?
____

e. Who does he not like?
____

f. What does Maria look like?
____

3. Complete with the missing words

Mi chiamo Francesca e ____otto anni. Sono indiana ma vivo ____ Verona. Nella mia familia ci ______sei persone. Vado d'accordo ____mio nonno perché ___ molto simpatico __ buono. Mio padre____ i capelli corti e ____ occhi verdi.

4. Find someone who? – answer the questions below about all 5 texts

a. Who has a granny who is very good?
____

b. Who is 15 years old?
____

c. Who celebrates their birthday on the 5th May?
____

d. Who is African?
____

e. Who gets on well with her mother?
____

f. Who has brown eyes and very short hair?
____

g. Who is muscular and strong?
____

Unit 6. Describing my family: TRANSLATION

1. Faulty translation: spot and correct any translation mistakes (in the English) you find below

a. Nella mia famiglia siamo in quattro:
In my family I have fourteen people

b. Mia madre Lina e mia sorella Katia:
My mother Lina is my cousin Katia

c. Non vado d'accordo con mio padre:
I get on very well with my father

d. Mio zio ha la barba:
My uncle has a moustache

e. Ivan è molto simpatico e gentile:
Ivan is very unfriendly and fun

2. From Italian to English

a. Mi piace mio nonno.

b. Mia nonna è molto brava.

c. Mio cugino ha i capelli rasati.

d. Vado d'accordo con mio fratello maggiore.

e. Non vado d'accordo con mia cugina perché è noiosa e chiacchierona.

f. Mi piace mio zio perché è generoso.

g. Mio padre è simpatico e divertente.

h. Mio fratello minore è sportivo e gentile.

i. Non vado d'accordo con mio cugino Luca perché è stupido e cattivo.

3. Phrase-level translation

a. He is nice

b. She is generous

c. I get on well with...

d. I do not get along well with...

e. My uncle is fun

f. My little brother

g. I like my cousin Daniela

h. She has short and black hair

i. He has blue eyes

j. I don't like my granddad

k. He is very stubborn

l. ...because she is generous

4. Sentence-level translation

a. My name is Federico Bellini. I am nine years old. In my family there are four people.

b. My name is Carla. I have blue eyes. I get on well with my brother.

c. I do not like my brother because he is stubborn and stupid.

d. My name is Peter. I live in Scotland. I like my uncle David because he is kind.

e. I do not get on well with my aunt because she is boring and talkative.

f. In my family we are five. I like my father because he is friendly and polite.

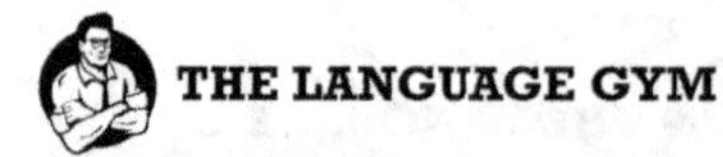

Unit 6. Describing my family: WRITING

<table>
<tr><td colspan="2">

1. Split sentences

Mio padre è	capelli neri
Mia madre è	d'accordo con
Ha gli	mio zio
Ha i	simpatico
Non mi piace	occhi neri
Mi piace molto	mia zia
Vado	generosa

</td><td colspan="2">

2. Rewrite the sentences in the correct order

a. nella sei famiglia sono ci mia persone

____

b. vado con fratello d'accordo mio

____

c. è alto zio mio e magro

____

d. mia occhi gli madre ha azzurri

____

e. mia simpatica e zia è chiacchierona

____

</td></tr>
</table>

3. Spot and correct the grammar and spelling errors

a. Nella mia familia ce

b. Vado dacordo con…

c. No mi piace mi zia…

d. Mia sorella e bello

e. Non andare d'accordo con…

f. Mio padre e generosa

g. Ho i occhi azurri

h. Mio fratella sono gentile

i. Ha il capello corti e ricci

j. Io essere simpatica

4. Anagrams

a. fagliami =

b. patiantica =

c. ducateo =

d. blela =

e. inligtelente =

f. mispatica =

g. votispor =

h. vertendite =

5. Guided writing – write 3 short paragraphs describing the people below in the first person:

Name	Age	Family	Description	Likes	Dislikes
Piero	12	4 people	mother: brown eyes, long blond hair	older brother because fun	cousin Gemma because unfriendly
Leo	11	5 people	father: green eyes, short black hair	grandma: because very generous	uncle Emilio: because stubborn
Mike	10	3 people	grandpa: blue eyes, very short grey hair	younger sister: because polite and kind	aunt Carolina: very strong but talkative

6. Describe this person in the third person (*lui*/he):

Name: Uncle Antonio

Hair: blond, crew-cut

Eyes: blue

Opinion: get on well

Physical: tall and strong

Personality: nice, fun, generous.

UNIT 7
Talking about pets

Grammar Time: AVERE (pets and description)
Questions skills: Age / Descriptions / Pets

In this unit will learn how to say in Italian

- what pets you have at home
- what pet you would like to have
- what their name is
- some more adjectives to describe appearance and personality
- key question words

You will also learn how to ask questions about
- Name / age / appearance / quantity

You will revisit the following
- Introducing oneself
- Family members
- Describing people
- The verb *'Avere'* (to have) in the present indicative

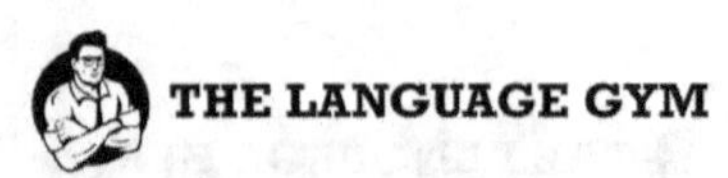

Talking about pets
'Che animale hai in casa?'
What pet do you have at home?

In casa ho *At home I have* **Non ho** *I don't have* **Il mio amico Fabio ha…** *My friend Fabio has…*	**un cane** *a dog* **un cavallo** *a horse* **un coniglio** *a rabbit* **un criceto** *a hamster* **un gatto** *a cat* **un pappagallo** *a parrot* **un pesce** *a fish* **un porcellino d'India** *a guinea pig* **un ragno** *a spider* **un serpente** *a snake* **un topo** *a mouse* **un uccello** *a bird*	**che si chiama Alfredo** *that is called Alfredo* **è** *he/it is*	**piccolo** *small* **grande** *big* **arancione** *orange* **bianco** *white* **giallo** *yellow* **marrone** *brown* **rosso** *red* **verde** *green* **buffo** *funny* **carino** *cute* **divertente** *fun* **intelligente** *clever* **noioso** *boring*
Mi piacerebbe avere *I would like to have* **Non mi piacerebbe avere** *I wouldn't like to have*	**una gallina** *a chicken* **una giraffa** *a giraffe* **una scimmia** *a monkey* **una tartaruga** *a turtle*	**che si chiama Mya** *that is called Mya* **è** *she/it is*	**piccola** *small* **grande** *big* **arancione** *orange* **bianca** *white* **gialla** *yellow* **marrone** *brown* **nera** *black* **rossa** *red* **verde** *green* **buffa** *funny* **carina** *cute* **divertente** *fun* **intelligente** *clever* **noiosa** *boring*

Unit 7. Talking about pets: VOCABULARY BUILDING

1. Complete with the missing word

a. In casa ho un u______________ *[I have a bird at home]*

b. Non ho un c______________ *[I don't have a rabbit]*

c. Mi piacerebbe avere un c________ *[I'd like to have a dog]*

d. Non mi piacerebbe avere una t________________in casa *[I wouldn't like to have a turtle at home]*

e. Abbiamo un g__________ *[We have a cat]*

f. Non ho un s________________ *[I don't have a snake]*

g. H_______ un ragno in casa *[I have a spider at home]*

h. Mi p______________ avere un criceto
[I'd like to have a hamster]

2. Match up

1. un gatto	a .a mouse
2. un cane	b. a hamster
3. un cavallo	c. two fish
4. un uccello	d. a cat
5. un pesce	e. a turtle
6. una tartaruga	f. a fish
7. un criceto	g .a guinea pig
8. un pappagallo	h. a dog
9. due pesci	i. a parrot
10. un topo	j. a bird
11. un porcellino d'India	k. a horse

3. Translate into English

a. Ho un can**e**.

b. La mia amica Giovanna ha un pappagallo.

c. Io ho due pesci.

d. Non ho animali in casa.

e. Ho tre cani.

f. Mi piacerebbe avere un criceto.

g. In giardino abbiamo una tartaruga.

h. Il mio gatto ha cinque anni.

4. Add the missing letter

a. Il mio ca_e

b. Una tartar_ga

c. Un pap_agallo

d. Due pe_ci

e. Un pes_ e

f. Un ga _to

g. Un cric_to

h. Un uccel_o

5. Anagrams

a. anec = cane

b. attgo =

c. tagarutar =

d. scepe =

e. penteser =

f. poto =

g. gnora =

h. nicoglio =

6. Broken words

a. I_ c_______ h____ u__ c________ = *[At home I have a dog]*

b. Il mio a________ h___ u___ p_______ = *[My friend has a fish]*

c. M__ f__________ h___ u___ t________________
= *[My brother has a turtle]*

d. N____ h___ u___ c____________ = *[I don't have a rabbit]*

e. H___ u_____ g____________ = *[I have a chicken]*

f. Alex h__ u__ p__________ d'______ = *[Alex has a guinea pig]*

g. H____ u__ p______ a__________ = *[I have a blue fish]*

7. Complete with a suitable word

a. Ho dieci ______________ in casa.

b. Il mio pesce si ___________ Rex.

c. Mio nonno _______ un cane.

d. Mio fratello ha ______ criceto.

e. In _________ ho due animali.

f. Ho ______ gallina e una _________
in giardino.

g. Non ho un _____________ in casa.

h. In casa ho due _______________.

Unit 7. Talking about pets: READING

Mi chiamo Elisa. Ho otto anni e vivo a Edimburgo. Nella mia famiglia siamo in quattro: i miei genitori, mio fratello minore che si chiama Leo ed io. Leo è molto antipatico e fastidioso. Abbiamo due animali: un cane che si chiama Artù e un gatto che si chiama Zeus. Artù è molto veloce. Zeus è antipatico, proprio **come** *[like]* mio fratello!

Mi chiamo Robert e sono inglese. Ho nove anni e vivo a Verona. Ci sono quattro persone nella mia famiglia. Mio fratello maggiore si chiama Jack. Lui ha dodici anni ed è un simpaticone *[funny guy]*. Abbiamo due animali: un pappagallo che si chiama Rico e un gatto che si chiama Max. Rico è molto buffo. Max è un simpaticone, come mio fratello!

Mi chiamo Kumar e sono un bambino dello Sri Lanka. Ho nove anni e abito a Milano. La mia famiglia è composta da cinque persone: i miei genitori, due fratelli che si chiamano Arjuna e Hashan, ed io. Arjuna è molto chiacchierone. Hashan è molto serio e lavoratore. In casa abbiamo due animali: il criceto Sam e la tartaruga Bella. Il criceto è buffo e vivace. Bella è molto seria, come mio fratello Hashan.

Mi chiamo Li Xiang e vivo a Prato, vicino Firenze. Ho dieci anni. Nella mia famiglia ci sono cinque persone: i miei genitori, le mie sorelle che si chiamano Shan e Mei ed io. Shan è molto generosa e gentile. Mei è un po' testarda e noiosa. Abbiamo due animali: un coniglio che si chiama Busy e un criceto che si chiama Lazy. Busy è molto tranquillo e carino. Lazy è rumorosa e **vivace** *[lively]*.

1. Find the Italian for the following in Elisa's text

a. two pets

b. which is called

c. a cat

d. very fast

e. like my brother

f. my parents

g. my name is

h. is unfriendly

i. we are four

2. Find someone who? – answer the questions below about Elisa, Robert, Li Xiang and Kumar

a. Who has a cat?

b. Who has a parrot?

c. Who has a hamster?

d. Who has a guinea pig?

e. Who has a rabbit?

f. Who has a dog?

3. Answer the following questions about Kumar's text

a. Where does Kumar live?

b. What is his brother Hashan like?

c. Who is fun and lively?

d. Who is like Hashan?

e. Who is Arjuna?

f. Who is Bella?

g. Who is Sam?

5. Fill in the blanks

Mi c______ Gianni. Ho undici a______ , sono italiano e v___ a Roma. Nella mia famiglia s____ in sei: i miei g______, due sorelle che si c______ Ale e Marta. Ale ___ molto chiacchierona e gentile. Marta è u___ po' pigra _____ antipatica. Ho due a_______ in casa: un pesce c_____ si chiama Maya e un gatto che s___ chiama Swift. Swift___ divertente e vivace. Maya è m______ pigra, c_______ m____ s________ Marta!

4. Fill in the table below

Name	Gianni	Robert
Age		
City/Nationality		
Pets		
Description of pets		

Unit 7. Talking about pets: TRANSLATION

1. Faulty translation: spot and correct any translation mistakes you find below

a. Nella mia famiglia ci sono quattro persone e due animali: *In my family there are four people and three pets.*

b. Abbiamo due animali in casa, un cane e una scimmia: *At home we have two pets: a dog and a rabbit.*

c. Il mio amico Paco ha una tartaruga che si chiama Speedy. Speedy è molto buffa: *My friend Paco has a duck called Speedy. Speedy is very boring.*

d. Mio fratello ha un cavallo che si chiama Dylan: *My sister has a parrot called Dylan.*

e. Mia madre ha una gallina che si chiama Lella: *My father has a frog called Lella.*

f. Ho un gatto che si chiama Sleepy. Sleepy è molto vivace: *I have a dog called Sleepy. Sleepy is very beautiful.*

2. Translate into English

a. Un gatto simpaticone =

b. Un cane buffo e veloce =

c. Una gallina rumorosa =

d. Una tartaruga pigra =

e. Un cavallo intelligente =

f. Una scimmia vivace =

g. Un criceto curioso =

h. Ho due animali =

i. Non abbiamo animali in casa =

j. Mi piacerebbe avere un cane =

k. Non mi piacerebbe avere un pesce =

l. Ho un porcellino d'India ma mi piacerebbe avere un serpente =

3. Phrase-level translation [En to It]

a. a boring dog=

b. a lively parrot =

c. at home =

d. we have =

e. a beautiful horse =

f. a curious cat =

g. a funny monkey=

h. I have =

i. I don't have =

j. I would like to have =

4. Sentence-level translation [En to It]

a. My brother has a horse who is called Rayo.

b. My sister has a big turtle who is called Nicole.

c. I have a fat hamster called Pancione.

d. At home we have three pets: a fish, a rabbit and a parrot.

e. I have a rat called Stuart.

f. At home we have two pets: a dog and a hamster

g. I have two fish which are called Nemo and Dory

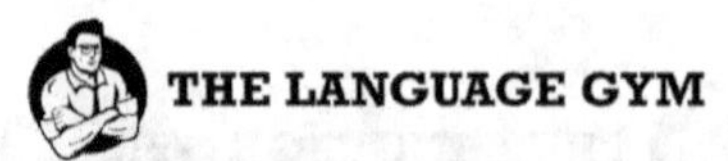

Unit 7. Talking about pets: WRITING

1. Split sentences

Ho un cane che	bianca
In casa abbiamo	avere un cavallo
Ho una gallina	si chiama Speedy
Ho un gatto	una scimmia
Mi piacerebbe	due animali
Mio fratello ha	casa
Non ho animali in	nero

2. Rewrite the sentences in the correct order

a. animali abbiamo In tre casa

b. un piacerebbe avere Mi topo

c. un Ho gatto un cane e

d. criceto amico nero Il mio ha Luigi un

e. Kiki verde un che Abbiamo si uccello chiama

f. due Abbiamo azzurri pesci

g. ha chiama sorella un che si Mia pappagallo Mango

3. Spot the mistake and rewrite the correct sentence[note: in several cases a word is missing]

a. In casa un cane e un gatto

b. Ho criceto nera

c. Piacerebbe avere un serpente

d. Mi avere una scimmia simpatica

e. Il amico Piero a due pesci

f. Il mio cavallo chiama Graham

g. Ho una cavallo bianco

h. In casa abiamo tre cane

4. Anagrams

a. neca =

b. miascim =

c. valloca =

d. llagina =

e. glioconi =

f. tocrice =

g. cellocu =

6. Describe this person in the third person:

Name: Massimo

Hair: blond, short

Eyes: green

Personality: very nice

Physical: tall, muscular

Pets: a dog, a cat and two fish
and would like to have a spider

5. Guided writing – write 3 short paragraphs (in 1st person)describing the pets below using the details in the box

Name	Animal	Age	Colour	Character or appearance
Gabriele	dog	4	white	affectionate
Gianfranco	monkey	6	black	funny
Dylan	horse	1	brown	beautiful

Grammar Time 3: AVERE (Part 2)
(Pets and description)

1. Translate

a. I have: io h __

b. You have: tu h __ __

c. She has: lei h__

d. We have: noi a__ __ __ __ __ __

e. You all have: voi a__ __ __ __

f. They have: loro h__ __ __ __

2. Translate into English

a. Ho un cavallo molto bello e veloce.

b. Mio fratello ha un gatto abbastanza brutto.

c. Mia madre ha un cane molto simpatico.

d. I miei genitori hanno un serpente nero.

e. In giardino abbiamo una gallina molto rumorosa.

f. In casa Cristina ha una tartaruga pigra.

3. Complete

a. I have a guinea pig: *Ho un p__________________ d'India.*

b. It is two years old: *H______ due anni.*

c. We have a turtle. It is 4 years old: *A___________ una tartaruga. H__ quattro anni.*

d. My sister has a dog: *Mia sorella ha u__ cane*

e. My uncles have two cats: *I miei zii h__________ due gatti*

f. They are three years old: *Loro h__________ tre anni*

g. My brother and I have a snake: *Mio fratello ed io a______________ un serpente*

h. Do you have pets?: *Voi a______________animali?*

i. What animals do you all have?: *Che animali a______________?*

4. Translate into Italian

a. I have a guinea pig. It is three years old.

b. We don't have pets at home.

c. My dog is three years old. It is very big.

d. I have three brothers. They are nice and funny.

e. My cousins have a horse and a chicken.

f. My auntie has blond, curly and long hair. She is very pretty.

g. My brother and I have black hair and green eyes. We have a rabbit.

Question Skills 1: Age / Descriptions / Pets

1. Match question and answer

1. Quanti anni hai?	a. Sono di Palermo
2. Perché non vai d'accordo con tua madre?	b. Sto bene, grazie
3. Come sono i tuoi capelli?	c. Ho quindici anni
4. Di dove sei?	d. Il verde
5. Di che colore sono i tuoi occhi?	e. Perché è severa
6. Qual è il tuo colore preferito?	f. Il cane
7. Come stai?	g. Sono simpatico e chiacchierone
8. Hai animali in casa?	h. Sì, perché è paziente
9. Qual è il tuo animale preferito?	i. Il venti giugno
10. Dove vivi?	j. Sono rossi
11. Come sei di carattere?	k. Sono azzurri
12. Come sei fisicamente?	l. Sì, due. Un gatto e un pappagallo.
13. Vai d'accordo con tuo padre?	m. Vivo a Londra, in Inghilterra.
14. Quando è il tuo compleanno?	n. Sono basso e un po' magro.

2. Complete with the missing words

a. Di _______ sei?
[Where are you from?]

b. _______ è Maria (di carattere)?
[What is Maria like (personality-wise)?]

c. _______ anni ha tuo padre?
[How old is your father?]

d. _______ stai? Sto _______, grazie.
[How are you? I am well, thank you]

e. _______ è il tuo compleanno?
[When is your birthday?]

f. _______ è il tuo cane?
[What is your dog like?]

g. _______ animali hai?
[How many pets do you have?]

3. Translate the following question words into English

a. Quale?

b. Quando?

c. Dove?

d. Come?

e. Di dove?

f. Chi?

g. Quanti?

h. Cosa?

i. Perché?

5. Translate into Italian

a. What is your name?

b. How old are you?

c. What is your hair like?

d. What is your favourite animal?

e. Do you get on with your father?

f. Why don't you get on with your sister?

g. How many pets do you have?

h. Where are you from?

4. Complete

a. Q_______ a_______ hai?

b. D_ d_______ sei?

c. D_______ v_______?

d. C___ sei d_ c_______?

e. H_______u___ a_________ in casa?

f. C_______ s_______?

g. V__ d'_______ c_____ t___ p______?

UNIT 8
Saying what jobs people do, why they like/dislike them and where they work

Grammar Time:- ARE verbs like lavorare + ESSERE

In this unit will learn how to say:

- What jobs people do
- Why they like/dislike those jobs
- Where they work
- Adjectives to describe jobs
- Words for common jobs
- Words for types of buildings
- The full conjugation of the verb 'Lavorare' (to work) in the present indicative

You will revisit the following:
- Family members
- The full conjugation of the verb 'Essere' (to be)
- Description of people and pets

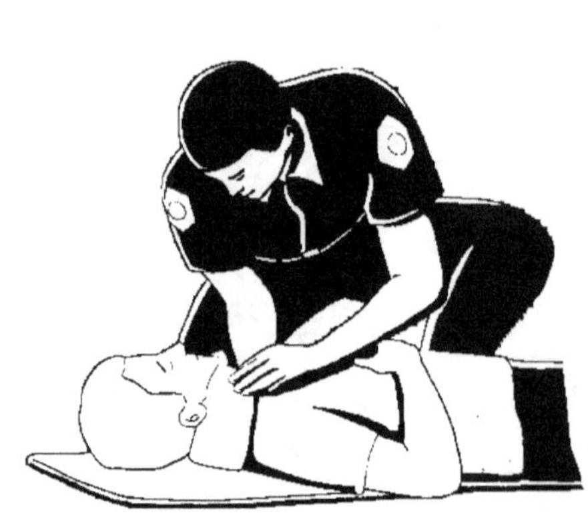

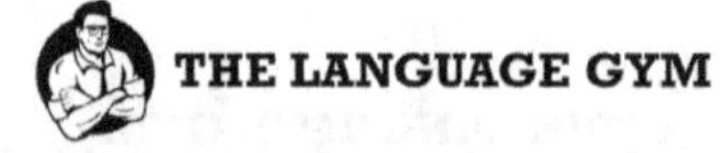

UNIT 8
Saying what jobs people do, why they like/dislike them and where they work
'Che lavora fa tuo/tua...?'
What job does your...do?

		attore *actor*		**ben pagato** *well-paid*	**Lavora in...** *He/she works in...*
		avvocato *lawyer*	**gli/le piace** *he/she likes it*		
		casalingo *house-husband*		**difficile** *difficult*	
		contabile *accountant*			**un'azienda** *a company*
Mio padre *My father*	**è** *he is*	**contadino** *farmer*		**dinamico** *dynamic*	
		cuoco *chef*			**una fabbrica** *a factory*
		infermiere *nurse*	**non gli/le piace** *he/she doesn't like it*	**divertente** *funny*	
Mio fratello *My brother*		**impiegato** *office-worker*			**campagna** *the countryside*
		uomo di affari *business man*		**facile** *easy*	
	lavora come *works as*	**ingegnere** *engineer*			**città** *the city*
Mio zio *My uncle*		**meccanico** *mechanic*			
		dottore *doctor*	**perché è...** *because it is...*		**un garage** *a garage*
		parrucchiere *hairdresser*			
		professore *teacher*		**gratificante** *rewarding*	**una fattoria** *a farm*
				interessante *interesting*	**un hotel** *a hotel*
		attrice *actress*	**(lui/ lei) ama il suo lavoro** *he/she loves his/her job*		
		avvocatessa *lawyer*			
Mia madre *My mother*		**casalinga** *house-wife*		**mal pagato** *low-paid*	**un ristorante** *a restaurant*
	è *she is*	**contabile** *accountant*			
		contadina *farmer*		**noioso** *boring*	**una scuola** *a school*
Mia sorella maggiore *My older sister*		**cuoca** *chef*			
		infermiera *nurse*			
		impiegata *office-worker*	**(lui/ lei) odia il suo lavoro** *he/she hates his/her job*	**stimolante** *exciting*	**un teatro** *a theatre*
	lavora come *works as*	**ingegnere** *engineer*			
		donna di affari *business woman*		**stressante** *stressful*	**un ufficio** *an office*
Mia zia *My aunt*		**meccanica** *mechanic*			
		dottoressa *doctor*			
		parrucchiera *hairdresser*			**Lavora da casa** *He/she works from home*
		professoressa *teacher*			

Unit 8. Saying what jobs people do: VOCABULARY BUILDING

1. Complete with the missing word

a. Mio padre è _________________ [My father is a lawyer]

b. Mia zia è _________________ [My aunt is a teacher]

c. Mio fratello lavora come _____________________
[My brother works as a mechanic]

d. Mia madre è _______________ [My mother is a doctor]

e. Mia sorella _________ lavora come _______________
[My older sister works as an engineer]

f. Mia zia è _______________ [My aunt is an accountant]

g. Mio _______ è _______________ [My uncle is a nurse]

2. Match up

1. è noioso	a. it's stressful
2. è dinamico	b. it's fun
3. è difficile	c. it's hard
4. è divertente	d. it's dynamic
5. è stimolante	e. it's rewarding
6. è stressante	f. it's boring
7. è facile	g. it's interesting
8. è gratificante	h. it's easy
9. è interessante	i. it's exciting

3. Translate into English

a. Mia madre è meccanica

b. Le piace molto il suo lavoro

c. Lavora in un garage

d. Mio fratello è contabile

e. Non gli piace il suo lavoro

f. Mio cugino è contadino

g. Lui ama il suo lavoro

h. Perché è divertente

4. Add the missing letter

a. È f_cile

b. Gli _iace

c. Ing_gnere

d. _ottoressa

e. È s_ressante

f. L_vora come

g. È in_ermiere

h. Pr_fessore

5. Anagrams

a. aDonndiafrifa =

b. cavvoAto =

c. toreDot =

d. totreA =

e. triceAt =

f. Cobintale =

g. uoCco =

h. pieImgato=

6. Broken words

a. M__ p________ è c_____________
= [My dad is a house husband]

b. G__ p________ i_ s___ l____________ = [He likes his job]

c. M__ f___________ è c__________ = [My brother is a chef]

d. L________ i__ c____________, è c________________
= [He works in the countryside, he is a farmer]

e. Lui a______ i___ s____ l________ = [He loves his job]

f. P________ è d_____________ = [Because it is dynamic]

g. ___ m______ g_____________ = [It is very rewarding]

7. Complete with a suitable word

a. Mia madre è _________________

b. Lei ___________ il suo lavoro

c. Gli piace perché è ____________

d. Lavora da _________________

e. Mio ___________ è parrucchiere

f. Non ____ piace il suo lavoro

g. Perché è molto ________________

h. ____ zia è dottoressa

i. ______ odia il suo ____________

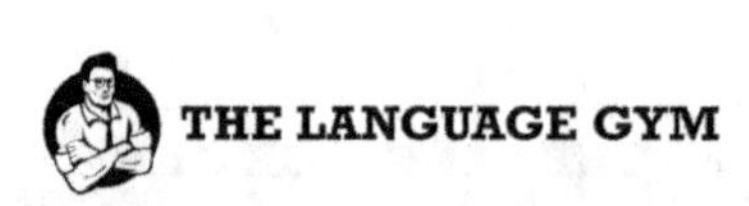

Unit 8. Saying what jobs people do: READING

Mi chiamo Filippo. Ho venti anni e vivo a Lecce, nel sud dell'Italia. Siamo in tre nella mia famiglia. Ho un cane molto divertente che si chiama Fluffy. Mio padre lavora come medico in ospedale. Lui ama il suo lavoro perché è gratificante. Mia madre Daniela è impiegata, lavora in un ufficio. A volte, è un lavoro noioso ma va d'accordo con i suoi colleghi.

Mi chiamo George. Vivo con la mia famiglia a Bergamo, nel nord dell'Italia. Che lavoro fa mio padre? Mio padre è avvocato. Gli piace il suo lavoro perché è interessante. Purtroppo, a volte è un po' stressante. Mia madre è infermiera e le piace abbastanza il suo lavoro perché è molto dinamico. Ho un cane che si chiama Dido. È affettuoso e buffo. Non mi piacciono i gatti!

Mi chiamo Fabio. Sono di Viareggio, in Toscana. Vado molto d'accordo con mia madre. È timida ma molto simpatica. Mia madre è ingegnere ed è molto impegnata. Nel futuro mi piacerebbe essere ingegnere, come mia madre! Odio mio zio, è intelligente ma cattivo. Mio zio è un uomo di affari ma odia il suo lavoro perché è difficile e viaggia molto. Ho una tartaruga che si chiama Speed. È lenta ma molto buffa.

Mi chiamo Camilla. La mia famiglia è composta da quattro persone . Mia madre si chiama Valeria ed è cuoca, lavora in un ristorante cinese in centro. Le piace il suo lavoro perché è dinamico. Mio padre è casalingo ma non gli piace molto, perché non è ben pagato ed è noioso! In casa non ho un animale ma mi piacerebbe avere un cavallo. Mio cugino fa il cuoco. Lui ha un cavallo che si chiama Apollo, è grande e veloce. **Che forte!***[Cool!]*

1. Find the Italian for the following in Filippo's text

a. I am 20

b. I have a dog

c. my dad works as…

e. in a hospital

f. he loves his work

g. it is rewarding

h. sometimes

i. a boring job

j. gets on well with colleagues

2. Answer the questions on ALL texts (in Italian)

a. Who is Apollo?

b. Whose mum is a nurse?

c. Why does Cristian love teaching in a school?

d. Whose father is a doctor?

e. Who has a turtle?

f. What is George's dog like?

3. Answer the following questions about Fabio's text

a. Where does Fabio live?

b. What is his mum like [personality]?

c. Why does he hate his uncle?

d. What job does his uncle do?

e. Who is Speed and what is she like?

f. What job would Fabio like to do and why?

4. Fill in the blanks

M__ chiamo Marina. Ho tredici a__ e v___ a Rieti, nel centro dell'Italia. Nella mia f______ ci sono cinque persone. Mio cugino Cristian ha trent'anni ed è molto div____e. Cristian è pr_____ e lavora in una s____ secondaria. Vive a Liverpool, in Inghilterra. Ama il suo l_______ perché è int______ e gra____. In casa ho __ animale piccolo ma carino. È un ra__: una tarantola!

5. Fill in the table below

Name	Marina [Pets]	Cristian [Jobs]
Age		
City		
Pets/Job		
Description of pets/job		

Unit 8. Saying what jobs people do: TRANSLATION

1. Faulty translation: spot and correct [IN THE ENGLISH] any translation mistakes you find below

a. Mio padre lavora come attore e gli piace molto perché è emozionante. Lavora in un teatro: *My father works as a cook and he really likes his job because it is interesting. He works in a school.*

b. Mia zia lavora come donna di affari in un ufficio. Le piace ma è difficile: *My aunt works as a business woman in a hair salon. She hates it but it's hard.*

c. Il mio amico Nuccio è infermiere. Lavora in un ospedale e gli piace il suo lavoro: *My friend Nuccio works as a doctor. He lives in a hospital and hates his work.*

d. Mio zio Gianfranco è cuoco in un ristorante italiano e lo trova divertente: *My uncle Gianfranco is a lawyer in an Italian firm and he finds it fun.*

e. Mia madre Susan è contabile e lavora da casa. Odia il suo lavoro perché è ripetitivo: *My mother Susan is an actress and works in an office. She loves her work because it is dynamic.*

3. Phrase-level translation [En to It]

a. my big brother =

b. works as =

c. a farmer =

d. he likes =

e. his job =

f. because it's dynamic =

g. and fun =

h. but it's tough =

2. Translate into English

a. Mio zio lavora come =

b. Mio padre è contabile =

c. Sono casalingo =

d. Sono infermiere =

e. *Faccio <u>la</u> cuoca=

f. *Faccio <u>l</u>'avvocato =

g. Le piace il suo lavoro=

h. Lavora in una fabbrica =

i. Lavora in un teatro =

j. Lavora in un'azienda =

k. È gratificante =

l. È difficile ma stimolante =

Author's note: *Faccio means "I do". You can say you do a job, however the verb **fare** "to do" must be followed by a definite article: *Faccio <u>la</u> cuoca*

4. Sentence-level translation [En to It]

a. My brother is a mechanic

b. My father is a business man

c. My uncle is a farmer and hates his job

d. My sister works from home

e. At home I have a snake called Sally

f. We have a friendly dog and a mean cat

g. My aunt is a nurse. She likes her job…

h. …because it is rewarding

i. My mother works in a hospital

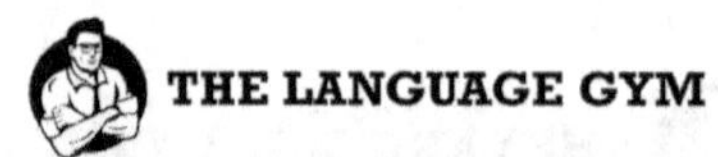

Unit 8. Saying what jobs people do: WRITING

1. Split sentences

1. Mio fratello	*a. donna di affari*
2. Mia zia lavora	*b. è avvocato*
3. Mia madre lavora come	*c. il professore*
4. Gli piace perché	*d. ma gratificante*
5. Lei odia	*e. in un'azienda*
6. Faccio	*f. il suo lavoro*
7. È difficile	*g. è stimolante*

2. Rewrite the sentences in the correct order

a. Le suo il lavoro piace molto

b. Lavora in un contabile come ufficio

c. casa da Mia lavora madre

d. come zio contadino Mio lavora

e. lavora Mio fratello un teatro in

f. Mio odia suo nonno lavoro il

g. mia amica La lavora un ristorante in

3. Spot the mistake and rewrite the correct sentence [note: in several cases a word is missing]

a. Mia zia e casalinga

b. È un lavoro noiosa e dinamica

c. Mi sorella lavora avvocatessa

d. Lei odia il suo lavoro perche e dificile

e. Faccio il dottore un ospedale en città

f. Le piace molto suo lavoro perché è facile

g. Mio padre odio il sua lavoro

h. Gli piace perché lavoro in campagna con l'animali.

4. Anagrams

a. eaTotr =

b. tiGracafinte =

c. Ritipetivo =

d. eL iaPce =

e. dinotaCon =

f. ranteRisto =

g. Psorfesossare =

6. Describe this person in Italian in the 3rd person

Name: Magdalena

Hair: blond + green eyes

Physical: tall and slim

Personality: hard-working, nice

Job: nurse

Opinion: likes her job a lot

Reason: stressful but rewarding

5. Guided writing – write 3 short paragraphs describing the people below using the details in the box [in 1st person]

Person	Relation	Job	Like/ Dislike	Reason
Giorgio	My dad	Mechanic	Loves	Active and interesting
Luciano	My brother	Lawyer	Hates	Boring but well-paid
Lucas	My aunt	Farmer	Likes	Tough but exciting

Grammar Time 4: The present indicative of "Lavor**are**" and other ARE verbs

io	**lavor<u>o</u>**	*I work*
tu	**lavor<u>i</u>**	*you work*
lui / mio fratello / mio padre	**lavor<u>a</u>**	*he works*
lei / mia sorella / mia madre	**lavor<u>a</u>**	*she works*
noi / mio padre ed io	**lavor<u>iamo</u>**	*we work*
voi	**lavor<u>ate</u>**	*you all work*
loro / le mie sorelle / i miei fratelli	**lavor<u>ano</u>**	*they work*

io lavoro **tu lavori** **lui/lei lavori**	**come** *as*	**casalingo/a**	*house-husband/wife*
		contadino/a	*farmer*
		cuoco/a	*chef*
		contabile	*accountant*
		infermiere/a	*nurse*
		impiegato/a	*office-worker*
		ingegnere	*engineer*
		meccanico/a	*mechanic*
		parrucchiere/a	*hairdresser*
		uomo/donna di affari	*businessman/businesswoman*
		avvoc<u>ato</u>/avvocat<u>essa</u>	*lawyer*
		dott<u>ore</u>/dottor<u>essa</u>	*doctor*
		profess<u>ore</u>/professor<u>essa</u>	*teacher*
		att<u>ore</u>/att<u>rice</u>	*actor/actress*
		scritt<u>ore</u>/scritt<u>rice</u>	*writer*

Drills

1. Match up

lavora	*I work*
lavoro	*You work*
lavorano	*He/she works*
lavorate	*We work*
lavoriamo	*You guys work*
lavori	*They work*

2. Complete with the correct option

a. Mio fratello _____________ come parrucchiere

b. I miei genitori non _______________

c. Mia sorella ed io ___________ come impiega**te**

d. La mia amica __________ come dottoressa

e. Mia madre _______________ come ingegnere

f. Voi _______________ come impiega**ti**

g. Perché tu non __________________?

h. Io non _____________ . Sono disoccupato.

lavoriamo	**lavora**	**lavorate**	**lavori**
lavorano	**lavoro**	**lavora**	**lavora**

3. Cross out the wrong option

	A	B
I miei genitori	lavorano	lavorate
Mio fratello	lavora	lavoro
Mio padre	lavori	lavora
I miei zii	lavoriamo	lavorano
Le mie zie	lavorano	lavorare
Tu ed io	lavoro	lavoriamo
Noi	lavori	lavoriamo
Voi	lavorate	lavoro
I miei cugini	lavorano	lavora
Io e lei	lavorate	lavoriamo

4. Complete the verb *Lavorare*

a. Mio fratello ed io non lavor_ _ _ _

b. I miei genitori lavor_ _ _

c. Mio padre lavor_ come avvocato

d. A volte i miei fratelli non lavor_ _ _

e. Tu non lavor_ mai !

f. Mia madre lavor_ da casa

g. Voi lavor _ _ _ come professori

h. Io lavor_ in un negozio di moda

i. Ma voi, quando lavor _ _ _?

5. Complete with the correct form of *'lavorare'*

a. I miei genitori _________________ come avvocati   *[My parents work as lawyers]*

b. Mia madre _______________ come profesoressa   *[My mother works as a teacher]*

c. Tu _______________ come contabile   *[You work as an accountant]*

d. Mio zio _________________ come contadino   *[My father works as a farmer]*

e. Mio fratello non __________________ , è disoccupato *[My brother doesn't work, he is unemployed]*

f. Le mie sorelle non __________________ nemmeno *[My sisters don't work either]*

g. Mio cugino _______________ come pompiere   *[My uncle works as a fireman]*

h. I miei amici ed io non __________________   *[My friends and I don't work]*

i. (io) _______________ in un ristorante   *[I work in a restaurant]*

j. Mia zia _______________ in un negozio di abbigliamento *[My aunt works in a clothing store]*

k. Dove _______________ (tu)?   *[Where do you work?]*

Verbs like LAVOR<u>ARE</u>

Amare: to love

Ascoltare: to listen to

Cenare: to have dinner

Giocare: to play (sport)

Mangiare: to eat

Parlare: to speak

Praticare: to practise

Studiare: to study

Viaggiare: to travel

6. Complete the sentences using the correct form of the verbs in the grey box on the left

a. Am__ i miei nonni   *[I love my grandparents]*

b. Cen__ con la sua famiglia   *[He has dinner with is family]*

c. Lei pratic__ lo sci   *[She practises skiing]*

d. Tu parl__ spagnolo?   *[Do you speak Spanish?]*

e. No, io parl__ italiano   *[No, I speak Italian]*

f. Voi studi__ _ _ matematica?   *[Do you all study mathematics?]*

g. Io ascolt__ musica rock   *[I listen to rock music]*

h. Noi mangi__ _ _ la pizza a cena   *[We eat pizza for dinner]*

Grammar Time 5: ESSERE (Part 2)
(Present indicative of "Essere" and jobs)

Present Indicative of 'Essere'		Jobs (nouns)	
		Singular	Plural
MASCULINE			
io	**sono** *I am*	**attore** *actor* **assistente di volo** *flight attendant*	assistenti di volo attori
tu	**sei** *you are*	**avvocato** *lawyer* **calciatore** *footballer*	avvocati calciatori
lui mio fratello mio padre	**è** *he is*	**commesso** *salesperson* **contabile** *accountant* **contadino** *farmer*	commessi contabili contadini
noi mio padre ed io	**siamo** *we are*	**cuoco** *chef* **dipendente** *shop assistant* **dottore/medico** *doctor*	cuochi dipendenti dottori/medici
voi	**siete** *you all are*	**infermiere** *nurse* **ingegnere** *engineer*	infermieri ingegneri
loro i miei fratelli i miei genitori	**sono** *they are*	**meccanico** *mechanic* **parrucchiere** *hair dresser* **professore** *teacher* **operaio** worker **scienziato** *scientist*	meccanici parrucchieri professori operai scienziati
FEMININE			
io	**sono** *I am*	**attrice** **avvocatessa**	attrici avvocatesse
tu	**sei** *you are*	**calciatrice** **commessa**	calciatrici commesse
lei mia sorella mia madre	**è** *she is*	**contabile** **contadina** **cuoca**	contabili contadine cuoche
noi mia madre ed io	**siamo** *we are*	**dipendente** **dottoressa** **infermiera**	dipendenti dottoresse infermiere
voi	**siete** *you all are*	**ingegnere** **meccanica**	ingegnere meccaniche
loro le mie sorelle le mie zie	**sono** *they are*	**operaia** **parrucchiera** **professoressa** **scienziata**	operaie parrucchiere professoresse scienziate

Drills

1. Match

Sono	She/he is
Siamo	You are
Sono	We are
Sei	I am
È	They are
Siete	You all are

3. Translate into English

a. Siamo parrucchieri

____

 b. Sono poliziotti

____

c. Sei pompiere o contadino?

____

d. Tracy lavora come modella

____

e. Sono operai in un cantiere [building site]

____

f. Io sono poliziotto

____

g. Voi siete infermiere

____

h. Noi siamo scienziate.

____

i. Mio padre ed io siamo attori

____

j. Voi non siete professori

____

k. Io non sono attrice, sono scrittrice

____

____

2. Complete with the missing forms of ESSERE

a. Mia madre ed io _________ dottoresse

b. I miei fratelli _________ operai

c. Mia sorella ______ infermiera

d. I miei genitori ed io _________ giardinieri [gardeners]

e. Tu _________ avvocato?

f. Io _________ pompiere

g. Loro non _________ poliziotti [policemen]

h. Voi ragazze_________ modelle? [models]

i. Voi ragazzi _________ attori, vero?

j. I miei zii _________ cuochi in un ristorante in centro

4. Translate into Italian (easier)

a. My father is a doctor

b. My parents are policemen

c. My uncle is a lawyer

d. I am a teacher

e. My cousins are mechanics

f. My aunt is a scientist

g. My friend Valentino is an actor

5. Translate into Italian (harder)

a. My brother is tall and handsome. He is an actor.

b. My older sister is very intelligent and hard-working. She is an engineer.

c. My younger brother is very sporty and active. He is a footballer.

d. My mother is very strong and hard-working. She is a scientist.

e. My father is very patient, calm and organized. He is an accountant.

UNIT 9
Comparing people's appearance and personality

In this unit will learn how to say in Italian:
- More/less … than
- As … as
- New adjectives to describe people

You will revisit the following:
- Family members
- Pets
- Describing animals' appearance and character

UNIT 9
Comparing people

Io	**sono** *am*		**affettuoso/a** *affectionate* **bello/a** *good-looking*		**Dylan** **Gianfranco**
Lei **Lui** **Mia cugina** **Mio nonno** **La mia amica Sara** **Il mio amico Ben** **Il mio cavallo** **Il mio cane** **Il mio ragazzo** *bf* **La mia ragazza** *gf* **Francesca** **Mario**	**è** *is*	**più..** *more* **meno...** *less* **tanto...** *as*	**chiacchierone/a** *chatty* **rumoroso/a** *noisy* **diligente** *hard-working* **divertente** *funny* **gentile** *kind* **giovane** *young* **grosso/a** *fat* **intelligente** *intelligent* **noioso/a** *boring* **pigro/a** *lazy* **serio/a** *serious* **sportivo/a** *sporty* **tonto/a** *silly* **tranquillo/a** *relaxed* **vecchio/a** *old*	**di...** *than* **di...** *than* **quanto...** *as*	**Simona** **Stefano** **me** *me* **te** *you* **noi** **voi** **loro** **mia madre** **mia sorella** **mio fratello** **mio padre** **mia zia** **mio zio**
I miei fratelli **I miei genitori** **I miei zii** **Le mie sorelle** **Le mie amiche** **Le mie zie**	**sono** *are*		**affettuosi/e** **gentili** **giovani** **sportivi/e** **tranquilli/e**	**del mio gatto** *than my cat* **della mia tartaruga** *than my turtle*	

Author's note: 1 The adjectives above ending in '**o**' change to '**a**' with feminine nouns. Ex. *Io sono bello/ Mia sorella è bella* 2 Feminine adjective ending in '**a**' change into '**e**' in the plural. *Ex. Le mie sorelle sono belle* 3 Adjectives ending in '**e**' do not change in the feminine. However, they change to '**i**' in the plural.
Ex: Mio fratello è intelligente / I miei fratelli sono intelligenti

 **THE LANGUAGE GYM**

Unit 9. Comparing people : VOCABULARY BUILDING

1. Complete with the missing word

a. Mio padre è più alto _______ mio fratello maggiore   *[My father is taller than my older brother]*

b. Mia madre è ________ chiacchierona di mia _________   *[My mother is less chatty than my aunt]*

c. Mio ________ è più basso di _____ padre   *[My grandfather is shorter than my father]*

d. I miei cugini sono più ___________ di _________   *[My cousins are lazier than us]*

e. Il mio cane _____ più ___________ del mio ________   *[My dog is more noisy than my cat]*

f. Mia zia è ________ bella di _______ madre   *[My aunt is less pretty than my mother]*

g. Mio ___________ è più ________________ di me   *[My brother is more hard-working than me]*

h. Il mio maestro ___ più ________________del mio pesce *[My teacher is more chatty than my fish]*

i. Mio fratello minore è ________ alto ________ me   *[My brother is as tall as me]*

2. Translate into English

a. i miei cugini sono

b. più affettuosi

c. meno simpatici

d. più diligente

e. di mia sorella

f. tanto forte quanto

g. è più bello

h. della mia migliore amica

i. sono meno alto

j. è più vecchio

k. siamo più intelligenti

l. quanto mio zio

3. Spot and correct any English translation mistakes

a. Lui è più alto di me   *He is taller than you*

b. Lui è tanto serio quanto me   *He is as good-looking as me*

c. Lei è meno tranquillo delle sue sorelle   *He is less quiet than me*

d. Io sono meno grosso di mio zio   *I am stronger than my uncle*

e. Siamo meno giovani di voi   *We are shorter than us*

f. Tu sei tanto vecchia quanto lei   *She is as old as him*

g. Lara è tanto sportiva quanto Mara   *Lara is as sporty as Mara*

4. Complete with a suitable word

a. Mia madre è ________ alta ________ me.

b. ____ padre _____ più giovane di mio zio.

c. I miei genitori sono ______ alti quanto i _______ cugini.

d. I _____ fratelli ________ più sportivi delle mie sorelle.

e. Il mio _________ è meno affettuoso _______ mio cane.

f. I miei nonni _______ tanto tranquilli ________ il mio gatto.

g. La mia amica è ______ bella della _____ tartaruga.

h. Mio zio non _____ tanto forte ________ mia ___________.

5. Match the opposites

1. bello	a. basso
2. diligente	b. noioso
3. giovane	c. brutto
4. alto	d. tonto
5. divertente	e. meno
6. simpatico	f. pigro
7. più	g. vecchio
8. intelligente	h. antipatico

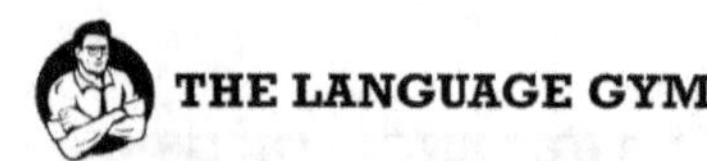

Unit 9. Comparing people : READING

Mi chiamo Fausto. Ho ventitré anni e vivo in Svizzera. Nella mia famiglia siamo in cinque: mamma, papà, i miei fratelli Ale e Stefano ed io. Stefano è più alto, bello e forte di Ale, però Ale è più intelligente e diligente di Stefano. I miei genitori si chiamano Antonio e Nina. **Entrambi** *[both]* sono molto carini, ma mio padre è più severo di mia madre. Inoltre, mia madre è più paziente e meno testarda di mio padre. Io sono tanto testardo quanto mio padre! In casa abbiamo due animali: un'anatra e un gatto. Sono entrambi molto simpatici, ma l'anatra è più rumorosa. Tanto rumorosa quanto me...

Mi chiamo Mauro Ferrari. Ho quindici anni e vivo a Montalcino, in Toscana. La mia famiglia è composta da cinque persone: mamma, papà, mio fratello Marco e mia sorella Barbara. Marco è più sportivo di Barbara, ma Barbara è più alta e forte.

I miei genitori si chiamano Fabio e Gabriella. Mi piace mio padre perché è meno severo di mia madre. Inoltre, mia madre è più antipatica di mio padre. In casa abbiamo due animali: un pappagallo e un criceto. Entrambi sono molto simpatici, ma il mio pappagallo è più chiacchierone. Tanto chiacchierone quanto me...

Mi chiamo Victoria. Ho venti anni e vivo a Siena con i miei genitori e le mie due sorelle Ava e Grace. Ava è più bella di Grace, ma Grace è più simpatica.

I miei genitori sono affettuosi e gentili, ma mia madre è più divertente di mio padre. Inoltre, mia mamma è più buffa del mio papà . Io sono tanto buffa quanto mio madre!

In casa abbiamo due animali: un cane e un coniglio. Entrambi sono molto grossi, ma il mio cane è più pigro. Tanto pigro quanto me...

1. Find the Italian for the following in Fausto's text

a. I live in:

b. Mum, dad:

c. Good-looking:

d. Hard-working:

e. Less stubborn:

f. More patient:

g. But:

h. Duck:

i. Two pets:

j. Very kind:

k. As stubborn as:

2. Complete the statements below based on Victoria's text

a. I am _______ years old

b. Ava is more __________ than Grace.

c. Grace is more _______

d. My parents are very __________ and ________.

e. My mum is __________ than my dad

f. I am as _____________ as my mother

g. We have _______ pets

h. My dog is _________ lazy

3. Correct any of the statements below [about Mauro Ferrari's text] which are incorrect

a. Mauro Ferrari ha tre animali

b. Marco è meno sportivo di Barbara

c. Marco è più alto di Barbara

d. Mauro è tanto chiacchierone quanto il criceto

e. Suo *[his]* padre è più severo di sua madre

4. Answer the questions on the three texts above

a. Where does Mauro Ferrari live?

b. Who is stricter, his mother or his father?

c. Who is as talkative as their parrot?

d. Who is as noisy as their duck?

e. Who has a stubborn father?

f. Who has a rabbit?

g. Who has an hamster?

h. Which one of Mauro's siblings is sportier?

i. Who is as funny as their mum?

Unit 9. Comparing people: TRANSLATION/WRITING

1. Translate into English

a. È così pigro come…

b. È più giovane di….

c. Meno gentile di…

d. Tanto sportivo quanto…

e. Sono meno chiacchierone di…

2. Gapped sentences

a. Mia mamma è _______ alta ______ mia zia
[My mum is taller than my aunt]

b. _____ padre _____ più _________ di mio fratello maggiore
[My father is stronger than my older brother]

c. I miei cugini _______ meno_____________ di noi
[My cousins are less sporty than us]

d. _______ fratello è _______tonto del suo ____________
[My brother is more stupid than his friend]

e. Mia nonna _____ ________ gentile _________ mio nonno
[My granmother is as kind as my grandfather]

f. Alberta è ________ diligente di __________
[Alberta is more hard-working than us]

g. Il mio gatto è meno ____________ del_____ cane
[My cat is less friendly than my dog]

h. Andrew _____ _________ testardo ______ sua moglie
[Andrew is more stubborn than his wife]

3. Phrase-level feminine translation [En to It]

a. My mother is…

b. Taller than…

c. As slim as…

d. Less stubborn than…

e. I am shorter than…

f. My parents are…

g. My cousins are…

h. As fat as…

i. They are as strong as…

j. My grandparents are…

k. I am as lazy as…

4. Sentence-level translation [En to It]

a. My older sister is taller than my younger sister

b. My father is as stubborn as my mother

c. My teacher is more hard-working than me

d. I am less intelligent than my brother

e. My best friend is stronger and sportier than me

f. My tortoise is less fast than my hamster

g. My cousins are as friendly as my friends

h. My duck is noisier than my dog

i. Pedro is younger than Leonardo

j. Ronaldo is faster than Giorgio

k. We are as kind as my parents

Revision Quickie 2 : Family, Pets and Jobs

1. Match

1. Dipendente	a. Doctor
2. Avvocato	b. Waiter
3. Infermiere	c. Journalist
4. Cameriere	d. Nurse
5. Giornalista	e. IT worker
6. Medico	f. Employee
7. Commesso	g. Teacher
8. Informatico	h. Lawyer
9. Professore	i. Shop-assistant

2. Sort the words listed below in the categories in the table

a. operaio; b. alto; c. commesso; d. simpatico; e. basso;
f. cugino; g. professoressa; h. infermiere; i. zio; j. padre;
k. occhi; l. capelli; m. coniglio; n. pompiere; o. mamma; p.
fratello; q. pesce; r. castani; s. anatra; t. gatto;
u. informatico

Descrizioni	Animali	Lavori	Famiglia

3. Complete with the missing adjectives

a. Mio padre è ___________ *[fat]*

b. Mia madre è ___________ *[tall]*

c. Mio fratello è ___________ *[nice]*

d. La mia amica è ___________ *[generous]*

e. Mio cugino è ___________ *[mean]*

f. Il mio gatto è ___________ *[boring]*

4. Complete with the missing nouns

a. Mio padre lavora come ___________ *[accountant]*

b. Mia madre è ___________ *[scientist]*

c. Il mio migliore amico è ___________ *[footballer]*

d. Mia sorella è ___________ *[air hostess]*

e. Mio cugino è ___________ *[student]*

f. Io lavoro come ___________ *[doctor]*

g. Marta è ___________ *[shop assistant]*

h. Tu lavori come___________ *[singer]*

5. Match the opposites

1. alto	a. vivace
2. bella	b. tonto
3. grossa	c. basso
4. pigro	d. silenzioso
5. intelligente	e. brutta
6. rumoroso	f. impaziente
7. cattivo	g. magra
8. paziente	h. buono

7. Complete with the correct verb

a. Mia madre ____ alta *[My mother is tall]*

b. _____ i capelli neri *[I have black hair]*

c. ___________ come cantante *[I work as a singer]*

d. Mio padre ____ quaranta anni *[My father is 40]*

e. Quante persone ci _____ nella tua famiglia?
[How many people are there in your family?]

f. I miei amici ______ alti *[My friends are tall]*

g. Mio zio non ___________ *[My uncle doesn't work]*

h. Il mio cane ___ _______Joy *[My dog is called Joy]*

i. Mio zio e mia zia ___________ irlandesi
[My aunt and my uncle are Irish]

6. Complete the numbers below

a. Quatto__ _ _ _ _ [14]

b. Quara__ _ _ [40]

c. Sessa__ _ _ [60]

d. Cinqu__ _ _ _ [50]

e. Settan__ _ [70]

f. Nov__ _ _ _ [90]

UNIT 10
Saying what's in my school bag / classroom/ describing colour

Grammar Time: Avere & Agreements

In this unit will learn how to say:

- What objects you have in your schoolbag/pencil case/classroom
- Words for classroom equipment
- What you have and don't have

You will revisit the following:

- Colours
- How adjectives agree in gender and number with nouns
- Introducing yourself (e.g. name, age, town, country)
- Pets

UNIT 10. Saying what's in my school bag/classroom:
'Cosa c'è nella tua aula/nel tuo zaino?'
What is in your classroom/schoolbag?

Nella mia aula *In my classroom*   **Nel mio zaino** *In my schoolbag*

C'è/Non c'è *There is/There isn't* **Ho/Non ho** *I have/I don't have* **Ho bisogno/non ho bisogno di** *I need/ I do not need* **Posso avere…** *May I have…* **Ci sono/Non ci sono** *There are/There aren't* **Il mio amico Paolo ha** *My friend Paolo has* **Il mio amico Paolo non ha** *My friend Paolo does not have*	**un astuccio** *a pencil case* **MASC** **un banco** *a desk* **un computer** *a computer* **un diario** *a diary* **un dizionario** *a dictionary* **un foglio** *a sheet of paper* **un libro** *a book* **un pennarello** *a felt-tip pen* **un quaderno** *an exercise book* **un temperino** *a pencil sharpener* **MASC PLURAL** **dei quaderni** *some exercise books* **dei pennarelli** *some felt-tip pens*	azzurr**o** bianc**o** giall**o** grigi**o** ner**o** ross**o** marrone verde arancione blu rosa viola **per favore?** gial**li** ross**i**
	una calcolatrice *a calculator* **FEM** **una colla** *a glue stick* **una gomma** *a rubber* **una lavagna** *a whiteboard* **una matita** *a pencil* **una penna** *a pen* **una riga** *a ruler* **una sedia** *a chair* **FEM PLURAL** **delle forbici** *some scissors* **delle matite** *some pencils*	azzurr**a** bianc**a** giall**a** grigi**a** ner**a** ross**a** marrone verde arancione blu rosa viola gial**le** ros**se**

Author's note: *The words for colour* **blu, rosa, viola** *do not change in number or gender.*
Ex. La matita blu / le matite blu

Unit 10. Saying what's in my school bag: VOCABULARY BUILDING

1. Complete with the missing words

a. Nel mio zaino ho un ________________________
[In my schoolbag I have an exercise book]

b. Mi serve una ________ *[I need an eraser]*

c. Non ho ______ penna *[I don't have a pen]*

d. Il mio amico __________un foglio *[My friend has a paper]*

e. Ho una ____________________ *[I have a calculator]*

f. Posso ________ una______ per favore?
[May I have a ruler please?]

g. ______ ho una __________ *[I don't have a chair]*

h. Il mio __________ non ha delle ____________________
[My friend doesn't have scissors]

2. Match up

1. una gomma	*a. a pencil*
2. una matita	*b. a planner*
3. un diario	*c. I have a…*
4. una sedia	*d. a sharpener*
5. ho un	*e. a pen*
6. ho bisogno di	*f. I don't have a*
7. non ho un	*g. please*
8. un temperino	*h. an eraser*
9. una penna	*i. I need a*
10. per favore	*j. a chair*

3. Translate into English

a. Ho una gomma e una riga

b. Nel mio zaino c'è un libro

c. Posso avere un diario per favore?

d. Nel mio astuccio c'è una penna

e. Ci sono tre matite rosse

f. Ho bisogno di un dizionario per favore

g. C'è un computer sul *[on the]* banco

h. Ho due quaderni verdi

4. Add the missing letter

a. Un tempe_ino

b. Una g_mma

c. Mi serv_no

d. Nel mio as_uccio

e. Un _iario

f. Uno zai__o

g. Delle fo_bici

h. Una lava_na

5. Anagrams

a. tiMate = Matite

b. uccioAst =

c. raneAncio =

d. Bicano =

e. orFbici =

f. inoZa =

g. llaCo =

h. rdVee =

6. Broken words

a. N_____ m_____ z__________ h______ u__ a____________
= *[In my bag I have a pencil case]*

b. N___ m___ a__________ c___ s_______ d______m__________
= *[In my pencil case there are some pencils]*

c. N_____ h_____ u______ g__________ = *[I don't have an eraser]*

d. H_ b__________ d___ u_____ r________ = *[I need a ruler]*

e. C'_____ u_______ l______________ = *[There is a whiteboard]*

f. H__ d______ p_________ b______ = *[I have some blue pens]*

g. H___ b__________ d_ u__ p__________
= *[I need a felt tip pen]*

7. Complete with a suitable word

a. Ho un ____________

b. Nel mio __________ c'è una riga

c. Mi piace il colore ______________

d. Posso avere un_______ per _______

e. Un quaderno ______________

f. Una __________ rossa

g. La mia __________ha un diario

h. Ho __________ di una colla

i. La mia maestra ha un ____________

j. Ci sono dei ______________ gialli

Unit 10. Saying what's in my school bag: READING

Mi chiamo Eloïse. Ho dodici anni e vivo a Parigi, in Francia. Siamo in quattro nella mia famiglia. Ho un gatto bianco. Nel mio zaino ci sono molte cose: una matita rossa, una penna gialla, una riga blu e una gomma bianca. La mia amica Claudia ha solo una matita nel suo astuccio. Però è **fortunata** [lucky] perché ha un cavallo grigio!

Mi chiamo Andrea. Ho quindici anni e vivo a Perugia, nel centro dell'Italia. Siamo in tre nella mia famiglia. Ho un criceto molto buffo. Nella mia classe c'è una lavagna, un computer e trenta banchi. La mia classe è molto grande. Io ho due matite grigie, una gomma, un temperino e una riga nuova. Il mio amico ha matite di tanti colori.

Mi chiamo Lucas. Ho diciotto anni e vivo a Mallorca, in Spagna. Mi piace la mia scuola. Nella mia aula ci sono venti banchi e venti sedie. La mia è una bella classe perché i miei amici sono simpatici ed il mio professore è molto divertente. Però, non ho una penna, né una matita, né una riga, né una gomma. Non ho niente. Praticamente, ho bisogno di tutto. A casa ho una gatta bianca molto carina.

Mi c________ Leo. Ho otto a______ e v________ a Positano, in Italia. Nella mia a________ ci sono ____ computer, una l__________ e tanti b________. Nel ______ zaino ho un l_______, due penne, tre q________ e una m______. La mia **compagna** [classmate] Ariella ha molte p________ colorate ma non ha un d______. Mi piace molto il mio maestro perché ____ molto sim__________. A casa ____ un serpente verde!

Mi chiamo Emiliano. Ho undici anni e vivo a Buenos Aires, in Argentina. Parlo spagnolo. Nella mia famiglia ci sono quattro persone. Vado d'accordo con mia madre ma di meno con mio padre. Lui è un po' antipatico e fa l'avvocato. Nella mia classe non ci sono molte cose. C'è una lavagna ma non c'è un computer! Ci sono ventotto banchi, ma solo ventisette sedie. È un problema! Io ho una matita, una calcolatrice e un diario.

1. Find the Italian for the following in Eloïse's text

a. I am 12

b. I live in Paris

c. We are 4 people

d. a white cat

e. a red pencil

f. a yellow pen

g. there are many things

h. only has one

i. she is lucky

j. a grey horse

2. Find Someone Who – which person…

a. …has a blue ruler?

b. …has most tables in their class?

c. …has a class with one student always standing?

d. …has no school equipment?

e. …has a green snake?

f. …doesn't like their dad?

3. Answer the following questions about Lucas' text

a. Where does Lucas live?

b. Does he like his school?

c. How many tables and chairs are there in his class?

d. How does he describe his class and teacher?

e. What school equipment does he have?

f. What do you think is the meaning of the word 'né'?

g. What does he say about his pet?

4. Fill in the table below

Name	Leo	Andrea
Age		
City/town		
Items in bag/pencil case		

Unit 10. Saying what's in my school bag: TRANSLATION

1. Faulty translation: spot and correct [in the English] any translation mistakes you find below

a. Nella mia aula ci sono due lavagne e un computer. Non mi piace il mio professore = *In my class there is a whiteboard and a computer. I like my teacher.*

b. Non ho molte cose nel mio astuccio. Ho una matita rosa ma non ho una riga = *I have many things in my pencil case. I have a red pencil but I don't have an eraser.*

c. La famiglia del mio amico Emilio è composta da cinque persone. Lui ha bisogno di una matita nera e un diario = *My friend Emilio has five people in his family. He needs a black pen and a diary.*

d. Professoressa, posso avere un temperino e una gomma per favore?= *Mrs..., can I have a pencil sharpener and a ruler please?*

e. Nella mia classe ci sono trenta sedie e trenta banchi. Però non abbiamo dizionari! Prof, mi presta un dizionario? = *In my class there are thirty computers and thirty chairs. But we do not have rulers! Mr...can you lend me a ruler?*

2. Translate into English

a. Posso avere una gomma, per favore?

b. Ho una matita nera

c. Non ho un temperino grigio

d. Il mio amico ha un libro

e. Mi piace il mio professore

f. Dei fogli bianchi

g. Delle penne rosse

h. Non ho un dizionario di italiano

i. Prof, mi presta una matita per favore?

3. Phrase-level translation [En to It]

a. A red book=

b. A black calculator =

c. I don't have =

d. I need a... =

e. I like =

f. There are... =

g. Please, may I have... =

h. My friend has... =

i. In my schoolbag there is... =

4. Sentence-level translation [En to It]

a. There are 20 tables

b. There is a whiteboard

c. My teacher is nice

d. I have some blue pens

e. I have some orange pencils

f. I need an eraser and a sharpener

g. May I have a book, please?

h. My class is very big and pretty

i. My father is a teacher

Unit 10. Saying what's in my school bag: WRITING

1. Split sentences

1. Ho una	a. ha una penna
2. Il mio professore	b. banchi
3. La mia aula	c. quaderno per favore
4. Ci sono trenta	d. calcolatrice
5. Il mio amico non	e. è grande
6. Posso avere un	f. c' è un astuccio
7. Nel mio zaino	g. è simpatico

2. Rewrite the sentences in the correct order

a. Ho una calcolatrice di bisogno

b. una rossa matita Ho e una nera penna

c. mia molto grande aula è La

d. Il amico ha mio un libro blu

e. Non diario ho un né gomma una

f. casa Nella mia tartaruga ho una verde

g. Mio è medico padre e in un lavora ospedale

h. favore per Posso una gomma avere

3. Spot and correct the grammar and spelling [note: in several cases a word is missing]

a. Nella mia clase ci sono venti banco.

b. Io ho un matita gialla.

c. Nel mio astucio c' è sono due gomme.

d. La amica ha tre astucci colorati.

e. Ho bisogno de dizionario.

f. Il mio amico Fernando a due penne rosse.

g. Mia madre ingegnere e lavora in cittá.

h. Sono alto e forte. Ho il capello biondo e l'occhi azzurri.

4. Anagrams

a. ccioastu = astuccio

b. gnavala =

c. pucomret =

d. chiban =

e. peritemno =

f. zionadirio =

g. preforessossa =

6. Describe this person in Italian:

Name: Diego

Pet: A black horse

Hair: brown,short + blue eyes

School equipment: has pen, 2 pencils, ruler, eraser

Does not have: sharpener, paper, dictionary

Favourite colour: blue

5. Guided writing – write 4 short paragraphs describing the people below using the details in the box [I]

Person	Lives	Has	Hasn't	Needs
Natalia	Verona	Exercise book	Pen	Diary
Ivan	Pisa	Ruler	Pencil	A paper
Katia	Cosenza	Felt-tip	Sharpener	A glue stick

Grammar Time 6: <u>AVERE</u> (Part 3) + AGREEMENTS
Present indicative of *"Avere"* (to have) and agreement training

school items		**age**	
un astuccio	**una** calcolatrice	dodici	
un computer	**una** matita	tredici	
un dizionario	**una** penna	quattordici	
un libro	**una** sedia	quindici	
un quaderno		sedici	**anni**
un pennarello		diciassette	
		diciotto	
		diciannove	
		venti	

avere **(non)**	ho *I have*	**family**	
	hai *you have*	due nonni, due nonne	
	ha *he/she has*	un fratello, una sorella	
	abbiamo *we have*	due fratelli, due sorelle	
	avete *you all have*	un figlio, una figlia	
	hanno *they have*	un cugino, una cugina	
		un fratellastro, una sorellastra	
		uno zio, una zia	

school **lezione di**	arte alle otto	**pets**
	scienze alle nove	un cane
	spagnolo alle dieci	un cavallo
	italiano alle undici	un coniglio
	geografia alle dodici	un criceto
	storia all'una	un gatto
	matematica alle due	un pappagallo
	educazione fisica alle tre	un pesce
		una gallina
		una tartaruga
dei professori molto bravi		un uccello
dei professori molto antipatici		

Present indicative of *"Avere"* + Agreements: Verb drills (1)

1. Match up

1. Io ho	*a. we have*
2. Tu hai	*b. I have*
3. Lui/lei ha	*c. they have*
4. Noi abbiamo	*d. you have*
5. Voi avete	*e. he/she has*
6. Loro hanno	*f. you all have*

2. Complete with the missing word (pets/family members)

a. Non _______________ animali *[I don't have pets]*

b. _________________ un gatto grigio *[We have a grey cat]*

c. _________________ due tartarughe *[They have two turtles]*

d. _________________ fratelli? *[Do you have siblings?]*

e. _________________ animali? *[Do you guys have pets?]*

f. Matteo ____ un porcellino d'India *[Matteo has a guinea pig]*

g. Mio cugino non ______animali *[My cousin doesn't have pets]*

h. I miei cugini ________ tre cani *[My cousins have three dogs]*

3. Complete with the present indicative form of "avere"

io   _______________

tu   _______________

lui, lei   _______________

noi   _______________

voi   _______________

loro   _______________

4. Add in the correct ending

a. Mio cugino non h____ animali

b. I miei zii non ha________ due gatti

c. Oggi (io) h_____ lezione di storia

d. Alle dodici (noi) abb________ geografia

e. Mio fratello h_____ dieci anni

f. I miei genitori h_______ quaranta anni

g. Mio padre h____ i capelli bianchi

h. Le mie amiche han______ i capelli rossi

i. Giulio e Stefano, (voi) av_________ una matita rossa?

5. Complete with the missing form of "avere"

a. Mio nonno _______ settantadue anni.

b. Mia madre _______ i capelli lunghi e neri.

c. Tu _______ gli occhi azzurri, invece io _______ gli occhi verdi.

d. Mio zio Mario non _______ capelli, è calvo!

e. Tu _______ fratelli o sorelle?

f. Voi ________ una matita e una gomma.

g. Io non ______ animali, ma mio fratello _______ un criceto.

6. Translate into Italian

a. My father has blue eyes

b. I don't have pets

c. I don't have a pen

d. In my pencil case I have a ruler

e. Do you have any felt-tip pens?

f. I have a dog at home

g. My mother has a black cat

h. My younger sister has a red schoolbag

i. Do you guys have history today?

j. No, we have Italian at ten.

Present indicative of "Avere" + Agreements
Verb drills (2)

7. Translate the pronoun <u>and</u> verb into Italian as shown in the example

I have: **(Io) ho**

You have: (   )

She has: (   )

He has: (   )

We have: (   )

You all have: (   )

They have: (   )

They do not have: (   )

8. Translate into Italian. Topic: Pets and colours

a. We have a blue parrot

b. I have two green turtles

c. My brother has a white guinea pig

d. My uncles have a black horse

e. My sister has a red and black spider

f. We don't have pets at home

g. Do you have pets at home?

9. Translate into Italian. Topic: family members

a. I don't have brothers

b. We have two grandparents

c. My mother has no sisters

d. Do you have any brothers or sisters?

e. Do you guys have cousins?

f. I don't have any brothers

g. You have one brother and one sister

10. Translate into Italian. Topic: School bag

a. They have five pencils

b. You have a rubber and a pen

c. I have a green exercise book

d. She does not have a pencil sharpener

e. Do you have a dictionary?

f. My teacher has some blue felt-tip pens

g. We do not have a glue stick

11. Translate into Italian. Topic: Hair and eyes

a. I have black hair

b. We have blue eyes

c. She has curly hair

d. My mother has blond hair

e. Do you have grey eyes ?

f. They have green eyes

g. My brother has brown eyes

h. We do not have a beard

i. You all have beautiful eyes

j. My parents have red hair

k. You have no hair

l. My sister has very long hair

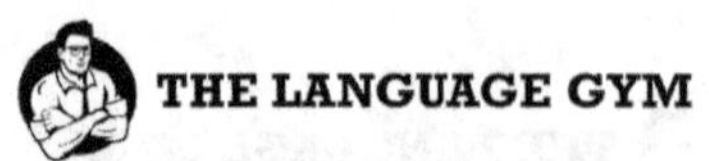

Grammar Time 7: Agreements (Part 1)

1. Complete the table

English	Italiano
Yellow	
	Rosa
	Grigio
Green	
Red	
	Viola
	Arancione
Black	
	Bianco
Blue	

2. Translate into English

a. Una matita gialla: _________________________________

b. Un astuccio nero: _________________________________

c. Due quaderni rosa: _________________________________

d. Tre pennarelli verdi:_________________________________

e. Una penna blu: _________________________________

f. Due gomme azzurre: _________________________________

g. Dei temperini arancioni: _________________________________

h. Dei fogli bianchi: _________________________________

i. Uno zaino rosso: _________________________________

j. Delle forbici bianche e nere:_________________________________

3. Provide the feminine version of each adjective in the table

Maschile	Femminile
Giallo	
Verde	
Azzurro	
Rosso	
Bianco	
Nero	
Arancione	
Rosa	

4. Complete with the missing adjective

a. Io ho uno zaino ___________ *[I have a red schoolbag]*

b. Non ho una penna _________ *[I don't have a black pen]*

c. Ho un astuccio ___________ *[I have an orange pencil case]*

d. Ho una riga ________________ *[I have a yellow ruler]*

e. Hai un foglio ___________ *[You have a white sheet of paper]*

f. Abbiamo due forbici _________ *[We have two red scissors]*

g. Ho una calcolatrice _________ *[I have a pink calculator]*

h. Tu hai un libro ____________ *[You have a green book]*

i. Posso avere una matita ___________? *[May I have a purple pencil?]*

5. Translate into Italian

a. a red chair

b. a black desk

c. a green schoolbag

d. a yellow pencil case

e. two green rulers

f. two blue scissors

6. Translate into Italian

a. I have a red pen and a blue diary

b. Felipe has a green schoolbag

c. Do you have a white pencil case?

d. Do you guys have any red markers?

e. I have a pink sheet of paper

f. We have a yellow schoolbag

g. My teacher has a black and white ruler

UNIT 11
Talking about food:
Likes / Dislikes / Reasons

Grammar Time: Mangiare /Bere

In this unit will learn how to say:

- What food you like/dislike and to what extent
- Why you like/dislike it (old and new expressions)
- New adjectives
- The full conjugation of 'mangiare' *[to eat]* and 'bere' *[to drink]*

You will revisit the following
- Time markers
- Providing a justification

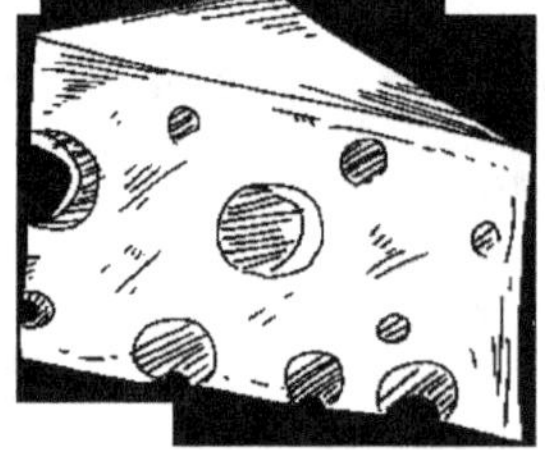

UNIT 11: Talking about food
Likes / Dislikes / Reasons Part 1
'Cosa ti piace mangiare/bere?'
What do youlike to eat/drink?

Singular			
Amo/Adoro *I love*	**il caffé** *coffee*		**caldo/a** *hot*
	il formaggio *cheese*		**delizioso/a** *delicious*
Mi piace molto *I like a lot*	**il latte** *milk*		**disgustoso/a** *disgusting*
	il miele *honey*		**dolce** *sweet*
Mi piace *I like*	**il pane** *bread*		**grasso/a** *oily, greasy*
	il pesce *fish*	**perché è** *because it is*	**insipido/a** *bland*
Mi piace un po' *I like a bit*	**il pollo arrosto** *roast chicken*		**malsano/a** *unhealthy*
	il riso *rice*		**piccante** *spicy*
Non mi piace *I don't like*	**il succo di frutta** *fruit juice*		**ricco/a di vitamine** *rich in vitamin*
	l'acqua *water*		**rinfrescante** *refreshing*
Odio *I hate*	**la carne** *meat*		**sano/a** *healthy*
	la cioccolata *chocolate*		**saporito/a** *tasty*
Preferisco *I prefer*	**la frutta** *fruit*		

Plural			
Amo/adoro *I love*	**i gamberi** *prawns*		**caldi/e** *hot*
	i pomodori *tomatoes*		**deliziosi/e** *delicious*
Mi piacciono molto *I like a lot*	**le arance** *oranges*		**disgustosi/e** *disgusting*
	le banane *bananas*		**dolci** *sweet*
Mi piacciono *I like*	**le cioccolate** *chocolates*		**grassi/e** *oily, greasy*
	le mele *apples*	**perché sono** *because they are*	**insipidi/e** *bland*
Mi piacciono un po' *I like a bit*	**le melanzane** *aubergines/eggplants*		**malsani/e** *unhealthy*
			piccanti *spicy*
Non mi piacciono *I don't like*	**le uova** *eggs*		**ricchi/ricche di proteine** *rich in protein*
	le verdure *vegetables*		**rinfrescanti** *refreshing*
Odio *I hate*	**gli hamburger** *burgers*		**sani/e** *healthy*
Preferisco *I prefer*			

Author's notes:
1 The adjectives above ending in '**o**' change to '**a**' with feminine nouns.
Ex. *Mi piace la frutta perché è deliziosa*
2 Adjectives ending in '**e**' do not change in the feminine. However, they change to '**i**' in the plural.
Ex: *La cioccolata è dolce / Le cioccolate sono dolci.*
3 When used in the plural, the adjectives in '**o**' change to '**i**' and the adjective in '**a**' change to '**e**'.
Ex.: *Mi piacciono i gamberi perché sono saporiti /Mi piacciono le verdure perché sono sane*

Unit 11. Talking about food (Part 1): VOCABULARY BUILDING (Part 1)

1. Match up

1. Le banane	*a. Eggs*
2. Le fragole	*b. Apples*
3. La carne	*c. Prawns*
4. Il pollo	*d. Milk*
5. L'acqua	*e. Fruit*
6. Il latte	*f. Water*
7. Le uova	*g. Burgers*
8. I gamberi	*h. Chicken*
9. Gli hamburger	*i. Meat*
10. La frutta	*j. Bananas*
11. Le mele	*k. Strawberries*

2. Complete

a. Mi piace molto il ___________ *[I like chicken a lot]*

b. Adoro i _______________ *[I love prawns]*

c. Mi piacciono le ___________*[I like strawberries]*

d. Amo il _____________ *[I love milk]*

e. Adoro le _______________ *[I love bananas]*

f. Preferisco l'______ minerale *[I prefer mineral water]*

g. Non mi piacciono i _________ *[I don't like tomatoes]*

h. Odio il _____________ *[I hate fish]*

i. Amo la ____________ *[I love fruit]*

j. Non mi piacciono le ___________ *[I don't like eggs]*

3. Translate into English

a. Mi piace la frutta

b. Odio le uova

c. Amo il pollo arrosto

d. Mi piacciono le mele

e. Odio la carne

f. Preferisco l'insalata verde

g. Non mi piacciono i pomodori

h. Odio il latte

4. Complete the words

a. Le uo_________

b. Le ban__________

c. La fr_________

d. Le verd____________

e. Gli hamb_____________

f. I gam_________

g. I pom____________

h. L'ac________

5. Fill the gaps with either *'mi piace'* or *'mi piacciono'* as appropriate

a. Non ___________________ le uova

b. ___________________ l'acqua

c. ___________________ il pollo

d. ___________________ gli hamburger

e. ___________________ le verdure

f. ___________________ la carne

g. ___________________ la frutta

h. ___________________ i gamberi

i. ___________________ la pasta

6. Translate into Italian

a. I like eggs

b. I love oranges

c. I hate tomatoes

d. I don't like prawns

e. I love fruit juice

f. I don't like vegetables

g. I really like milk

h. I like apples but I prefer oranges

i. I don't like cheese

Unit 11. Talking about food (Part 1): VOCABULARY BUILDING (Part 2)

1. Complete with the missing words. The initial letter of each word is given

a. Queste banane sono d________________
[These bananas are disgusting]

b. Queste mele sono d________________
[These apples are delicious]

c. Questo pollo è molto p________________
[This chicken is very spicy]

d. Non mi piace la c______________
[I don't like meat]

e. Questo caffè è molto d______________
[This coffee is very sweet]

f. Le salsicce sono m________________
[Sausages are unhealthy]

g. Le verdure sono s________________
[Vegetables are healthy]

h. Amo il ______________
[I love milk]

2. Complete the table

Italiano	English
Il latte	
	Roast chicken
Il pesce	
Le uova	
	Water
	Bread
I cereali	
Il pane tostato	
	Vegetables

3. Complete with 'mi piace' or 'mi piacciono' as appropriate

a. ________________ le mele

b. ________________ il latte

c. Non ________________ i cereali

d. ________________ il pane tostato

e. ________________ il succo di frutta

f. Non ________________ la pasta

g. ________________ il riso

h. Non ________________ il caffè

4. Broken words

a. N___ m___ p__________ l____ u________
[I don't like eggs]

b. A_________ l_____ m____________ *[I love apples]*

c. O______ g____ h__________________ *[I hate burgers]*

d. M___ p__________ m________ l___ c______________
[I really like chocolates]

e. I__ m____c_________ è c__________ *[My coffee is hot]*

f. I__ p____________ è s_________ *[Fish is healthy]*

g. I__ curry indiano è p____________ *[Indian curry is spicy]*

5. Complete each sentence in a way which is logical and grammatically correct

a. Le ______________ non sono sane

b. Le banane sono ______________

c. Non mi ____________ il latte

d. Mi __________ il pollo arrosto

e. ______________ il pesce perché è saporito

f. ______________ la carne rossa perché è malsana

g. ______________ le verdure perché sono ricche di vitamine

Unit 11. Talking about food (Part 1): READING

Ciao, mi chiamo Manuela. Cosa preferisco mangiare? Amo i frutti di mare, quindi mi piacciono molto i gamberi ed i calamari perché sono deliziosi. Mi piace molto il pesce perché è saporito e ricco di proteine. Soprattutto mangio il salmone, prodotto tipico scozzese, dove vivo. Mi piace abbastanza il pollo arrosto. Inoltre, amo la frutta specialmente uva e fragole. Non mi piacciono molto le verdure perché non sono saporite, ma fanno bene alla salute!

Salve, mi chiamo Alessandro. Cosa preferisco mangiare? Amo le verdure. Le mangio tutti i giorni. Le mie verdure preferite sono gli spinaci, le carote e le melanzane perché sono ricche di vitamine e minerali. Mi piace anche la frutta perché è sana, rinfrescante e deliziosa. Sono vegetariano. Odio la carne e il pesce. Anche se sono ricchi di proteine, non sono saporiti.

Ciao, mi chiamo Violetta. Cosa preferisco mangiare? Adoro la carne, soprattutto la carne di agnello, perché molto saporita. Mi piace molto il pollo arrosto piccante, lo trovo saporito ed è ricco di proteine. Mi piacciono abbastanza le uova. Sono sane e ricche di vitamine e proteine. Mi piace abbastanza la frutta, soprattutto le ciliegie. Sono molto deliziose. Però non mi piacciono per niente le mele.

Ciao, mi chiamo James. Cosa mi piace mangiare? Preferisco la carne. La adoro perché è saporita, soprattutto mi piacciono molto gli hamburger. Mi piace anche la frutta perché è dolce. Non mi piacciono le verdure. Odio i pomodori e le carote. Non mi piacciono le uova. Sono ricche di vitamine e proteine ma sono disgustose. Non mi piacciono le patate fritte perché sono malsane.

Salve, mi chiamo Fernando. Cosa mi piace mangiare? Amo la carne rossa perché è saporita e ricca di proteine. Non mangio molto pesce perché è disgustoso. Mi piacciono abbastanza i calamari fritti, però non fanno bene alla salute. Mi piace moltissimo la frutta, soprattutto le banane, perché sono deliziose, ricche di vitamine e non sono care. Non mi piacciono le mele e odio le arance. Non mangio verdure.

1. Find the Italian for the following in Manuela's text

a. I love seafood

b. I really like prawns

c. Are delicious

d. because it is tasty

e. I eat salmon

f. I quite like

g. Moreover

h. Above all

i. They are not tasty

2. Fernando or Manuela? Write *F* or *M* next to each statement below

a. I love seafood - *M*

b. I hate oranges

c. I like fruit a lot

d. I don't like vegetables

e. I prefer salmon

f. I quite like squid

g. I prefer bananas

h. I don't eat much fish

i. I love red meat

3. Complete the following sentences based on Alessandro's text

a. Alessandro loves_________________________________

b. He eats them _________________________________

c. His favourite vegetables are _________________,
_________________ and _________________

d. He also likes _________________ because it is
_________________ and _________________

e. He hates _____________ and _________________

4. Fill in the table below about James

Loves	Likes a lot	Hates	Doesn't like

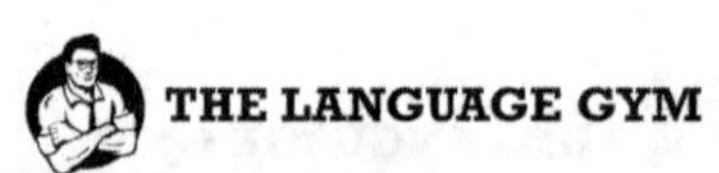

Unit 11. Talking about food (Part 1): Translation 1

1. Faulty translation: spot and correct [IN THE ENGLISH] any translation mistakes you find below

a. Adoro i gamberi: *I hate prawns*

b. Odio il pollo e la zuppa: *I like meat and soup*

c. Mi piace il miele: *I don't like honey*

d. Amo le arance e l'uva: *I love apples and grapes*

e. Le uova sono disgustose: *Eggs are tasty*

f. Le banana sono ricche di vitamine: *Bananas are rich in protein*

g. Il pesce fa bene alla salute: *Fish is unhealthy*

h. Preferisco la cioccolata calda: *I prefer hot water*

i. Le cioccolate fanno male alla salute: *Chocolates are healthy*

j. Mi piace il riso perché non ha glutine: *I hate rice because it is gluten-free*

k. Il pane è salato: *Fried squid is salty*

l. Il curry indiano è piccante: *Indian curry is sweet*

2. Translate into English

a. I gamberi sono saporiti e sani.

b. Il pesce è delizioso e ricco di vitamine.

c. Il pollo è ricco di proteine.

d. Amo il riso perché non ha glutine.

e. La carne rossa è malsana.

f. La frutta è rinfrescante e dolce .

g. Le uova sono saporite e ricche di proteine.

h. Preferisco l'acqua minerale.

i. La zuppa è buona e salutare.

3. Phrase-level translation [En to It]

a. Spicy chicken:

b. This coffee:

c. I quite like:

d. Very sweet:

e. A disgusting apple:

f. Some delicious oranges:

g. I don't like:

h. I love pizza because:

i. It is refreshing:

j. Mineral water:

k. It is bland:

4. Sentence-level translation [En to It]

a. I like spicy chicken a lot

b. I like oranges because they are healthy

c. Meat is tasty but unhealthy

d. This coffee is hot

e. Eggs are disgusting but healthy

f. I love oranges. They are delicious and rich in vitamins

g. I love fish. It is tasty and rich in protein

h. Vegetables are disgusting

i. I prefer fruit because is refreshing

j. This tea is sweet

THE LANGUAGE GYM

Unit 11. Talking about food (Part 1): Translation 2

Paragraph 1	**Tick a box each time you spot the correct translation in the text**				**Translate the paragraph into English**
Ciao, mi chiamo Albert e sono australiano. Faccio colazione alle sette. Mi piace mangiare la frutta perché è sana. A pranzo mangio un panino al formaggio o una zuppa di verdure. Di solito bevo acqua o una limonata. La sera ceno a casa. Amo le salsicce perché sono saporite.	For lunch I eat	I have breakfast	or a vegetable soup	In the evening	__________
	because it is healthy	at seven	and Italian fluently	I love sausages	__________
	Hi, my name is Albert	a cheese sandwich	because they are tasty	I usually drink	__________
	and I am Australian	water or lemonade	I like eating fruit	I have dinner at home	__________
Paragraph 2					
Salve, io sono Gloria. Normalmente a colazione mangio cereali e bevo un caffè in cucina. Di solito pranzo verso l'una, mangio un'insalata o una pizza. Mi piace moltissimo. Non mangio mai patate fritte perché penso che siano malsane. Odio il pesce perché è insipido.	Hello, I am Gloria	I never eat	I really like it	and I drink	__________
	I usually have lunch	because I think that	Normally for breakfast	they are unhealthy	__________
	chips	in the kitchen	it is bland	I eat cereals	__________
	a coffee	a salad or a pizza	I hate fish because	around 1pm, I eat	__________
Paragraph 3					
Buonasera, mi chiamo Yan. Sono cinese ma parlo italiano. Di solito non faccio colazione perché non ho tempo. A pranzo mangio sempre riso con verdure e pollo e bevo un té. Mi piacciono le cioccolate anche se preferisco le banane o le mele. La sera con la mia famiglia ceniamo verso le sette.	I am Chinese	and I am 14	I like chocolates	and I drink tea	__________
	Good evening, my name is Yan	For lunch	but I speak Italian	I usually don't have breakfast	__________
	vegetables and chicken	we have dinner around 7	because it is big	I eat rice with	__________
	bananas and apples	because I do not have time	even if I prefer	In the evening with my family	__________

Unit 11. Talking about food (Part 1): WRITING

1. Split sentences

Amo il pollo [1]	minerale
Odio le verdure perché	arrosto [1]
Preferisco la	è dolce
Questo caffè	sono disgustose
Mi piacciono	saporiti ma malsani
I calamari fritti sono	le mele
Adoro l'acqua	pizza

2. Rewrite the sentences in the correct order

a. il Amo arrosto pollo = _Amo il pollo arrosto_

b. le verdure Odio

c. caffè Questo amaro è

d. frutta bene fa La alla salute

e. minerale l' Preferisco acqua

f. rinfrescanti sono arance Le

g. Mi sono le piacciono uova perché deliziose

h. piace carne rossa è non Mi salutare la ma sana

i. pesce il Adoro arrostito

j. La è ricca frutta vitamine di

k. cibo Mi piccante il piace

3. Spot the mistake and rewrite the correct sentence (there may be missing words)

a. Mi piace le patate fritte e le gamberi =

b. Non piacciono le verdure =

c. Il pollo e saporito è picante =

d. Adoro il cafe caldo =

e. Preferisco la insalada verde =

f. Odio a carne e il pescie=

4. Anagrams

a. tteLa

b. berimGa

c. rneCa = Carne

d. saInlata

e. canPicte

f. Dilesozio

g. mineViat

5. Guided writing – write 4 short paragraphs describing the people below using the details in the box [I]

Person	Loves	Quite likes	Doesn't like	Hates
Loretta	Pizza because tasty	Milk because healthy	Red meat	Eggs because disgusting
Eddie	Chicken because healthy	Oranges because sweet	Fish	Meat because unhealthy
Angela	Honey because sweet	Fish because tasty	Fruit	Vegetables because bland

6. Write a paragraph on Sara in Italian [using the third person singular]

Name: Sara

Age: 18

Description: tall, good-looking, sporty, friendly

Occupation: student

Food she loves: chicken

Food she likes: vegetables

Food she doesn't like: red meat

Food she hates: fish

Grammar Time 8: MANGIARE/BERE
Present Tense
Talking about food Part 1

Bere *to drink*		
(Io) bev<u>o</u> *I drink*		**acqua** *water*
		aranciata *orangeade*
(Tu) bev<u>i</u> *you drink*		**caffè** *coffee*
		cioccolata calda *hot chocolate*
(Lui/lei) bev<u>e</u> *he/she drinks*		**latte** *milk*
		limonata *lemonade*
(Noi) bev<u>iamo</u> *we drink*		**succo di mela** *apple juice*
(Voi) bev<u>ete</u> *you all drink*	**a volte** *sometimes*	**tè** *tea*
		vino *wine*
(Loro) bev<u>ono</u> *they drink*	**ogni tanto** *from time to time*	
Mangiare *to eat*		**carne** *meat*
		cioccolata *chocolate*
	raramente *rarely*	**insalata verde** *green salad*
		formaggio *cheese*
(Io) mang<u>io</u> *I eat*		**frutta** *fruit*
	spesso *often*	**pane** *bread*
(Tu) mang<u>i</u> *you eat*		**pesce** *fish*
		pollo arrosto *roast chicken*
(Lui/lei) mang<u>ia</u> *he/she eats*		**riso** *rice*
(Noi) mang<u>iamo</u> *we eat*		**arance** *oranges*
		banane *bananas*
(Voi) mang<u>iate</u> *you all eat*		**cioccolate** *chocolates*
		gamberi *prawns*
(Loro) mang<u>iano</u> *they eat*		**hamburger** *burgers*
		mele *apples*
		pomodori *tomatoes*
		uova *eggs*
		verdure *vegetables*

Author's Note: mai *[never]* needs to have an additional at the start of the sentence:
Non bevo mai acqua – *I never drink water*
Non mangio mai gamberi – *I never eat prawns*

The adverbs (apart from **mai** which needs to be used as shown above) can also be placed at the **start** of the sentence, such as **"Ogni tanto io mangio riso"** *From time to time I eat rice,* AND at the **end "Io mangio riso ogni tanto"** *I eat rice from time to time.*

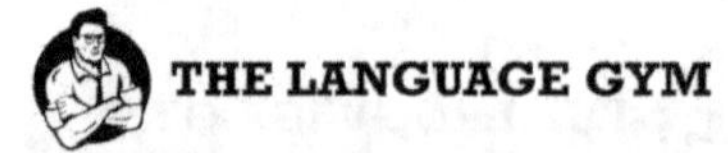

1. Match

a. Mangio	1. *They eat*
b. Mangi	2. *She eats*
c. Mangia	3. *We eat*
d. Mangiamo	4. *You guys eat*
e. Mangiate	5. *You eat*
f. Mangiano	6. *I eat*

2. Translate into English

a. A volte mangio pasta   f. Non mangiamo mai insalata

b. Lui beve un succo di mela   g. Spesso tu mangi del riso

c. Ogni tanto bevo del vino   h. Voi bevete caffè?

d. Noi mangiamo pesce   i. Cosa mangiate?

e. Beviamo sempre acqua   j. Non bevo mai latte

3. Spot and correct the mistakes

a. Mio padre mangio pasta al pomodoro

b. Mio fratello ed io non mangiare verdure

c. Mia madre mai bevi cioccolata calda

d. I miei fratelli bevete molto succo frutta

e. (io) Mai bere café

f. Mia sorella mangi speso carne

g. (voi) Mangiano carne di cavallo?

h. Cosa bevo tu?

4. Complete with the verb *"bere"* or *"mangiare"*

a. Mio padre _______________ molta frutta

b. (io) Non _____________ mai succo di kiwi

c. (Tu) _________ pollo?

d. Mia madre ed io ____________ molta pasta

e. I miei genitori ____________ molta acqua

f. Mia sorella _______ molta cioccolata calda

g. Noi non _______________ mai vino

h. (voi) Cosa _____________ a colazione?

5. Translate into Italian

a. I eat pasta

b. We drink orange juice

c. What do you eat?

d. What do you guys drink?

e. We eat a lot of meat

f. They don't eat a lot of fish

g. She never eats vegetables

h. We drink lots of mineral water

6. Translate into Italian

a. I never eat red meat. I don't like it because it is unhealthy.

b. I rarely eat sausages. I don't like them because they are fatty.

c. I drink fruit juice often. I love it because it is delicious and healthy.

d. I eat cheese from time to time. I love it because it is very tasty.

e. I rarely eat vegetables. They are tasty but I don't like them because they are disgusting.

f. I never drink tea or coffee because I don't like them.

UNIT 12
Talking about food:
Likes/ Dislikes / Reasons

Grammar Time: Agreement (food)

In this unit you will consolidate all that you learnt in the previous unit and learn how to say:
- What meals you eat every day
- What you eat at each meal
- The full present indicative conjugation of *'mangiare'*, *'pranzare'*, *'cenare'*
- 'The', 'This' and 'these' in Italian

You will revisit the following:
- The full present indicative conjugation of regular ARE verbs
- Noun-to-adjective agreement

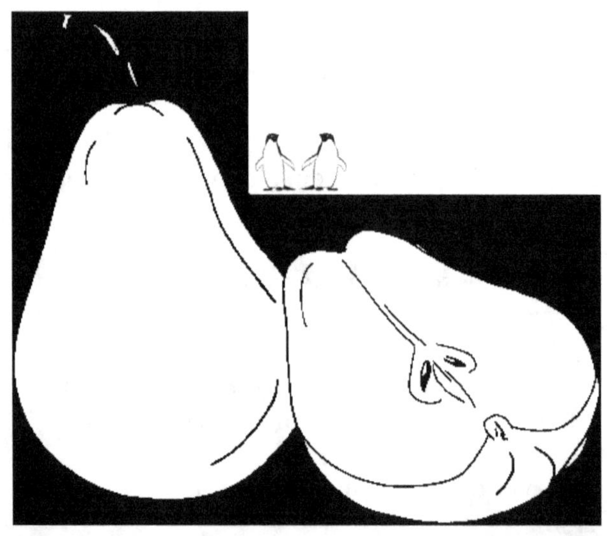

Unit 12 Part 2
Talking about food: Likes/ Dislikes/ Reasons
'Cosa ti piace mangiare? Perché?'
What do you like to eat? Why?

A colazione *For breakfast* **A pranzo** *For lunch* **A merenda** *For snack* **A cena** *For dinner*		**mangio** *I eat* **bevo** *I drink*		**un cornetto** *a croissant* **una mela** *an apple* **un bicchiere d'acqua** *a glass of water* **un bicchiere di latte** *a glass of milk*	

		SINGULAR		
Mi piace/Mi piacciono *I like* **Non mi piace/ Non mi piacciono** *I don't like* **Amo/Adoro** *I love* **Preferisco** *I prefer* **Odio** *I hate*	**moltissimo** *very much* **molto** *a lot* **un po'** *a bit* **per niente** *at all*	**il panino al formaggio** *cheese sandwich* **il panino al prosciutto** *ham sandwich* **il tonno** *tuna* **l'insalata mista** *a mixed salad* **la mela/pera** *an apple/a pear* **la pizza** *a pizza* **la zuppa** *a soup* **il caffè** *a coffee* **il succo di arancia** *an orange juice* **una tazza di tè** *a cup of tea*	**perché è** *because it is*	**amaro/a** *bitter* **aspro/a** *acidic, sour* **delizioso/a** *delicious* **disgustoso/a** *disgusting* **dolce** *sweet* **insipido/a** *bland* **malsano/a** *unhealthy* **nutriente** *nutritious* **piccante** *spicy* **rinfrescante** *refreshing* **ricco/a di vitamine** *rich in vitamins* **saporito/a** *tasty* **sano/a** *healthy* **succoso/a** *juicy*
		PLURAL		
		i biscotti *biscuits* **i calamari** *squid* **i dolci** *cakes* **i frutti di mare** *seafood* **i gamberi** *prawns* **i pomodori** *tomatoes* **le arance** *oranges* **le mele** *apples* **le pesche** *peaches* **le salsicce** *sausages* **le verdure** *vegetables*	**perché sono** *because they are*	**amari/e** **aspri/e** **deliziosi/e** **disgustosi/e** **dolci** **insipidi/e** **nutrienti** **piccanti** **saporiti/e** **sani/e**

Unit 12. Talking about food – Likes/Dislikes (Part 2): VOCABULARY

1. Match

1. L'acqua	a. sandwich
2. Il pesce	b. water
3. Il riso	c. roast chicken
4. Il panino	d. fish
5. Il pollo arrosto	e. cheese
6. La carne	f. icecream
7. I calamari	g. prawns
8. I gamberi	h. strawberries
9. Il gelato	i. sausages
10. Il formaggio	j. rice
11. Le salsicce	k. squid
12. Le fragole	l. vegetables
13. Le verdure	m. meat

2. Complete with the missing words

a. Adoro l' _______________ = [I love salad]

b. Mi piacciono molto le__________= [I like vegetables a lot]

c. Mi piaciono i f _______ d__m_______ = [I like seafood]

d. A colazione mangio una _________
= [For breakfast I eat an apple]

e. Questo ________è delizioso = [This chicken is delicious]

f. Questa ________ è molto succosa =[This meat is very juicy]

g. Preferisco le _______________ = [I prefer sausages]

h. Mi piace ____________ il miele = [I like honey very much]

i. Mi _______________ i dolci = [I like cakes]

3. Complete with the missing letters

a. L' a_ _ _ _ = water

b. La _ _ _ ne = meat

c. Il to_ _ _ = tuna

d. S _ _ _ = healthy

e. Il _ _ _ _ggio= cheese

f. Il pa _ _ _ _ = sandwich

g. Gli sp _ _ _ _ _ = spinach

h. La fr_ _ _ _ _= strawberry

i. Suc _ _ _ _= juicy

j. Col_ _ _ _ _ _ = breakfast

k. Ce_ _ _ = dinner

l. Il r _ _ _ = rice

m. Il gel _ _ _ = ice cream

n. Disg_ _ _ _ _= disgusting

o. Molti_ _ _ _ _ = very much

p. Bu_ _ _ = good

q. Il p_ _ _ = bread

r. Pi _ _ _ _ _ e = spicy

4. Match

1. Nutriente	a. Good
2. Fritto	b. Delicious
3. Succoso	c. Juicy
4. Saporito	d. Healthy
5. Salutare	e. Nutritious
6. Buono	f. Disgusting
7. Delizioso	g. Fried
8. Grasso	h. Sweet
9. Disgustoso	i. Fatty
10. Dolce	j. Tasty

5. Sort the items below into the appropriate category

a. delizioso	e. buono	i. mela	m. agnello	q. salmone	u. latte
b. dolce	f. gamberi	j. fragola	n. bistecca	r. pollo	v. pesca
c. saporito	g. yogurt	k. gelato	o. insipido	s. nutriente	w. carota
d. banana	h. malsano	l. succoso	p. sano	t. spinaci	x. formaggio

frutta	verdura	aggettivi	pesce o carne	latticini [dairy products]

Unit 12. Talking about food – Likes/Dislikes (Part 2): READING

Mi chiamo Robert, vivo in Inghilterra. Cosa mangio? Spesso mangio poco a colazione. Solo una mela o una banana e un cappuccino.

A pranzo, mangio un panino al prosciutto e delle patate fritte. Bevo acqua o una coca cola. Le patate fritte non sono sane, ma le adoro perché sono saporite.

Nel pomeriggio mangio un gelato a merenda o della frutta. Adoro le pesche perché sono succose.

A cena di solito mangio del pesce con le verdure, mi piacciono i frutti di mare. A volte mangio un'insalata. Mi piacerebbe mangiare del formaggio ma mia madre dice che non è sano. Lei odia il formaggio.

Mi chiamo Stefano. Cosa mangio? Normalmente a colazione non mangio molto. Solo un uovo e una tazza di tè. Il tè mi piace dolce, con molto zucchero. A volte bevo succo di pera. A pranzo mangio pollo arrosto con verdure e bevo acqua minerale. Mangio molte verdure perché sono nutrienti e sono sane. Mi piacerebbe mangiare più spesso i gamberi perché mi piacciono moltissimo. Dopo la scuola, a merenda, mangio il pane tostato col miele e un succo di arancia. Amo il miele perché è delizioso e ricco di vitamine. A cena mangio molto. Di solito mangio il riso, bistecca con patate e frutta. A volte mangio un piatto di pasta perché è ricca di carboidrati.

1. Find the Italian for the words below in Stefano's text.

a. for breakfast : a c_______________

b. a cup of tea: u___t_______d_ t___

c. sugar: z_____________

d. pear juice: s_______d__p_______

e. for lunch: a p_______________

f. they are healthy: s____ s___

g. after school: d______s__________

h. toast : p________t___________

i. rich in vitamins: r________ d____ v_____________

j. for dinner: a c_____________

k. a plate of pasta: u__p_____ d_p_____

2. Complete the following sentences based on Stefano's text

a. Normally, at breakfast I do not eat _______. Only an _____ and a cup of ______

b. I like my tea __________ with a lot of _____________

c. For _________ I eat ______ ______ with __________ and I drink _________ ________

d. I eat a lot of vegetables because they are ________ and good for ____________

e. As a snack I eat________ with ______ and drink an ____ ______________

f. Usually I eat ________, __________ with potatoes and _________

g. Sometimes I eat a________ of pasta because it is rich in _____________

3. Find the Italian for the following in Robert's text

a. I live in England.

b. I often have a small breakfast

c. ham sandwich

d. chips are not healthy

e. but I love them

f. I eat an ice cream

g. I like seafood

h. I would like to eat

i. my mother says

j. they are juicy

k. in the afternoon

l. I usually eat

m. it is not healthy

n. she hates cheese

4. Who says this: Robert, Stefano, or both?

a. I would love to eat cheese – *Robert*

b. I love honey

c. I drink pear juice

d. I don't eat much for breakfast

e. I would like to eat prawns more often

f. I have toasts with honey

g. I love peaches

h. Chips are not healthy

i. I usually eat rice

j. I drink mineral water

k. His mother hates cheese

l. I have a cappuccino at breakfast

Mi chiamo Luca, vivo a Melbourne, in Australia. Cosa mi piace mangiare? Normalmente al mattino mangio molto: una banana, due o tre uova, pane con prosciutto, una spremuta d'arancia e una tazza di caffè. Il caffè mi piace dolce. A pranzo, di solito, mangio solo del pollo con patate o verdure e bevo acqua minerale o succo di frutta. Adoro il pollo perché è sano e ricco di proteine. A volte mangio asparagi. Mi piacciono perché sono amari ma sono ricchi di vitamine. Nel pomeriggio, dopo scuola, faccio merenda con pane, burro e marmellata e bevo una tazza di tè. A cena mangio molto di più. Di solito mangio pasta, carne con verdure e gelato o torta di mele come dolce. Mi piacerebbe mangiare della cioccolata, perché è deliziosa, però mia madre dice che fa male.

5. Answer the following questions on Luca's text

a. How much does he eat at breakfast?

b. What does he eat/drink? [4 things]

c. How does he like coffee?

d. What juice does he drink at lunch?

e. What does he have with chicken?

f. Why does he like asparagus?

g. What does he have for snack in the afternoon?

h. What desserts does Luca eat?

i. Why doesn't his mother allow him to eat chocolate?

---

6. Find in Luca's text the following:

a. a word for dessert, starting with G:

b. a vegetable starting with A:

c. a drink starting with S:

d. a type of cold meat starting with P:

e. a fruit starting with B:

f. a dairy product starting with B:

g. an adjective starting with D:

h. a container starting with T:

i. a verb starting with M:

j. a fruit starting with A:

k. an adjective starting with S:

l. a meal starting with C:

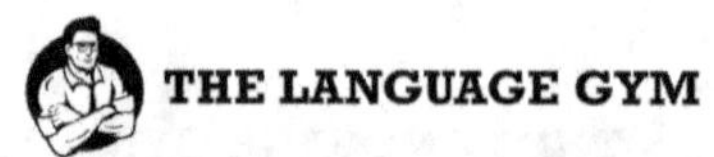

Unit 12. Talking about food – Likes/Dislikes (Part 2): WRITING

1. Split sentences

Mangio sempre pollo	con il latte
Mangio cereali	con il burro
Mangio il pane tostato	arrosto
Mi piace l'insalata	frutta preferita
La carne rossa è	piccante
Il curry è	o caffè
L'uva è la mia	verde
Bevo té	deliziosa ma malsana

2. Complete with the correct option

a. Amo i _________________, soprattutto le cozze.

b. Normalmente __ _________ mangio una zuppa.

c. Mangio sempre ____________ a colazione.

d. A volte preparo _______ arrosto con mia madre.

e. _______ alle sette con la mia famiglia.

f. Normalmente, mangio un frutto a ___________.

g. Mi piace molto il _______ perché è dolce

h. Il caffè è _________, ma è buono.

i. Non mi _________il latte, che schifo!

j. La frutta è nutritiva e ___________.

ceno	pollo	a pranzo	merenda	amaro
miele	frutti di mare	cereali	piace	sana

3. Spot and correct the grammar and spelling mistakes [note: in several cases a word is missing]

a. Normalmente a pranzo io mangiare un panino

b. Bevo aqua o succo fruta.

c. La carne rosa non è sana, pero mi piacce.

d. Adoro il succo darancia.

e. Nel pomeriggio a merenda magio pane marmellata.

f. Beviamo una taza de caffe con late.

g. Mi piace moltissimo il capacino perché è delizioso.

h. A cena mangio pasta o piza con prosutto.

i. Non mi piaciono per niente le verdure, anche se sono sano.

j. La mia frutta preferito è la mela. È deliciosa!

5. Sentence level translation EN - IT

a. I love fruit juice because it is sweet and refreshing.

b. I don't like salmon because it is disgusting.

c. At tea time I eat a cheese sandwich.

d. I always drink milk with honey. I like it because it's sweet.

e. I like fish, especially seafood.

4. Guided writing – write 3 short paragraphs in the first person [I] using the details below

Person	Lunch [usually]	Opinion	Sometimes	Meal
Matthew	chicken and rice	likes because it is tasty	cake or ice cream	dinner
Bridget	fish and chips	delicious but unhealthy	cereals and fruit	breakfast
Luciana	salad or soup	really healthy and light	toast and jam	snack

Grammar Time 9: ARE Verbs (Part 2)
PRANZARE, CENARE, MANGIARE

PRANZARE to eat for lunch	al ristorante at the restaurant		MANGIARE to eat	
	a mensa at the canteen	e *and*		una mela
Pranz**o** *I have lunch*	a casa *at home*	di solito *usually*	mangi**o** *I eat*	un panino
Pranz**i** *you*	a casa di mia madre at my mum's house		mang**i** *you*	una pizza
Pranz**a** *he/she*			mang**ia** *he/she*	
Pranz**iamo** *we*		sempre *always*	mang**iamo** *we*	l'agnello
Pranz**ate** *you all*	a mezzogiorno at midday		mang**iate** *you all*	
Pranz**ano** *they*	all'una *at one*	spesso *often*	mang**iano** *they*	lasagne
CENARE to eat for dinner	alle due *at two*			pasta
				salsicce
Cen**o** *I have dinner*	alle sei *at six*			spaghetti
Cen**i** *you*	alle sette *at seven*			verdure
Cen**a** *he/she*	alle otto *at eight*			
Cen**iamo** *we*				
Cen**ate** *you all*				
Cen**ano** *they*				

Author's note: Pranzare, cenare and *mangiare* belong to the group of regular verbs ending in –are, in the infinitive form. What patterns do you notice in the Present Tense?

DRILLS

1. Complete with the missing letters

a. (io) Mangi__ cereali a colazione

b. Mia madre pranz__ all'una

c. I miei genitori pranz__ _ _ alle due

d. Mio nonno mangi__ pollo arrosto

e. Noi mangi__ _ _ molta frutta

f. (Io) Cen__ sempre alle sei

g. Cosa mang__ tu?

h. Loro cen__ _ _ _ alle sette?

i. Noi pranzi__ _ _ in cucina.

j. A mezzogiorno voi pranz__ _ _ a scuola.

k. Mio fratello pranz__ alle tre in campagna

l. Tu cen__ alle otto con la tua famiglia.

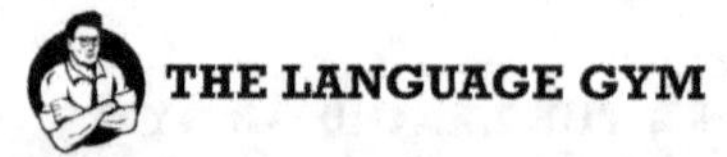

2. Complete with the missing forms of *'Mangiare'*

a. (Io) Non ___________ molto. Prendo solo un panino.

b. Mia madre ___________ sempre la frutta.

c. I miei genitori _____________ pesce a cena.

d. Mia sorella a colazione _____________ cereali con latte.

e. E voi, cosa _______________ a pranzo?

f. Ciao Marco, cosa ___________ (tu) a merenda?

g. Noi non _______________ mai il formaggio, è disgustoso!

3. Spot and correct the errors with the verbs *'Pranzare'* and *'Cenare'*

a. (Io) Non pranziamo a casa

b. Mia madre ceno alle sei

c. Mio fratello ed io ceni alle sette

d. Mio padre pranzate in ufficio

e. Voi pranzano a scuola

f. Loro cena sempre alle cinque

g. La mia amica tutti i giorni pranzo a mezzogiorno.

4. Translate into English

a. Mia madre è dottoressa, lei pranza in ospedale.

b. Mia sorella mangia la cioccolata tutti i giorni.

c. A volte io ceno alle sei a casa di mia madre.

d. Normalmente io pranzo a mensa verso l'una.

e. Che cosa mangiate? Mangiamo un'insalata mista.

f. Noi di solito ceniamo alle sette.

g. Voi mangiate sempre pane tostato a colazione.

h. Di solito loro cenano al ristorante.

5. Translate into Italian

a. I have dinner – C______________________

b. We have lunch – P______________________

c. She eats – M______________________

d. They have lunch – P______________________

e. He has dinner – C______________________

f. They have dinner – C______________________

g. I have lunch – P______________________

h. You all eat – M______________________

6. Translate into Italian

a. For breakfast I eat two eggs and one sausage. Also, I drink a coffee with milk.

b. My friend Paolo has lunch at school. He only eats a ham sandwich and an apple.

c. We have dinner at six. We eat a steak or fish with potatoes.

d. At noon I drink a cup of coffee with my friend.

e. My friend Carlo never eats red meat. He only eats fish or chicken.

f. My parents have lunch at home, but my brother has lunch in the garden.

g. I like fruit. I eat oranges every day. Sometimes I have dinner at the restaurant.

h. I always eat at the canteen.

Grammar Time 10: AGREEMENTS (Part 2) (Food)

Il *the*	**caffè**　　　**MASC SING**			**amar**<u>**o**</u>
	cappuccino			**buono**
	pane			**delizioso**
	tè			**dolce**
	succo di frutta			**fresco**
				malsano
Lo *the*	**s**<u>**p**</u>**aghetto**		**è**	**saporito**
	<u>**z**</u>**ucchero**		*is*	**salato**
Quest<u>**o**</u> *this*				**sano**
La *the*	**carne**　　　**FEM SING**			**amar**<u>**a**</u>
	frutta			**buona**
	marmellata			**deliziosa**
	mela			***dolce**
Quest<u>**a**</u> *this*	**pasta**			**fresca**
	pizza			**malsana**
				saporita
				salata
				sana
	MASC PLURAL			**amar**<u>**i**</u>
I *the*	**biscotti**			**buoni**
	grissini			**deliziosi**
	panini			**dolci**
				freschi
Gl<u>**i**</u> *the*	**spaghetti**		**sono**	**malsani**
	zuccheri		*are*	**saporiti**
Quest<u>**i**</u> *these*				**salati**
				sani
	FEM PLURAL			**amar**<u>**e**</u>
	carote			**buone**
L<u>**e**</u> *the*	**fragole** *strawberries*			**deliziose**
	mele			**dolci**
	salsicce			**fresche**
Quest<u>**e**</u> *these*	**verdure**			**malsane**
				saporite
				salate
				sane

*__Author's note:__ adjectives ending in –e, like dolce sweet, do not change in the feminine but they change into –i in the plural. Ex: 'il gelato è dolce'; 'i gelati sono dolci'. **La** becomes **l'** before a vowel: l'acqua, l'uva.*

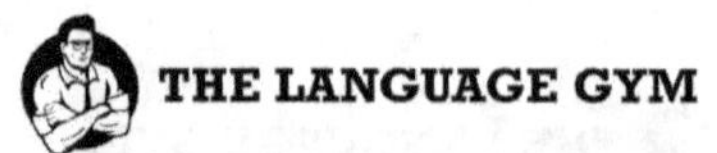

1. Choose the correct option as shown in the example

	A	**B**
Questo pesce è	<u>sano</u>	sana
Questo pane è	delizioso	deliziosa
Questa carne è	grasso	grassa
Il latte è	fresco	fresca
La pizza è	salato	salata
Questa mela è	sano	sana
Questi panini sono	buone	buoni
Queste fragole sono	dolce	dolci

2. Write the opposite version of the adjectives below

Maschile	Femminile
	disgustosa
delizioso	
	amara
dolce	
fresco	
	sana
saporiti	
	salate

3. Translate into English

a. Questi gamberi sono salati

b. Questo agnello è buono

c. Questo pollo è molto saporito

d. Questa mela non è molto fresca

e. Questi biscotti sono dolci

f. Queste salsicce sono malsane

g. Questa pizza è un po' salata

4. Tick off the correct sentences and correct the incorrect ones

a. Questi gamberi sono buono

b. Questo agnello è saporito

c. Questo pollo sono molto salati

d. Questa mela è molto deliziosa

e. Gli spaghetti sono saporiti

f. Queste salsicce sono molto grasso

5. Complete

a. Il pesce è disgustos___

b. Le mele sono san___

c. La carne rossa è malsan___

d. I biscotti sono troppo dolc___

e. Gli spaghetti sono saporit___

f. Queste fragole sono delizios___

g. Queste banane sono fresch___

h. Questo caffè è amar___

6. Translate into Italian

a. This fish is disgusting

b. These prawns are delicious

c. This coffee is too sweet

d. These sausages are very fatty

e. These vegetables are very tasty

f. These oranges are very healthy

g. This pasta is very good

h. This fruit is refreshing

Question Skills 2: Jobs/School bag/Food

1. Translate into English

a. Dove pranzi a mezzogiorno?

b. Che lavoro fa tua madre?

c. Cosa c'è nel tuo zaino?

d. Qual è il tuo **cibo** *[food]*preferito?

e. Cosa ti piace bere?

f. A che ora ceni con la tua famiglia?

g. Ti piace il caffè?

h. Perché non mangi verdure?

i. Mangi spesso il gelato?

j. Di che colore è il tuo astuccio?

k. Perché mangi la frutta?

l. Di solito cosa mangi a colazione?

2. Match the answers below to the questions in activity 1

1. Si, mi piace molto.

2. Mi piace bere il succo d'arancia.

3. A colazione di solito mangio un cornetto alla marmellata.

4. Si, lo mangio spesso. È delizioso.

5. Perché non mi piacciono.

6. La pizza margherita.

7. Perché è fresca e dolce.

8. Io e la mia famiglia ceniamo alle sette.

9. Ci sono due libri, una matita e un tablet.

10. Mia madre è poliziotta.

11. A mezzogiorno pranzo a scuola.

12. Il mio astuccio è verde.

3. Provide the questions to the following answers

a. Non mangio carne.

b. Mangio sempre le verdure perché sono sane.

c. Lavoro come dentista.

d. Amo la frutta perché è deliziosa e sana.

e. Pranzo a scuola.

f. A volte mangio pesce a cena.

g. Vivo a Edimburgo.

h. Sono di Roma.

i. Non ho animali.

j. La mia bibita *[drink]* preferita è la limonata.

k. Mio padre è un avvocato.

l. Nel mio astuccio ci sono due penne e una gomma.

4. Complete

a. C______ c'__ n____ t___ zaino?

b. C___ l_________fai? Faccio il cuoco.

c. A c___ o___ c______ con la tua famiglia?

d. C_____ m______ a colazione?

e. Q____ è l__ t__ bevanda p____________?Il latte!

f. Q_____ è i__ t___ c_____ preferito? La pasta!

g. D__ d______ sei? Sono di Leeds.

h. D______ p______ normalmente? A scuola!

UNIT 13
Talking about clothes and accessories I wear, how frequently and when

Grammar Time 11: -ARE Verbs (Part 2) Indossare + Agreements

Revision Quickie 3: Jobs, food, clothes and numbers 20-100

In this unit you will learn how to:

- Say what clothes you wear in various circumstances and places
- Describe various types of weather
- Give a wide range of words for clothing items and accessories
- Use a range of words for places in town
- Make the full present indicative conjugation of *'portare'* (to wear)

You will revisit:
- Time markers
- Frequency markers
- Colours
- Self-introduction phrases
- Present indicative of *'Avere'*
- Noun-to-adjective agreement

UNIT 13
Talking about clothes
'Che vestiti porti di solito?'
What clothes do you usually wear?

				SING FEM	
A volte *Sometimes*			**borsa** *bag*		**bianca** *white*
		una *a*	**camicia** *shirt*		**gialla** *yellow*
Di solito *Usually*			**canottiera** *tank top/ vest*		**nera** *black*
			cintura *belt*		**rossa** *red*
Mai** *Never*			**collana** *necklace*		**verde** *green*
			cravatta *tie*		***blu** *blue*
Raramente *Rarely*			**giacca** *jacket*		**rosa** *pink*
			gonna *skirt*		**viola** *purple*
Sempre *Always*	**porto/ indosso** *I wear*		**maglietta** *a T-shirt*		**cara** *expensive*
			sciarpa *scarf*		**comoda** *comfy*
			tuta *tracksuit*		**firmata** *designer*
			uniforme *uniform*		**sportiva** *sporty*

				SING MASC	
	non porto/non indosso *I don't wear*		**berretto** *baseball cap*		**bianco** *white*
Quando fa caldo *When it is hot*		**un** *a*	**cappotto** *coat*		**giallo** *yellow*
			costume *swimsuit*		**caro** *expensive*
			maglione *jumper*		**firmato** *designer*
			cappello *hat*		**sportivo** *sporty*
Quando fa freddo *When it is cold*			**completo** *suit*		
			vestito *dress*		

			PLURAL MASC	
		calzini *socks*		**bianchi** *white*
		pantaloni *trousers*		**gialli** *yellow*
In casa *At home*		**pantaloni corti** *shorts*		**cari** *expensive*
		sandali *sandals*		**firmati** *designer*
In palestra *At the gym*	**porta/ indossa** *he/she wears*	**jeans** *jeans*		**sportivi** *sporty*
		vestiti *clothes*		
In spiaggia *At the beach*		**occhiali da sole** *sun glasses*		
		stivali *boots*		

			PLURAL FEM	
A scuola *At school*		**scarpe** *shoes*		**azzurre** *light blue*
In ufficio *In the office*		**scarpe coi tacchi** *high heel shoes*		**bianche** *white*
		scarpe da ginnastica *sports shoes*		**care** *expensive*

Author's note: *Bear in mind that the words for colour **blu, rosa, viola** do not change in number or gender. *Ex. Le scarpe rosa/ I pantaloni blu.*

** The adverb "**mai**" should be used after the verb, mainly in the negative form. Ex. *"Non indosso mai"*

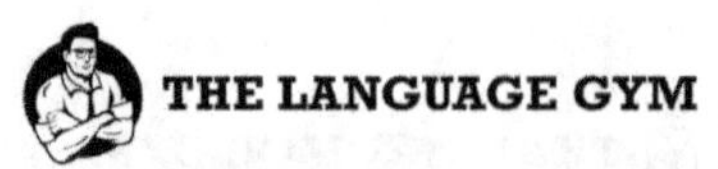

Unit 13. Talking about clothes: VOCABULARY BUILDING

1. Match up

1. stivali	a. a baseball cap
2. una maglietta	b. trainers
3. un vestito	c. some trousers
4. scarpe da ginnastica	d. a suit
5. dei pantaloni	e. a T-shirt
6. un completo	f. boots
7. un berretto da baseball	g. a dress

2. Translate into English

a. Indosso una maglietta nera.

b. Indosso un vestito grigio.

c. Non porto scarpe da ginnastica.

d. Mia madre porta un cappello blu.

e. Non porto un orologio.

f. Non indosso mai orecchini.

g. Indosso una tuta e una canottiera.

h. Non porto mai un completo.

i. Sempre indosso sandali.

j. Non porto mai un cappello

k. Mio fratello sempre indossa i jeans

l. Io porto sempre gli occhiali da sole.

5. Complete each sentence in a way which is logical and grammatically correct

1. Raramente porto una sciarpa _______________.

2. Non porto un __________________ verde.

3. Indosso sempre una _______________ bianca.

4. A scuola, a volte indosso un'____________ grigia.

5. In palestra non porto mai una _____________.

6. Di solito in spiaggia indosso ___________ neri.

3. Complete with the missing word

a. In casa _____ una ____________________
[At home I wear a T-shirt]

b. A scuola indosso un' ________________ n_______
[At school I wear a black uniform]

c. In palestra ___________ una tuta ________
[At the gym I wear a pink tracksuit]

d. In spiaggia _________ un _________
[At the beach I wear a swimsuit]

e. Porto sempre un ________ nero e ________
_________ bianche *[I always wear a black dress and white high heels shoes]*

f. Raramente _______ scarpe ___ ______________
[I rarely wear sports shoes]

g. Non ________ mai un completo
[I never wear a suit]

4. Anagrams [clothes and accessories]

a. un colleppa

b. un ologioro

c. una parscia

d. una gliematta

e. un pocapott

f. una nonga

g. un stucome

h. leso da liocchia

i. gliomane

j. stitove

k. persca

l. feunimor

6. Complete with the missing letters

a. Porto sti_____ neri *[I wear black boots]*

b. In c________ *[At home]*

c. Ho un__________ *[I have a watch]*

d. Porto una cr________ rossa
[I wear a red tie]

e. Indosso un com__________ azzurro
[I wear a blue suit]

f. Lui porta un be___________ da baseball
[He wears wears a baseball hat]

g. Mia sorella indossa sempre vestiti n_____
[My sister always wears black dresses]

Unit 13. Talking about clothes: READING

Mi chiamo Paloma. Sono spagnola. Sono di San Roque. Ho quindici anni. Sono sportiva e ho molti vestiti di colori e stili differenti. Preferisco i vestiti di buona qualità (*of good quality*) ma non troppo cari. Di solito in casa indosso una tuta. Ho tre o quattro tute diverse. Quando vado a scuola, indosso qualcosa di comodo: un maglione, dei jeans **aderenti** *[skinny]* e delle scarpe da ginnastica.

Mi chiamo Claudia. Sono francese. Ho tredici anni, ho i capelli lunghi e castani. Amo comprare (to buy) vestiti, soprattutto scarpe. Ho molte scarpe e firmate. Mi piacciono i vestiti italiani perché sono di buona qualitá. Quando fa freddo di solito porto un cappotto e dei pantaloni neri. A volte porto una giacca sportiva. Quando fa caldo, in spiaggia porto dei pantaloncini corti, una canottiera e dei sandali.

Mi chiamo Hilda. Sono tedesca. Ho dodici anni. Mi piace molto la moda italiana. Mi piacerebbe comprare una borsa Prada o Armani perché le borse firmate sono belle e di buona qualitá. Di solito però indosso vestiti sportivi: una tuta o un maglione, perché sono comodi. Ho **un armadio** *[a wardrobe]* grande. Mi piacerebbe comprare un paio di scarpe coi tacchi, quando sono grande!

Mi chiamo Giulia, sono italiana ma vivo in Scozia. Ho quattordici anni. In casa di solito indosso una maglietta e dei jeans. Ho molti maglioni e giacche. Quando vado a scuola, indosso un'uniforme: camicia bianca, gonna grigia, cravatta verde e scarpe nere. Sono molto sportiva. Quando vado in palestra indosso una tuta e delle scarpe da ginnastica. Quando fa freddo porto un cappotto rosso e una sciarpa blu.

1. Find the Italian for the following in Paloma's text

a. I am from

b. Very sporty

c. Many clothes

d. Good quality clothes

e. A tracksuit

f. When I go to school

g. Something comfy

h. Different styles

i. A jumper

j. Trainers

2. Find the Italian for the following in Giulia's text

a. I live in Scotland

b. At home I usually wear

c. T-shirt and jeans

d. I have many jumpers

e. When I go

f. I wear a uniform

g. Grey skirt

h. Black shoes

i. I am sporty

j. When it is cold

3. Complete the following statements about Claudia's text

a. She is __________ and she is __________ years old

b. She loves buying __________, especially __________

c. She has many branded __________ and __________

d. When it's cold she wears a __________ and __________ __________

e. Sometimes she wears a __________ __________

4. Answer in Italian the questions below about Hilda

a. Come si chiama?

b. Di dov'è?

c. Quanti anni ha?

d. Cosa le piace molto?

e. Cosa indossa di solito?

5. Find someone who...

a. ...loves branded clothes

b. ...is from Germany

c. ...wears a sports jacket

d. ...would like to buy high heels when she is older

e. ...has many jackets and jumpers

f. ...has a lot of t-shirts and jeans at home

g. ...wears skinny jeans for school

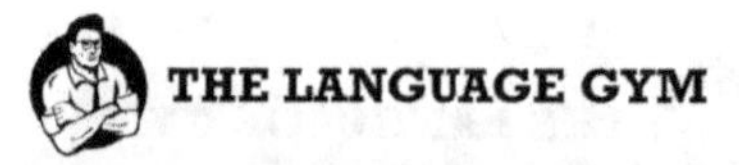

Unit 13. Talking about clothes: WRITING

1. Split sentences

A casa porto	porto una maglietta
Quando fa	una tuta comoda
In palestra	porto scarpe con i tacchi
Quando fa caldo	freddo porto una sciarpa
Non indosso mai jeans	indosso dei pantaloncini
In ufficio	Levi's
Indosso pantaloni	nera
Lei porta una camicia	neri

2. Complete with the correct option

a. In __________ indosso vestiti belli ma comodi.

b. A scuola lei ___________ un'uniforme verde.

c. In palestra porto delle ________ da tennis.

d. In spiaggia indosso un _______________

e. Quando _____ caldo porto una ____________

f. In casa mia madre porta ______ tuta.

g. Mia sorella indossa una ________ firmata

h. ________ fa freddo, indosso un ____________

cappotto	borsa	una	porta	quando
scarpe	casa	fa	costume	maglietta

3. Spot and correct the grammar and spelling mistakes [note: in several cases a word is missing]

a. Quando freddo mia nonna indossa uno sciarpa.

b. In casa porto una tuta comodo.

c. Ho molte scarpe nera.

d. Mio fratello porta bereto bianco.

e. A scuola un' uniforme elegante.

f. Mi piacciono i vestito firmati.

g. Di solito indossare vestiti buona qualità.

h. Porto sempre una gona rosso.

5. Describe this person in Italian using the 3rd person

Name: Giacomo

Lives in: London

Age : 20

Pet: A black dog

Hair: blond + green eyes

Always wears: white shirt

Never wears: shorts

At the gym wears: an Adidas tracksuit

4. Guided writing – write 3 short paragraphs in the first person [I] using the details below

Person	Lives	Always wears	Never wears	Likes
Amparo	Madrid	coat	skirt	belt
Charlotte	Sydney	white t-shirt	coats	sunglasses
Flavia	Milan	black dress	shorts	designer bag

Grammar Time 11: ARE Verbs (Part 3)
PORT**ARE** + A**VERE** + AGREEMENTS

PORT**ARE** to wear			MASC	
(Io) porto *I wear*	un a	**berretto** *baseball cap*		**bianco** *white*
(Tu) porti *you wear*		**cappotto** *coat*		**giallo** *yellow*
(Lei/lui) porta *he/she wears*		**costume** *swimsuit*		**nero** *black*
(Noi) portiamo *we wear*		**cappello** *hat*		**caro** *expensive*
(Voi) portate *you all wear*		**completo** *suit*		**comodo** *comfy*
(Loro) portano *they wear*		**gilè** *waistcoat*		**firmato** *designer*
		maglione *jumper*		**sportivo** *sporty*
		vestito *dress*		
		borsa *bag*	**FEM**	
AVERE *to have*	una a	**camicia** *shirt*		**bianca** *white*
(Io) ho *I have*		**canottiera** *tank top/vest*		**gialla** *yellow*
(Tu) hai *you have*		**cintura** *belt*		**rossa** *red*
(Lei/lui) ha *he/she has*		**collana** *necklace*		**verde** *green*
(Noi) abbiamo *we have*		**cravatta** *tie*		**rosa** *pink*
(Voi) avete *you all have*		**giacca** *jacket*		**viola** *purple*
(Loro) hanno *they have*		**gonna** *skirt*		**cara** *expensive*
		maglietta *shirt*		**comoda** *comfy*
		sciarpa *scarf*		**firmata** *designer*
		tuta *tracksuit*		**sportiva** *sporty*
		uniforme *uniform*		

DRILLS

1. Complete with the missing verb endings

a. (io) Non port__ mai una tuta

b. Che vestiti port__ (tu) di solito?

c. Mio fratello h___ molte magliette

d. I miei genitori h______ vestiti firmati

e. Il mio professore di arte indoss__ un gilè

f. Voi port_____ un'uniforme a scuola

g. In spiaggia (noi) port________ un costume

h. (io) H___ molti jeans e pantaloni

i. Che scarpe av____________? (voi)

j. Mia madre ed io ab________ molti vestiti cari

k. Lei port__ una borsa firmata

l. Quando fa freddo (tu) port__ una sciarpa

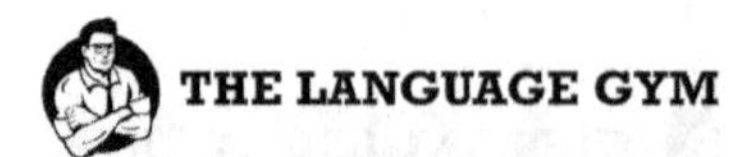

2. Complete with the missing verbs

a. Mia madre _________ molti vestiti di marca *[My mother has a lot of branded clothes]*

b. I miei fratelli _______________ sempre magliette *[My brothers always wear t-shirts]*

c. La mia professoressa di solito __________ una gonna *[My teacher usually wears a skirt]*

d. I miei professori ____________ sempre giacca e cravatta *[My teachers always wear a blazer and tie]*

e. La mia amica ____ molte borse e scarpe coi tacchi *[My friend has many bags and high heels shoes]*

f. Io e il mio amico Pablo _____________ molte camicie nere. Nel mio armadio _________ molti jeans.
[My friend Pablo and I have many black shirts. In my wardwrobe there are many jeans]

g. I miei genitori _____________ molti vestiti sportivi *[My parents wear a lot of sporty clothes]*

h. Voi non ____________ scarpe da ginnastica blu *[You all don't have blue trainers]*

3. Complete with the correct form of 'Portare'

a. (io) Port_ una maglietta.

b. Mia madre port_ un vestito elegante.

c. I miei fratelli non port_______ berretti.

d. Noi port_______ sempre jeans e legging.

e. Le mie amiche port_______ legging neri.

f. Che vestiti port__ tu?

g. (noi) Non port__________ mai un cappello.

h. In palestra (io) port___ una tuta comoda.

4. Complete with the correct form of 'Avere'

a. (io) Non h___ una cintura marrone.

b. Noi non abb_______ vestiti firmati.

c. Mio fratello ____ molte magliette bianche.

d. La mia amica Giovina_____ molte scarpe coi tacchi e borse.

e. Mio fratello _______ tante cravatte rosse.

f. Mia nonna non ____ vestiti eleganti.

g. Voi __________ un berretto da baseball nero.

5. Translate into English

a. Non indosso mai giacche sportive.

b. Lui indossa sempre pantaloni verdi.

c. Non abbiamo cappelli e borse.

d. Lei porta sempre dei pantacollant neri.

e. Tu hai molte scarpe di marca.

f. Voi indossate scarpe da ginnastica Nike.

g. Che vestiti porti a scuola?

h. In palestra a volte porto pantaloncini.

i. In spiaggia non indosso mai calzini.

j. Portiamo un'uniforme per andare a scuola.

6. Translate into Italian

a. Do you have baseball caps?

b. We have many shoes.

c. I don't have an elegant dress.

d. My father has many suits and ties.

e. My mother never wears jeans.

f. I never wear trainers.

g. What clothes do you usually wear?

h. They never wear uniforms.

i. At the gym I wear a tracksuit.

j. Do you wear sports clothes often?

Revision Quickie 3: Jobs, food, clothes and numbers 20-100

1. Complete (numbers)

a. 100 = ce

b. 90 = no

c. 30 = tr

d. 50 = ci

e. 80 = ot

f. 60 = se

g. 40 = qu

2. Translate into English (food and clothes)

a. la sciarpa

b. la bibita

c. il cibo

d. la gonna

e. il panino

f. l'acqua

g. la carne

h. i frutti di mare

i. la colazione

j. il cappotto

k. le scarpe

l. le verdure

m. il succo d'arancia

n. la cena

3. Write in a word for each letter in the categories below as shown in the example

LETTERA	Vestiti e accessori	Cibo o bibita	Numeri	Lavori
S	sciarpa	salsicce	sessanta	soldato
C				
V				
T				
O				

4. Match

indosso	I like
ho	I drink
sono	for lunch I have
ci sono	I live
mangio	I work
bevo	I have
pranzo	for dinner I have
lavoro	there is
ceno	I am
vivo	there are
c'è	I wear
mi piace	I eat

5. Translate into English

a. Non indosso mai gonne lunghe.

b. Mangio sempre pane con marmellata a merenda.

c. Lavoro come assistente di volo.

d. Bevo spesso caffè con latte.

e. Mi piace una bibita fresca.

f. A volte pranzo all'una con mia sorella.

g. Di solito ceno **verso** *[around]* le sette.

h. Non ho vestiti cari, né firmati.

i. Nel mio armadio ci sono molte magliette e jeans.

UNIT 14
Saying what I and others do in our free time

Grammar Time: Giocare, Fare, Andare

In this unit you will learn how to say:

- What activities you do using the verbs **'giocare'** (play), **'fare'** (do) and **'andare'** (go)
- Other free time activities

You will revisit:
- Time and frequency markers
- Weather
- Expressing likes/dislikes
- Adjectives
- Pets

UNIT 14
Saying what I (and others) do in our free time
'Che cosa fai nel tuo tempo libero?'
What do you do in your free time?

A volte *Sometimes* **Nel mio tempo libero** *In my free time* **Tutti i giorni** *Every day*	**gioco** *I play* **mi piace giocare** *I like playing*	**a**	pallone/calcio pallacanestro pallavolo scacchi tennis	*football* *basketball* *volleyball* *chess* *tennis*
		alla	playstation	*PlayStation*

Venerdì *Friday* **Sabato** *Saturday* **Domenica** *Sunday* **Quando fa bel tempo** *When the weather is good* **Quando fa brutto tempo** *When the weather is bad*	**faccio** *I do*	**atletica** **arrampicata** **ciclismo** **corsa** **i compiti** **equitazione** **ginnastica** **nuoto** **trekking**	*athletics* *rock climbing* *cycling* *jogging* *homework* *horse riding* *gymnastics* *swimming* *hiking*
	vado *I go*	**a casa del mio amico** *to my friend's house* **a sciare** *skiing* **al centro sportivo** *to the sports centre* **al cinema** *to the cinema* **al parco** *to the park* **in bicicletta** *on a bike ride* **in discoteca** *clubbing* **in montagna** *to the mountains* **in piscina** *to the pool* **in palestra** *to the gym* **in spiaggia** *to the beach*	

Author's Note: When using **"sempre"** *[always]*, we place it after the verb.
E.g. Gioco **sempre** a calcio *[I always play football]*

Unit 14. Free time: VOCABULARY BUILDING – Part 1

1. Match up

1. Gioco a pallavolo	a. I do horse-riding
2. Gioco a golf	b. I play volleyball
3. Faccio equitazione	c. I play basketball
4. Gioco a carte	d. I play golf
5. Faccio ciclismo	e. I go swimming
6. Faccio nuoto	f. I play football
7. Gioco a calcio	g. I go cycling
8. Gioco a pallacanestro	h. I play cards

2. Complete with the missing word

a. Gioco a ____________ [I play chess]

b. ___________ equitazione [I go horse riding]

c. ___________ a carte [I play cards]

d. Mi piace fare _______________ [I like doing gymnastics]

e. Gioco a __________________________ [I play basketball]

f. Faccio __________________ [I do athletics]

g. Mi piace fare _______________ [I like going swimming]

h. Faccio ______________________ [I go rock climbing]

i. Faccio _______________ [I do weights]

j. Non faccio i ________________ [I don't do my homework]

gioco	pesi	atletica	arrampicata	faccio
compiti	ginnastica	scacchi	pallacanestro	nuoto

3. Translate into English

a. Nel mio tempo libero gioco a calcio.

b. Spesso gioco a pallacanestro

c. A volte faccio arrampicata.

d. Raramente faccio equitazione.

e. Quando fa bel tempo vado a pesca.

f. Tutti i giorni mi piace fare ciclismo.

g. Raramente vado in discoteca.

h. Domenica vado al cinema.

i. Quando fa bel tempo, vado in spiaggia

j. Faccio i compiti tutti i giorni.

k. A volte, vado a casa del mio amico.

4. Broken words

a. Faccio eq________________ [I go horse-riding]

b. Faccio n________________ [I go swimming]

c. Vado a p________________ [I go fishing]

d. Vado in b________________ [I go on a bike ride]

e. Gioco a s________________ [I play chess]

f. Vado in d________________ [I go clubbing]

g. Gioco a c________________ [I play cards]

h. Faccio a________________ [I do rock climbing]

5. 'Vado', 'Gioco' or 'Faccio'?

a. _________ a pallacanestro

b. _________ in bicicletta

c. _________ a carte

d. _________ nuoto

e. _________ in montagna

f. _________ a tennis

g. _________ pesi

h. _________ equitazione

6. Bad translation – spot any translation errors and fix them

a. Non vado mai in discoteca: *I often go clubbing*

b. Spesso gioco a carte: *I play chess often*

c. Raramente faccio trekking: *I go swimming rarely*

d. Quando fa bel tempo gioco a golf: *when the weather is nice I go hiking*

e. Vado in bici due volte a settimana: *I go biking every day*

f. Spesso gioco a scacchi: *I never play chess*

g. Sempre faccio arrampicata: *I never go hiking*

h. Spesso vado in piscina: *I go swimming from time to time*

Unit 14. Free time: READING

Mi chiamo Thomas Weidner. Sono tedesco. Nel mio tempo libero faccio molto sport. Il mio sport preferito è l'arrampicata. Faccio arrampicata tutti i giorni. Quando fa brutto tempo **sto a casa** [*I stay at home*] e gioco a scacchi o a carte. Mi piace giocare ai videogiochi su Playstation o Xbox. Gioco sempre alla Playstation.

Mi chiamo Verónica. Sono spagnola, di Barbastro. Ho i capelli rossi. Sono molto simpatica e divertente, ma non sono molto sportiva. Preferisco leggere libri [*reading books*], giocare ai videogiochi o a scacchi e ascoltare musica. Quando fa bel tempo, tuttavia, corro nel parco del **mio quartiere** [*my area*] o gioco a tennis con mio fratello. Non mi piace andare in palestra, né in piscina. Odio il nuoto perché non mi piace l'acqua.

Mi chiamo Nicola. Sono inglese. Nel mio tempo libero mi piace molto leggere libri e giornali. Mi piace anche giocare a carte e a scacchi. Non sono molto sportiva ma a volte vado in palestra e faccio pesi. Inoltre, quando fa bel tempo faccio trekking in campagna con il mio cane. Il mio cane si chiama Doug ed è grande e bianco.

Mi chiamo Annie. Sono francese. Adoro andare in bicicletta. Vado in bici tutti i giorni con i miei amici. È il mio sport preferito. A volte faccio arrampicata, nuoto o trekking. Non mi piace né il tennis né il calcio. Odio anche il nuoto. Mi piace giocare sul telefonino e **inviare** [*to send*] WhatsApp ai miei amici. Due volte alla settimana vado in discoteca col mio fidanzato. Amo ballare.

1. Find the Italian for the following in Thomas' text

a. I do a lot of sport

b. My favourite sport

c. Climbing

d. Every day

e. When the weather's bad

f. I play chess

g. Always

h. I play on the PlayStation

2. Find the Italian in Annie's text for

a. I love biking

b. with my friends

c. sometimes

d. I do swimming

e. I go clubbing

f. I go rock climbing

g. with my boyfriend

h. playing on the phone

3. Complete the following statements about Verónica

a. She is ______________ from ____________________

b. She is very ______________ and ____________________

c. She plays videogames or ____________________

d. When the weather is nice she ____________________

e. She also plays tennis with her____________________

f. She doesn't enjoy the gym nor the ______________

4. List 8 details about Nicola

1. ____________________

2. ____________________

3. ____________________

4. ____________________

5. ____________________

6. ____________________

7. ____________________

8. ____________________

5. Find someone who…

a. …enjoys reading newspapers

b. …hates swimming

c. …does a lot of sport

d. …does weight lifting

e. …goes clubbing twice a week

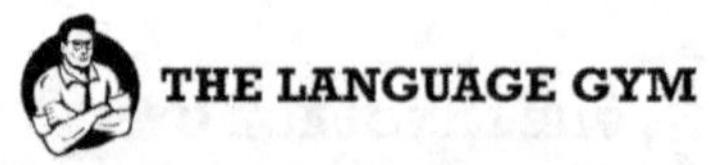

Unit 14. Free time: TRANSLATION

1. Gapped translation

a. Non vado mai in discoteca: *I ______________ go clubbing*

b. Spesso gioco a pallacanestro: *I often play ________________*

c. Gioco a tennis due volte alla settimana: *I play tennis ________________________________*

d. Gioco a __________________: *I play volleyball*

e. Tutti i giorni gioco a __________: *every day I play cards*

f. A volte, vado al parco: ______________, *I go to the park*

g. Non faccio mai pesi: *I never do ____________________*

h. Quando ____ bel tempo faccio __________: *When the weather is nice, I go jogging*

2. Translate to English

a. Due volte a settimana

b. A volte

c. Quando fa brutto tempo

d. A casa del mio amico

e. Al centro sportivo

f. Tutti i giorni

g. Faccio arrampicata

h. Vado in spiaggia

i. Vado a pesca

3. Translate into English

a. Non vado mai a pesca con mio padre

b. Gioco a carte con mio fratello

c. Faccio trekking con mia madre

d. Gioco a pallone con la mia migliore amica

e. Raramente gioco alla playstation con mio cugino

f. Spesso vado al cinema con la mia ragazza *[girlfriend]*

4. Translate into Italian

a. Bike: B______________________

b. Rock climbing: A________________

c. Basketball: P____________________

d. Fishing: P______________________

e. Weights: P______________________

f. Videogames: V__________________

g. Chess: S______________________

h. Cards: C______________________

i. Hiking: T____________________

j. Jogging: C____________________

5. Translate into Italian

a. I 'do' jogging

b. I play chess

c. I 'do' rock climbing

d. I 'do' swimming

e. I 'do' horse riding

f. I do weights

g. I do my homework

h. I play videogames

i. I 'do' cycling

j. I 'do' gymnastics

Unit 14. Free time: WRITING

1. Split sentences

Vado al centro	parco
Spesso gioco	volte a settimana
Vado a casa	sportivo tutti i giorni
Faccio corsa nel	a pallavolo
Gioco a	bicicletta
Faccio sport due	della mia amica
A volte vado in	in palestra
Faccio pesi	carte

2. Complete the sentences with a suitable word

a. Non __________ ginnastica

b. A volte ____________ a pallavolo

c. Raramente __________ arrampicata

d. Spesso _________ equitazione

e. Gioco a tennis __________ _____ giorni

f. Vado a _________ del mio amico John.

g. Nel mio __________ libero mi piace nuotare.

h. Mi __________ giocare a rugby

i. Gioco _____ golf una volta a settimana

3. Spot and correct mistakes
[note: in some cases a word is missing]

a. Facio ecquitazione:

b. Giooco a palavolo:

c. Vado a casa mio amico:

d. Tutti giorni vado bicicletta:

e. Faccio gli compiti:

f. Vado a piscina:

g. Gioco a calicio:

h. mi piace gioco a tennis:

4. Complete the words

a. Sca________________

b. Pallac______________

c. Ginn______________

d. Video____________

e. Equi______________

f. Atle________________

g. Pall________________

h. Pisc________________

5. Write a paragraph for each of the people below in the first person singular (I):

Name	Sport I do	How often	Who with	Where	Why I like it
Giovanni	Hiking	every day	with my friend	in the countryside	it's fun
Dylan	Weight-lifting	often	with my friend James	at home	it's healthy
Simona	Jogging	when the weather is nice	alone	in the park	it's relaxing

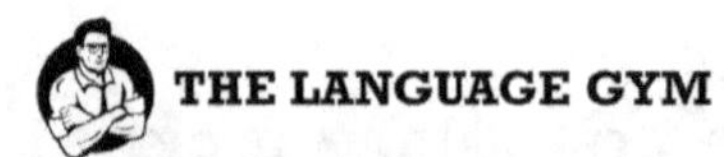

	Giocare *to play*	
A volte *Sometimes* **Due volte a settimana** *Twice a week* **Tutti i giorni** *Every day* **Raramente** *Rarely*	**(io) gioco** *I play* **(tu) giochi** *you play* **(lui/lei) gioca** *he/she plays* **(noi) giochiamo** *we play* **(voi) giocate** *you all play* **(loro) giocano** *they play*	**a carte** *cards* **a calcio/pallone** *football* **a hockey** *hockey* **a pallacanestro** *basketball* **a scacchi** *chess* **a tennis** *tennis*
	Fare *to do*	
Quando ho tempo *When I have time* **Quando fa brutto tempo** *When the weather is bad* **Quando fa bel tempo** *When the weather is good*	**(io) faccio** *I do* **(tu) fai** *you do* **(lui/lei) fa** *he/she does* **(noi) facciamo** *we do* **(voi) fate** *you all do* **(loro) fanno** *they do*	**arrampicata** *rock climbing* **ciclismo** *cycling* **i compiti** *homework* **corsa** *jogging* **equitazione** *horse riding* **nuoto** *swimming* **una passeggiata** *a walk*
	Andare *to go*	
Lunedì *Monday* **Martedì** *Tuesday* **Mercoledì** *Wednesday* **Giovedì** *Thursday* **Venerdì** *Friday* **Sabato** *Saturday* **Domenica** *Sunday*	**(io) vado** *I go* **(tu) vai** *you go* **(lui/lei) va** *he/she goes* **(noi) andiamo** *we go* **(voi) andate** *you all go* **(loro) vanno** *they go*	**a pesca** *fishing* **al centro sportivo** *to the sports centre* **al cinema** *to the cinema* **al mare** *to the seaside* **al parco** *to the park* **in bicicletta** *on a bike ride* **in discoteca** *clubbing* **in montagna** *to the mountains* **in palestra** *to the gym* **in piscina** *to the pool* **in spiaggia** *to the beach*

1. Match

Faccio	He/she does
Fai	We do
Fa	You do
Facciamo	I do
Fate	They do
Fanno	You all do

3. Write the correct form of GIOCARE (to play)

a. I play: _______________________

b. You play: _______________________

c. She plays: _______________________

d. We play: _______________________

e. You guys play: _______________

f. They play: _______________________

g. My brothers play: ______________

h. You and I play: _______________

i. He and I play: _______________

5. Spot and correct the translation errors

a. Vado a pesca [You go fishing]

b. Vai in chiesa [We go to church]

c. Andiamo al centro commerciale

[You guys go to the shopping mall]

d. Non vado mai a casa di Marta

[We never go to Marta's house]

e. Vanno al cinema una volta a

settimana

[She goes to the cinema once a week]

f. Lei va a sciare in inverno

[She goes skiing at the weekend]

2. Complete with the correct ending

a. (io) Non facci___ mai i compiti.

b. Mio padre gioc___ spesso a pallone con me.

c. Che sport fa__ tu?

d. (noi) lunedì gioch________ a tennis.

e. (voi) Cosa fa____ domenica?

f. I miei amici gioc_____ sempre alla Playstation.

g. (tu) Non gioc___ mai ai videogiochi.

h. Mio fratello maggiore f___ atletica tutti i giorni.

i. I miei cugini non f__ ginnastica, gioc_____ a golf.

j. Mia madre ed io, il sabato, facc________ nuoto.

4. Complete with the first person of FARE, ANDARE and GIOCARE: *faccio, vado, gioco*

a. A volte ___________ a pallavolo.

b. _________ sport tutti i giorni.

c. _________ a pallavolo.

d. Raramente _________ a carte.

e. Non ________ mai ciclismo, ________ equitazione.

f. _________ alla playstation tutti i giorni.

g. Quando fa bel tempo________ al mare.

h. ________ arrampicata quando ho tempo.

i. La domenica ________ allo stadio con mio padre.

j. _________ sempre i compiti nel pomeriggio.

6. Complete the forms of ANDARE below

a. V___ in palestra [I go to the gym]

b. V____ in chiesa [They go to church]

c. A______ in spiaggia [We go to the beach]

d. V____ in piscina [They go to the swimming pool]

e. Dove v__? V___ a casa

 [Where are you going? I am going home]

f. Tu v__ a teatro [You go to the theatre]

g. V__ andate allo stadio? [Do you all go to the stadium?]

7. Complete with _fa, gioca_ or _va_ as appropriate

a. Mia madre ___________ molto sport.

b. Mio padre ________ in chiesa raramente.

c. Mio fratello _______ alla moschea tutti i venerdì.

d. Mio nonno non _________ mai a carte con me.

e. Mio fratello maggiore __________ karate.

f. La mia amica Sara _______ sempre in bici.

g. Mio fratello minore ________ sempre ciclismo.

h. Mia zia _____ una **passeggiata** _[walk]_ tutti i giorni.

8. Complete with _fanno, giocano_ or _vanno_ as appropriate

a. I miei amici ____________ a pallacanestro

b. I miei fratelli non ___________ sport

c. Le mie sorelle ___________ a pallone

d. Mamma e papá _____________ a carte

e. I miei cugini spesso _____________ a golf

f. I miei professori_________ in piscina tutti i giorni.

g. I miei zii __________ in chiesa molto raramente

h. Loro ____________ arrampicata una volta alla settimana.

i. Loro ___________ ciclismo in estate?

j. I miei amici Luke e Paul _____________ alla Xbox tutte le sere.

k. I miei nonni non ____________ in piscina, loro _________ al parco a fare una passeggiata.

9. Translate into English

a. Non giochiamo mai a pallone.

b. Luigi fa i compiti tutti i giorni.

c. A volte vado in chiesa la domenica.

d. Mio fratello va a scuola di calcio il sabato .

e. Quando fa bel tempo faccio una passeggiata.

f. Ogni martedì vado in palestra a fare pesi.

g. Quando fa brutto tempo gioco con la Xbox a casa.

10. Translate into Italian.

a. We never go to the swimming pool

b. They do sport rarely

c. She plays basketball every day

d. When the weather is nice, I do jogging

e. I rarely do cycling

f. I often do rock climbing

g. My father and I often play badminton

h. My sister plays tennis twice a week

i. I go to the swimming pool on Saturday

j. When the weather is bad I go to the gym

k. They rarely do their homework

l. We never play football, we play volleyball.

UNIT 15
Talking about free time and giving opinions

GRAMMAR TIME: Giocare/ Fare/ Andare
Question skills: Clothes / Free time/ Opinions

In this unit you will learn how to say:
- What free-time activities you do and give your opinion
- Where you do them and who with
- Words for places in town

You will also learn how to ask and answer questions about:
- Clothes
- Free time

You will revisit:
- Sports and hobbies
- The verbs 'fare', 'andare' and 'giocare' in the present indicative
- Pets
- Places in town
- Clothes
- Family members
- Numbers from 1 to 100
- Weather

Unit 15
Talking about free time and giving opinions
Cosa fai nel tuo tempo libero?
What do you do in your free time?

Nel mio tempo libero *In my free time* **Durante le vacanze** *During my holidays* **In estate** *In the summer* **In inverno** *In the winter* **Il fine settimana** *At the weekend* **La domenica** *On Sunday* **A volte** *Sometimes* **Spesso** *Often* **Sempre** *Always* **Tutti i giorni** *Everyday*	**gioco** *I play* **la mia amica Maria gioca** *my friend Maria plays*	**a carte** *cards* **a pallone** *football* **a tennis** *tennis* **ai videogiochi** *videogames* **con i miei amici** *with my friends* **con i suoi amici** *with his/her friends*	**perché è** *because it is* **anche se è** *even if it is* **secondo me è** *according to me it is* **a mio parere è** *in my opinion it is* **penso che è** *I think it is* **mi piace perché è** *I like it because it is* **non mi piace perché è** *I do not like it because it is*	**appassionante** *thrilling* **difficile** *difficult* **dinamico/a** *dynamic* **divertente** *fun* **emozionante** *exciting* **facile** *easy* **fantastico/a** *fantastic* **faticoso/a** *tiring* **interessante** *interesting* **noioso/a** *boring* **pericoloso** *dangerous* **rilassante** *relaxing*
	faccio *I do* **il mio amico Leo fa** *my friend Leo does*	**arrampicata** *rock climbing* **ciclismo** *cycling* **corsa** *jogging* **nuoto** *swimming*		
	vado *I go* **il mio amico Andrew va** *my friend Andrew goes*	**a sciare** *skiing* **al cinema** *to the cinema* **al parco** *to the park* **allo stadio** *to the stadium* **in palestra** *to the gym* **in bici** *on a bike ride*		
	ascolto musica *I listen to music* **leggo un libro** *I read a book* **guardo Netflix** *I watch Netflix* **prendo il sole** *I sunbathe* **suono il piano** *I play the piano*			

Unit 15. Talking about free time and opinions: VOCABULARY BUILDING 1

1. Match up

1. In estate	a. at the weekend
2. In inverno	b. during my holidays
3. Nel mio tempo libero	c. every day
4. Il fine settimana	d. sometimes
5. Durante le vacanze	e. in my free time
6. A volte	f. in summer
7. Tutti i giorni	g. in winter

2. Translate into English

a. Nel mio tempo libero

b. Il fine settimana

c. Ascolto sempre la musica

d. A volte guardo la televisione

e. In inverno vado a sciare

f. Durante le vacanze

g. In estate faccio nuoto

h. Prendo il sole

i. Leggo un libro

3. Complete with the missing word

a. Il ___________ settimana *[At the weekend]*

b. ____________ le vacanze *[During the holidays]*

c. Vado in bici tutti i _________________
[I go on the bike every day]

d. Nel mio tempo ____________ faccio nuoto
[In my free time I do swimming]

e. In inverno vado in __________________
[In the winter I go to the gym]

f. A __________ vado allo stadio con mio fratello
[Sometimes I go to the stadium with my brother]

g. La domenica mia madre ________ spesso al cinema
[On Sunday my mum often goes to the cinema]

h. La mia amica Sara ________ a pallone
[My friend Sara plays football]

4. Anagrams

a. emprse	g. rantedu
b. a tevol	h. le cavazen
c. sospes	i. uttit i nigior
d. vernoin in	j. li nefi tisetmana
e. ni testae	k. cogio
f. la menicado	l. ciofac

5. Bad translation- spot any translation errors and fix them

1. Il fine settimana vado al parco - *I go to the park every day*

2. La domenica il mio amico gioca a tennis- *On Sunday my friend plays the violin*

3. A volte guardo Netflix – *I often watch Netflix*

4. La mia amica Maria spesso va allo stadio - *My friend Maria never goes to the stadium*

5. In estate prendo il sole - *In summer I go skiing.*

6. Suono sempre il piano - *I play the piano in my free time*

6. Complete

a. Durante le ____________
[During the holidays]

b. Il fine ____________
[At the weekend]

c. _________ a tennis *[I play tennis]*

d. _________ un libro *[I read a book]*

e. Gioco con i miei __________
[I play with my friends]

f. _____ mio tempo libero
[In my free time]

g. _________ il violino
[I play the violin]

h. Spesso ____________ musica
[I often listen to music]

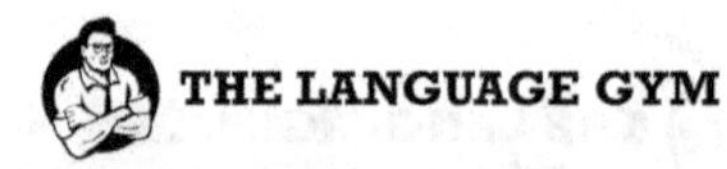

Unit 15. Talking about free time and opinions: VOCABULARY BUILDING 2

1. Match up

1. faticoso	a. fun
2. emozionante	b. relaxing
3. divertente	c. in my opinion
4. io penso che	d. easy
5. a mio parere	e. tiring
6. rilassante	f. I think that
7. secondo me	g. exciting
8. facile	h. according to me

2. Complete with the missing word

a. Gioco sempre a pallone ___________ é divertente
[I always play football because it is fun]
b. Penso che il nuoto è ________________
[I think that swimming is tiring]
c. A volte vado allo stadio perché è ______________
[I sometimes go to the stadium because it's exciting]
d. A mio_____________ è facile. *[In my opinion it's easy]*
e. ___________ me è noioso. *[According to me it's boring]*
f. Gioco con i miei amici perché è _________________
[I play with my friends because it's fantastic]
g. Caterina suona il violino ________ ____ è difficile
[Caterina plays the violin even if it's difficult]
h. Vado a sciare perché è a______________
[I go skiing because it's thrilling]

3. Translate into English

a. Perché è facile

b. A mio parere è noioso

c. Secondo me è divertente

d. Anche se è faticoso

e. Penso che è dinamico

f. Mi piace molto perché è

appassionante

g. Non mi piace perché é difficile

4. Anagrams [adjectives]

a. fotisaco

b. vertedinte

c. nappantessioa

d. cifdifile

e. sonoio

f. zioemontena

g. cilefa

h. namidico

i. sticofanta

j. ressaintente

k. santerilas

l. loperisoco

5. Broken words

a. S_________ i_ p________ a_____ s_ è f____________
[I play the piano even if it's tiring]

b. M___ z____ F______ g_______ a c__________
[My aunt Franca plays cards]

c. V____ i_ b___ p_______ è d_________________
[I go on the bike because it's fun]

d. L_____ v__ a_ p________ c__ i s_____ a________
[Lina goes to the park with her friends]

e. M__ p______p______ è d_____________
[I like it because it is dynamic]

f. N___ m___p______ il n______ p_____ è p___________
[I don't like swimming because it's dangerous]

6. Complete

a. Faccio ____________ *[I go cycling]*

b. Mario ________ai videogiochi
[Mario plays videogames]

c. Lui ______ nuoto *[He does swimming]*

d. Vado ___ palestra *[I go to the gym]*

e. ______ in piscina *[I go to the pool]*

f. _________ che è facile *[I think it's easy]*

g. Prendo il____________ *[I sunbathe]*

h. __________ me è pericolosa
[According to me it's dangerous]

i. A mio ____________ *[In my opinion]*

Unit 15. Talking about free time and giving opinions: READING

Mi chiamo Pietro. Sono italiano. Ho dodici anni. Sono molto sportivo. Nel mio tempo libero faccio molto sport perché è fantastico! Di solito gioco a rugby o pallacanestro. Una volta alla settimana faccio arrampicata anche se, secondo me, è pericolosa! La domenica vado in palestra o vado al parco e indosso una tuta e delle scarpe da ginnastica. A volte però è un po' faticoso.

Ciao, mi chiamo Isabella e sono di Roma. Ho quindici anni. Nel mio tempo libero, quando fa freddo, vado in palestra perché è salutare. Quando fa caldo, invece, vado in bici o faccio una passeggiata. Tutti i giorni però faccio i compiti anche se è noioso! Poi guardo Netflix o ascolto musica, mi piace molto perché è emozionante. A casa di solito indosso jeans, o una tuta, quando leggo un libro nella mia camera.

Salve, mi chiamo Ana Laura. Vivo in Brasile. Ho sedici anni. Nel mio tempo libero amo cantare perché è emozionante. Il fine settimana vado al centro commerciale con le mie amiche. Quando esco di solito indosso una giacca sportiva e una minigonna. A volte vado al cinema con mia sorella. Mi piace perché, a mio parere, guardare un film é sempre interessante.

Mi chiamo Chloé. Sono francese. Ho quattordici anni. Durante le vacanze vado in spiaggia e faccio nuoto. La mattina, a volte, prendo il sole con mia sorella perché è rilassante. Nel pomeriggio leggo un libro o ascolto la musica. La sera vado al ristorante ed esco con i miei amici. Quando vado in discoteca indosso dei pantaloncini e una maglietta. Mi piace ballare in discoteca perché è emozionante. Mia sorella invece, in estate, gioca sempre a carte!

[invece = instead]

1. Find the Italian for the following in Pietro's text

a. I am Italian

b. I am 12

c. I am very sporty

d. in my free time

e. usually I play

f. I go to the park

g. according to me

h. it's dangerous

i. trainers

j. a bit tiring

2. Find the Italian for the following in Chloe's text

a. during the holidays

b. I swim

c. I go to the beach

d. it is relaxing

e. I go to a restaurant

f. a t-shirt

g. I wear shorts

h. it's exciting

i. instead

j. she always plays

3. Complete the following statements about Isabella's text

a. She is ________ years old
b. In her free time, when it ______, she goes to the ________
c. When it's hot, instead, she ___________ or goes for a walk with her _________ brother
d. Every day she does her __________ even if it is _______
e. Isabella watches _________ or she listens __ _______, she really likes it because it is __________
f. At home she wears _______ or a ________

4. Answer in Italian the questions below about Ana Laura

a. Dove vive Ana Laura?

b. Quanti anni ha?

c. Cosa fa nel suo tempo libero?

d. Dove va il fine settimana?

e. Cosa indossa?

f. Perché le piace guardare un film?

5. Find someone who...

a. reads a book in her bedroom ___________________

b. is from France ___________________

c. is very sporty ___________________

d. wears a miniskirt ___________________

e. does rock climbing ___________________

f. likes sunbathing ___________________

g. loves singing ___________________

Unit 15. Talking about free time and opinions: WRITING

1. Split sentences

Nel mio tempo	interessante
Durante le	il piano
Il fine	vacanze vado al mare
Vado allo	libero faccio corsa
La domenica gioco	stadio con mio fratello
A volte suono	fantastico
Penso che è	settimana
A mio parere è	a tennis

2. Complete with the correct option

a. Il fine ___________ il mio amico va allo stadio.

b. Spesso _________ il piano perché è rilassante.

c. Durante le _________ faccio nuoto con i miei amici.

d. In inverno _________ un maglione e una _______.

e. A _____ parere andare in palestra è faticoso.

f. _______ i giorni leggo un libro o gioco a carte.

g. La domenica la mia ________ Sara va ___ cinema.

h. Non faccio mai arrampicata perché è ___________

vacanze	indosso	suono	tutti	sciarpa
pericolosa	settimana	mio	amica	al

3. Spot and correct the grammar and spelling mistakes [note: in several cases a word is missing]

a. In inverno vado palestre con mia sorella

b. Durante le vacance vado in spiagia

c. Mi piace perché è interessante

d. A mio parere il ciclismo ha faticoso

e. Guardo la televisione tutto i giorni in salotto.

f. La domenica facio colazione in cucina con madre.

g. Spesso guardo Netflix, penso que è appassionante.

h. Di solito indosso un vestito nera perché e elegante

i. Nel mia tempo libero ascoltare musica

4. Guided writing – write 3 short paragraphs in the first person [I] using the details below

Name	Lives	Activity	With	Opinion
Stefano	Leeds	I go to the gym	my friend	exciting but tiring
Santino	Napoli	I play tennis	my brother	dynamic
Luciana	Glasgow	I listen to music	dog	fantastic

5. Describe this person in Italian using the 3rd person [he/she]

Name: Steven

Lives in: New York

Age : 13

Pet: a white dog

Weather: sunny and good weather

Always: goes to the park and does cycling

Opinion: because it is fun and relaxing

Grammar Time 13: Giocare, Fare, Andare + Essere and Avere

Giocare to play		
(io) gioco *I play*	**(noi) giochiamo** *we play*	**a carte** *cards* **a calcio/pallone** *football* **a pallacanestro** *basketball* **a scacchi** *chess*
(tu) giochi *you play*	**(voi) giocate** *you all play*	
(lui/lei) gioca *he/she plays*	**(loro) giocano** *they play*	

Fare to do		
(io) faccio *I do*	**(noi) facciamo** *we do*	**ciclismo** *cycling* **i compiti** *homework* **una passeggiata** *a walk*
(tu) fai *you do*	**(voi) fate** *you all do*	
(lui/lei) fa *he/she does*	**(loro) fanno** *they do*	

Andare to go		
(io) vado *I go*	**(noi) andiamo** *we go*	**al parco** *to the park* **al cinema** *to the cinema* **in bicicletta** *on a bike ride* **in piscina** *to the pool*
(tu) vai *you go*	**(voi) andate** *you all go*	
(lui/lei) va *he/she goes*	**(loro) vanno** *they go*	

Essere to be		
(io) sono *I am*	**(noi) siamo** *we are*	*Singular* *Plural* **alto/a** **alti/e** *tall* **bello(a)** **belli/e** *beautiful* **inglese** **inglesi** *English* **italiano/a** **italiani/e** *Italian*
(tu) sei *you are*	**(voi) siete** *you all are*	
(lui/lei) è *he/she is*	**(loro) sono** *they are*	

Avere to have		
(io) ho *I have*	**(noi) abbiamo** *we have*	**due fratelli** *2 brothers* **gli occhi scuri** *dark eyes* **i capelli castani** *brown hair* **undici anni** *11 years old* **un cane** *a dog*
(tu) hai *you have*	**(voi) avete** *you all have*	
(lui/lei) ha *he/she has*	**(loro) hanno** *they have*	

***Author's note:** the subject pronouns *"io", "tu", "lui", "lei", "noi", "voi", "loro"* are optional! They are useful to:
1) Add emphasis
2) Help know who we are talking about in the third person (he/she)

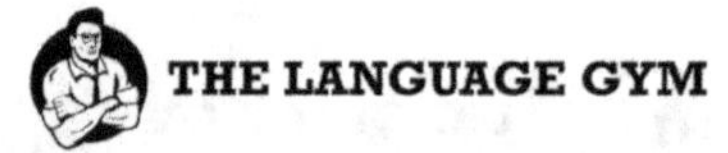

1. Complete with the one of the following verbs: *Ho – Vado – Sono – Gioco – Faccio*

a. ___________ sport

b. ___________ al parco

c. ___________ un gatto

d. ___________ a calcio

e. ___________ a carte

f. ___________ un cane

g. ___________ quindici anni

h. ___________ due animali

i. ___________ al cinema

j. ___________ arrampicata

k. ___________ ciclismo

l. ___________ a scacchi

m. ___________ a pallacanestro

n. ___________ gli occhi scuri

o. ___________ i capelli biondi

2. Rewrite the sentences in the first column in the third person singular

io	lui , lei
gioco a tennis	
vado al cinema	
ho un gatto	
sono alta	
faccio nuoto	

3. Translate into English

a. Facciamo ciclismo

b. Giochiamo a scacchi

c. Lei non fa niente

d. Loro vanno allo stadio

e. Abbiamo due cani

f. Siamo francesi

g. Non ha fratelli

h. Non sono di Londra

i. Non faccio niente

4. Complete

a. Io non v_________ mai in piscina

b. Mia madre a volte v_______ in chiesa

c. (Noi) A________ spesso al centro sportivo

d. Mio fratello h__ un gatto

e. Noi s_______ inglesi, tu s___ italiano

f. Io h___ i capelli rossi

g. Mio fratello ed io f___________ nuoto

5. Complete with the appropriate verb

a. (Io) Non _______ al cinema con i miei genitori

b. Mia sorella ed io ____________ al parco

c. Mia madre _______ quaranta anni

d. Mio cugino ______ molto alto e bello

e. I miei fratelli _________ sempre alla Xbox

f. (Lui) spesso ________ sport

g. Quando fa bel tempo Anna ____ al mare

6. Translate into Italian

a. I never play tennis with my dad

b. My mother never goes to church

c. My brother is tall and slim. He has blond hair and blue eyes

d. My uncle is forty years old

e. My sister goes to the gym every day

f. They never go to the swimming pool

g. My friends are generous and fun

Revision Quickie 4: Clothes/Free time/Opinions

1. Match

1. Faccio i compiti	*a. I go to church*
2. Faccio sport	*b. I go to the swimming pool*
3. Gioco a pallacanestro	*c. I go to the gym*
4. Gioco a carte	*d. I play volleyball*
5. Vado in chiesa	*e. I do the homework*
6. Vado in piscina	*f. I go swimming*
7. Vado in palestra	*g. I do rock climbing*
8. Gioco a pallavolo	*h. I do sport*
9. Faccio nuoto	*i. I go horse-riding*
10. Faccio equitazione	*j. I go to the beach*
11. Vado in spiaggia	*k. I play cards*
12. Faccio arrampicata	*l. I play basketball*

2. Opinions – Complete

a. A mio p_ _ _ _ _

b. S _ _ _ _ _ _ me

c. P_ _ _ o c_ _ è...

d. N _ _ m _ p_ _ _ _

e. A _ _ _ _ se...

f. È fa _ _ _ _ _ _ _ o

g. È ap _ _ _ _ _ _ _ _ _ e

h. Mi p_ _ _ _

i. Pr_ _ _ _ _ sco

3. Fill in the gaps in Italian

a. Il fine s____________normalmente faccio e______________ *[At the weekend I usually go horseriding]*

b. In i__________ la mia a_______ Lea v____ in p___________ *[In the winter my friend Leas goes to the gym]*

c. Non f_______ s____ perché a m____ p_______ è p___________ *[I don't do skiing because in my opinion it is dangerous]*

d. Quando v_______ al parco, p_________ una t____________ *[When I go to the park I wear a tracksuit]*

e. Q________ fa c_________, vado i_ p______________ *[When it is hot I go to the swimming pool]*

f. La d_____________ mio f _________ g________ a tennis *[On Sunday my brother plays tennis]*

g. Quando h__ t___________ v_________ i____ p______________ *[When I have time I go to the pool]*

4. Translate into Italian

a. At the weekend:

b. During my holidays:

c. I play basketball:

d. I do my homework:

e. I go rock climbing:

f. My friend plays videogames:

g. I go to the swimming-pool:

h. I go to the gym:

5. Translate into Italian

a. I wear a coat

b. We wear a uniform

c. They play basketball

d. She goes rock climbing

e. When I have free time

f. They go swimming

g. My parents do sport

h. She plays football often

Question Skills 3: Clothes/Free time/Opinions

1. Translate into English

a. Cosa indossi d'estate?

b. Quando vai al cinema?

c. Cosa fai nel tuo tempo libero?

d. Ti piace giocare con i tuoi amici?

e. Con chi giochi a pallacanestro?

f. Perché non ti piace il calcio?

g. Dove fai nuoto?

h. Qual è il tuo sport preferito?

i. Ti piace ascoltare la musica?

2. Complete with the missing question word:

a. _________ vivi?

b. ______ sport fai?

c. Ti _______ il ciclismo ?

d. _________ vai allo stadio?

e. _______ indossi per andare a scuola?

f. Con _______ giochi a tennis?

g. ______ ti chiami?

h. _________ non leggi un libro?

come	cosa	chi	quando
perché	dove	piace	che

3. Split questions

Dove vai la	in inverno?
Con chi	andare in bici?
Perché	nel tuo tempo libero?
Quando fai	domenica?
Ti piace	giochi a scacchi?
Qual è	i compiti?
Cosa indossi	non ti piace il tennis?
Cosa fai	il tuo sport preferito?

4. Translate into Italian

a. What? _____________________

b. Where? _____________________

c. How? _____________________

d. When? _____________________

e. Who? _____________________

f. Who with? _____________________

g. Do you like? _____________________

h. Why? _____________________

5. Write the questions to these answers

a. Indosso una giacca quando fa freddo

b. Faccio sport il fine settimana

c. Vado in piscina la domenica

d. Mi piace uscire con i miei amici

e. Guardo la televisione con mia madre

f. Indosso un'uniforme: camicia bianca e cravatta

g. Raramente vado a sciare, spesso faccio corsa

6. Translate into Italian

a. Where do you play tennis?

b. What do you do in your free time?

c. What do you wear to go to school?

d. What is your favourite sport?

e. Do you do like jogging?

f. When do you do your homework?

g. Why don't you play golf?

UNIT 16
Talking about my daily routine

In this unit you will learn how to say:

- What you do every day
- At what time you do it
- Sequencing events/actions (e.g. using 'then', 'finally')

You will revisit:
- Numbers
- Free time activities
- Nationalities
- Clothes
- Hair and eyes
- Food
- Jobs

UNIT 16
Talking about my daily routine
'Cosa fai di solito durante il giorno?'
What do usually do during the day?

Di solito *Usually*	**ceno** *I have dinner*	***all'una** 1*				**cinque** 5
	esco di casa *I leave my house*	**alle** *at*	**due** 2	**e** *past*	**dieci** 10	
Normalmente *Normally*	**faccio colazione** *I have breakfast*		**cinque** 5		**un quarto** *quarter*	
La mattina *In the morning*	**faccio i compiti** *I do my homework*		**sei** 6	**meno** *to*		
	faccio la doccia *I shower*	**verso le** *at around*	**sette** 7		**venti** 20	
Il pomeriggio *In the afternoon*			**otto** 8		**venticinque** 25	
La sera *In the evening*	**gioco sul telefonino** *I play on my phone*	**dalle...alle** *from...to*	**nove** 9	**e mezza** *half past*		
Lunedì *On Monday*	**guardo la televisione** *I watch tv*		**dieci** 10			
Martedì *On Tuesday*	**mi alzo** *I get up*	**poi** *then*	**undici** 11	**in punto** *o' clock / on the dot*		
			dodici 12			
Mercoledì *On Wednesday*	**mi rilasso** *I relax*	**a** *at*	**mezzogiorno** *12pm / noon / midday*			
Giovedì *On Thursday*	**mi riposo** *I have a rest*		**mezzanotte** *12 am / midnight*			
Venerdì *On Friday*	**pranzo** *I have lunch*					
Sabato *On Saturday*	**torno a casa** *I go back home*	**alle sette di mattina / del mattino** *at 7 in the morning*				
Domenica *On Sunday*	**vado a lavoro** *I go to work*					
	vado a letto *I go to bed*	**alle otto di sera / del pomeriggio** *at 8 in the evening*				
	vado a scuola *I go to school*					

Author's note: * before *una* (1 o'clock) *la* shortens to *l'* before vowel. This means that in Italian you would say: *all'una (at 1) / verso l'una (at about 1) / dalle dodici all'una... (from 12 until 1 p.m.)*

Unit 16. Talking about my daily routine: VOCAB BUILDING (Part 1)

1. Match up

1. Mi alzo	a. I have lunch
2. Vado a scuola	b. I have dinner
3. Vado a letto	c. I get up
4. Pranzo	d. I have breakfast
5. Ceno	e. I do my homework
6. Faccio colazione	f. I go to school
7. Faccio i compiti	g. I go back home
8. Torno a casa	h. I go to bed

2. Translate into English

a. Mi alzo alle sei del mattino

b. Vado a letto alle undici di sera

c. Pranzo a mezzogiorno

d. Faccio colazione alle sette

e. Torno a casa alle tre e mezza del pomeriggio

f. Ceno verso le nove e poi mi riposo

g. Guardo la televisione verso le quattro

h. Vado a scuola alle otto

i. Vado al lavoro verso le otto e un quarto

3. Complete with the missing words

a. ______________ a scuola *[I go to school]*

b. ______________ di casa *[I leave the house]*

c. ______________ a casa *[I come back home]*

d. ______________ la televisione *[I watch television]*

e. ______________ i compiti *[I do my homework]*

f. ________ ____ lavoro *[I go to work]*

g. ______________ sul telefonino *[I play on the phone]*

h. ______________ all'una *[I have lunch at one]*

4. Complete with the missing letters

a. ____ccio la doccia *[I have a shower]*

b. ____rno a ___asa *[I go back home]*

c. ____oco sul ______nino *[I play on the phone]*

d. ___nzo *[I have lunch]*

e. ___eno *[I have dinner]*

f. ___do a scuola *[I go to school]*

g. Mi ____zo *[I get up]*

h. Va___ a le_____ *[I go to bed]*

i. ______rdo la televisione *[I watch tv]*

5. Faulty translation – spot and correct any translation mistakes. Not all translations are wrong.

a. Mi alzo sempre alle sei : *I always shower at 6am*

b. Vado a letto a mezzanotte: *I go to bed at noon*

c. Lunedì faccio i compiti : *I do my homework on Tuesday*

d. Pranzo: *I have lunch*

e. Vado a scuola: *I come back from school*

f. Torno a casa: *I leave the house*

g. Guardo la televisione: *I watch television*

h. Esco di casa: *I leave school*

i. Sabato suono il pianoforte: *On Friday I play music.*

6. Translate the following days and times into Italian

a. Monday at 6.30am

b. Thursday at 7.30am

c. Sunday at 8.20pm

d. Wednesday at midday

e. Friday at 9.20am

f. Tuesday at 11.00pm

g. Saturday at midnight

h. Today at 5.15pm

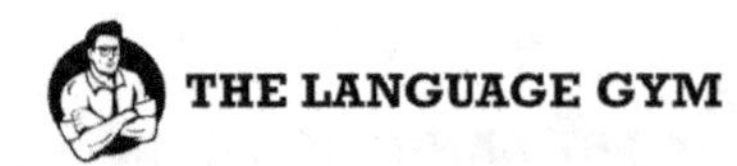

Unit 16. Talking about my daily routine: VOCAB BUILDING (Part 2)

1. Complete the table

Vado a letto	
	I relax
Mi alzo	
	I go back home
Alle otto e un quarto	
Pranzo	
	I have dinner
Gioco sul telefonino	
	I leave the house
Faccio colazione	
Vado a scuola	
	I do my homework
Mi vesto	

2. Complete the sentences using the words in the table below

a. Alle sette e ___________ *[At seven thirty]*

b. ________ le cinque *[At around five o'clock]*

c. Alle_________ del mattino *[At 8am]*

d. A _________________ *[At noon]*

e. Alle __________ e un quarto *[At 11.15]*

f. Verso le tre ________ venti *[At around 2.40]*

g. A _________________ *[At midnight]*

h. Verso _______ quattro *[At around four o'clock]*

i. ______ sette e venti *[At 7.20]*

j. Alle otto meno _________ *[At 7.55]*

cinque	mezza	alle	otto	mezzogiorno
undici	le	meno	verso	mezzanotte

3. Translate into English (numerical)

a. Alle otto e mezza   *At 8:30*

b. Alle nove e un quarto   ____________

c.Alle dieci meno cinque   ____________

d. A mezzogiorno   ____________

e. A mezzanotte   ____________

f. Alle undici meno cinque   ____________

g. Alle dodici e venti   ____________

h. Alle sei e mezza   ____________

4. Complete

a. Al_____ c________ e m_________ *[at 5:30]*

b. Ve_____ l__ o_____ e u__ q________
[at around 8:15]

c. A m_________________ *[at noon]*

d. Verso l__ o_____ m_____ un q______ *[at 7:45]*

e. A m_________________ *[at midnight]*

f. A_____ u________ e m_________ *[at 11:30]*

g. Dal_______ t_____ alle qu__________
[from 3 to 4]

5. Translate the following into Italian

a. I go to school at around 8 ____

b. I come back home at around 4 ____

c. I have dinner at 7:30 ____

d. I do my homework at around 5:30 ____

e. I have breakfast at 6:45 ____

f. I go to bed at midnight ____

g. I have lunch at midday____

Unit 16. Talking about my daily routine: READING (Part 1)

Mi chiamo Hiroto. Sono giapponese. Di solito durante il giorno faccio questo: mi alzo verso le sei, faccio la doccia e mi vesto. Dopo, faccio colazione con mio padre e mio fratello minore. Poi, mi lavo i denti e mi pettino. Verso le sette e mezza esco di casa e vado a scuola in bici. Torno a casa verso le quattro e guardo la televisione. Poi, vado al parco con i miei amici fino alle sei. Mi piace perché è divertente! La sera, dalle sei alle sette e mezza faccio i compiti e verso le otto, ceno con la mia famiglia. Non mangio molto. Solo un hamburger. Poi, guardo un film in tv e verso le undici, vado a letto.

Mi chiamo Raúl. Sono messicano. Di solito, mi alzo alle sei e un quarto. Poi faccio la doccia e faccio colazione con i miei fratelli. Dopo mi lavo i denti e preparo lo zaino. Verso le sette vado a scuola a piedi. Torno a casa verso le tre e mezza. Dopo mi riposo un po'. Normalmente navigo su internet, guardo una serie su Netflix o chatto con i miei amici su WhatsApp o Snapchat. Dalle cinque alle sei faccio i compiti. Secondo me è noioso. Ceno alle sette e mezza. Mangio riso o insalata. Poi guardo la tele e,verso le undici e mezza vado a letto.

Mi chiamo Andreas. Sono tedesco. Questa è la mia giornata tipica. Di solito, mi alzo **presto** [early], verso le cinque. Faccio una corsa e poi faccio la doccia e mi vesto. Dopo, verso le sei e mezza, faccio colazione con mia madre e mia sorella. Mangio frutta. Poi mi lavo i denti e preparo lo zaino. Verso le sette e un quarto vado a scuola. Torno a casa verso le tre e mezza. Nel pomeriggio di solito guardo la tele o chatto con i miei amici su internet. Dalle sei alle otto faccio i compiti. Poi, alle otto e un quarto, ceno con la mia famiglia. Dopo cena, gioco alla playstation fino a mezzanotte. A mio parere, é appassionante. Ma a mia madre non piace! Infine, vado a **dormire** [sleep].

1. Answer the following questions about Hiroto

a. Where is he from?

b. At what time does he get up?

c. With whom does he have breakfast with?

d. At what time does he leave the house?

e. Until what time does he stay at the park?

f. Why does he like it?

2. Find the Italian for the phrases below in Hiroto's text

a. At around eleven

b. With my friends

c. I go by bike

d. I go to the park

e. I shower and get dressed

f. I don't eat much

g. From six to seven thirty

h. I do my homework

3. Complete the statements below about Andreas' text

a. He gets up ___________ at around___________________

b. He comes back from school at ____________________

c. For breakfast he eats ______________________________

d. He has breakfast with _____________ and ______________

e. After getting up he _______________ and then showers

f. Then he brushes his teeth and prepares ___________

___________. Around 7.15 he ___________________ .

g. Usually he _________________________ until midnight,

but his mum _________________________________.

4. Find the Italian for the following chunks in Raúl's text

a. I am Mexican

b. I shower

c. With my brothers

d. I relax a bit

e. I eat rice or salad

f. I surf the internet

g. I have dinner at half past seven

Unit 16. Talking about my daily routine: READING (Part 2)

Mi chiamo Yang. Ho dodici anni. Sono cinese. Questa è la mia giornata tipica. Di solito, mi alzo verso le sei e mezza. Poi faccio la doccia e mi vesto. Poi, faccio colazione con mia madre e mio fratello, Li Wei. Dopo mi lavo i denti e preparo lo zaino. Verso le sette e mezza esco di casa e vado a scuola. Torno a casa verso le quattro e mi riposo un po'. Nel pomeriggio guardo la televisione, ascolto la musica o gioco sul telefonino perché penso che è rilassante. Dalle sei alle sette e mezza faccio i compiti. Dopo, alle otto, ceno con la mia famiglia. Non mangio molto. Infine guardo un film e verso le undici vado a letto.

Mi chiamo Anna. Sono italiana. La mia routine quotidiana è molto semplice. Di solito, mi alzo alle sei e un quarto. Poi faccio colazione con la mia sorella maggiore. Dopo mi lavo i denti e preparo lo zaino. Verso le sette vado a scuola in autobus. Torno a casa verso le due e mezza. Nel pomeriggio navigo su internet, guardo la televisione o leggo riviste di moda. A mio parere è fantastico! Verso le otto ceno con la mia famiglia. Mangio frutta o un'insalata. Poi leggo un libro o gioco sul tablet e, verso le undici e mezza, vado a letto.

Mi chiamo Kim, sono inglese. Ho quindici anni. La mia routine quotidiana è molto semplice. Normalmente, mi sveglio presto, verso le cinque e mezza. Faccio una corsa e poi mi lavo e mi vesto. Dopo, verso le sette, faccio colazione con mia madre e la mia sorellastra. Poi, mi lavo i denti e preparo lo zaino. Verso le sette e mezza esco di casa e vado a scuola. Torno a casa dopo le tre. Poi, mi riposo un po'. Di solito, ascolto la musica o chatto con i miei amici su WhatsApp. Dalle sei alle otto faccio i compiti. Alle otto e un quarto, ceno con la mia famiglia. Dopo, guardo un film in tv **fino a** *[until]* mezzanotte. Infine, vado a letto.

1. Find the Italian for the following in Yang's text

a. I am Chinese

b. my typical day

c. I shower

d. I prepare my bag

e. at around 7.30

f. I don't eat much

g. I watch television

h. I go to school

i. I do my homework

j. from six to seven thirty

k. I watch a movie

2. Translate these items from Kim's text

a. I am English

b. normally

c. around 5.30

d. with my mum and stepsister

e. I go back home

f. after three

g. I have dinner with my family

h. I rest a bit

i. I brush my teeth

j. I go for a run

3. Answer the following questions on Anna's text

a. What nationality is Anna?

b. At what time does she get up?

c. What three things does she do after school?

d. How does she go to school?

e. With whom does she have breakfast?

f. At what time does she go to bed?

g. What does she eat for dinner?

h. What does she do before going to bed?

4. Find someone who...

a. has breakfast with their older sister

b. doesn't watch television at night

c. reads fashion magazines

d. gets up at 5.30am

e. has breakfast with their brother and mother

f. chats with their friends online after school

g. does exercise in the morning

Unit 16. Talking about my daily routine: WRITING

1. Split sentences

Vado a scuola	casa
Torno a	compiti
Faccio i	in autobus
Guardo	sul telefonino
Gioco	alle dieci e mezza
Mi alzo	di casa
Vado a letto	verso le sei
Esco	la televisione

2. Complete with the correct option

a. Mi alzo _______ sette del mattino

b. Faccio _____ compiti

c. Guardo ______ televisione

d. _________ sul telefonino

e. Vado a ___________ alle undici

f. Torno _______ casa

g. Esco di _________

h. Vado a scuola _________ autobus

a	letto	alle	in
la	i	casa	gioco

3. Spot and correct the grammar and spelling mistakes [in several cases a word is missing]

a. Vado a squola in bici

b. Mi alzo a sette e mezza

c. Esco casa alle otto

d. Torno al casa

e. Vado scuola in autobus

f. Vado di letto verso le dieci

g. Ceno alle oto meno quarto

h. Faccio mio compiti alle cinque mezza

4. Complete the words

a. qu_______   *[Quarter]*

b. me______   *[Half]*

c. al_____ di_____   *[At 10]*

d. v______ l__ s____   *[At around six]*

e. al_____ o_______   *[At 8]*

f. ve________   *[Twenty]*

g. p___   *[Then]*

h. p__________   *[I have lunch]*

i. e__________ di casa *[I leave home]*

j. g__________   *[I play]*

5. Guided writing – write 3 short paragraphs in the first person [I] using the details below

Person	Gets up	Showers	Goes to school	Comes back home	Watches television	Has dinner	Goes to bed
June	6.30	7.00	8.05	3.30	6.00	8.10	11.10
Frank	6.40	7.10	7.40	4.00	6.30	8.15	12.00
Anita	7.15	7.30	8.00	3.15	6.40	8.20	11.30

Describe your daily routine using reflexive verbs.
'Qual'è la tua routine quotidiana?'
What is your daily routine?

A volte *From time to time*	**mi alzo** *I get up*	**all'** *at*	**una**	**e** *past*	**cinque** *5* **dieci** *10*
	mi asciugo i capelli *I dry my hair*	**alle** *at*	**due**		**quarto** *quarter*
Una volta alla settimana *Once a week*	**mi faccio la doccia** *I have a shower*		**tre**		
Due volte alla settimana *Twice a week*	**mi faccio il bagno** *I have a bath*		**quattro**	**meno** *to*	**venti** *20*
	mi faccio la barba/ **mi rado** *I shave*		**cinque**		**venticinque** *25*
Durante la settimana *During the week*	**mi lavo i denti** *I brush my teeth*	**verso le** *around*	**sei** **sette**		**mezza** *half*
Il fine settimana *At the weekend)*	**mi lavo il viso/** **mi lavo la faccia** *I wash my face*		**otto**		
Ogni giorno *Every day*	**mi metto l'uniforme** *I put on my uniform*		**nove** **dieci**	**in punto** *o' clock*	
Ogni mattina *Every morning*	**mi pettino i capelli** *I brush my hair* **mi preparo** *I get ready*		**undici** **dodici**		
Ogni tanto *From time to time*	**mi riposo** *I have a rest* **mi sveglio** *I wake up*	**a** *at*		**mezzogiorno** *midday* **mezzanotte** *midnight*	
Tutti i giorni *Every day*	**mi trucco** *I put make-up on*				
Quando posso *When I can*	**mi vesto** *I get dressed*				

Unit 16. Daily routine with reflexive verbs: Translation

Paragraph 1	Tick a box each time you spot the correct translation in the text				Write the translation
Hi, my name is Roberto. Every day I wake up at half past six, I have a shower and I put on my uniform. I have breakfast and I go to school at eight o'clock. From time to time I go back home at four because I go to my friends' house. Every afternoon I have a rest a bit in the sofa. I always go to bed at ten.	alle dieci	perché vado	mi metto l'uniforme	sempre	__________
	alle quattro	mi sveglio	Faccio colazione	vado a scuola	__________
	alle otto in punto	alle sei e mezza	Ogni giorno	torno a casa	__________
	Ciao, mi chiamo Roberto	mi faccio la doccia	a casa dei miei amici	un po' sul divano	__________
	Ogni pomeriggio	mi riposo	Vado a letto	ogni tanto	__________

Paragraph 2					
Good morning, my name is Karen. During the week I always get up at quarter past seven. I have a bath at quarter to eight, I dry my hair and I brush my teeth. I leave home at nine o'clock and I go to school by bus. Every day, I go back home at three, I play on the PlayStation, I relax and I go to bed.	sempre	mi riposo	alle tre	in autobus	__________
	torno a casa	esco di casa	mi lavo i denti	mi sveglio	__________
	mi asciugo i capelli	alle nove in punto	mi faccio il bagno	Buongiorno	__________
	alle sette e un quarto	durante la settimana	mi chiamo Karen	tutti i giorni	__________
	gioco alla PlayStation	alle otto meno un quarto	mi lavo i denti	vado a scuola	__________

Paragraph 3					
Hi, my name is Emma. Twice a week, during the week end, I have a rest and I get up at ten because I don't go to school. Five times a week, when I go to school, I wake up at seven o'clock and I comb my hair. I get back home at four, I relax and I play with my brother and my dog.	alle dieci	mi sveglio	mi rilasso	alle quattro	__________
	vado a scuola	alle sette in punto	mi pettino (i capelli)	Due volte alla settimana	__________
	Torno a casa	durante il fine settimana	Ciao, mi chiamo Emma	cinque volte alla settimana	__________
	e con il mio cane	non vado a scuola	quando	con mio fratello	__________
	perché	alle otto	e gioco	mi alzo	__________

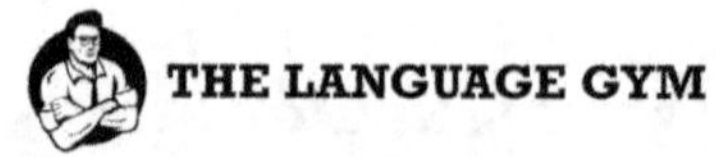

Grammar Time 14: Reflexive verbs

USEFUL VOCABULARY

Alzarsi	to get up
Chiamarsi	to be called
Farsi il bagno	to bathe
Farsi la barba	to shave
Farsi la doccia	to shower
Lavarsi	to wash
Lavarsi i denti	to brush one's teeth
Riposarsi	to rest
Pettinarsi	to comb one's hair
Prepararsi	to get ready
Truccarsi	to put on make-up

Present Indicative of ARE verbs ending in -SI

	Alzarsi	**Farsi la doccia**
(io)	**mi** alzo *[I get up]*	**mi** faccio la doccia *[I have a shower]*
(tu)	**ti** alzi *[you get up]*	**ti** fai la doccia *[you have a shower]*
(lui) **(lei)**	**si** alza *[he/she gets up]*	**si** fa la doccia *[he/she has a shower]*
(noi)	**ci** alziamo *[we get up]*	**ci** facciamo la doccia *[we have a shower]*
(voi)	**vi** alzate *[you all get up]*	**vi** fate la doccia *[you all have a shower]*
(loro/ essi)	**si** alzano *[they get up]*	**si** fanno la doccia *[they have a shower]*

1. Complete with <u>mi</u>, <u>si</u> or <u>ci</u>

a. (loro) _____ svegliano

b. (io) _____ faccio la doccia

c. (lei) _____ pettina

d. (noi) _____ laviamo

e. (lui) _____ lava i denti

f. (noi) _____ pettiniamo

g. (loro) _____ preparano

h. (tu) _____ alzi

2. Complete with the correct form of the verb

a. Lei (lavarsi) s____ l____________ i denti

b. Noi (farsi la doccia) c__ f_________l_d______ ogni giorno

c. Lui (preparasi) s___ p___________ tutte le mattine

d. Lui (farsi la barba) s___ f_____l___ b________ ogni mattina

e. Lei (truccarsi) _____ _______________

f. Loro (alzarsi) _____ _____________ presto

3. Translate into English

a. Mi sveglio verso le sei, peró mio fratello si sveglia alle sette. Mi faccio la doccia poco dopo.

b. Mia sorella si riposa prima di andare a scuola. Lei si pettina sempre e si trucca.

c. Mi faccio la barba tutti i giorni, mentre mio padre si fa la doccia tutti i giorni.

d. I miei genitori si svegliano presto. Dopo si lavano e fanno colazione prima di noi.

e. Mio padre é pelato *[bald]* quindi, non si pettina mai.

f. Mia madre ha i capelli rossi. Lei si pettina e si trucca un'ora prima di uscire di casa.

g. Non abbiamo una vasca da bagno in casa. Quindi, ci facciamo la doccia.

h. Mi lavo i denti cinque volte al giorno. Invece, mio fratello si lava i denti solo una volta al giorno.

Io mi alzo mezz'ora dopo mio padre, alle sei e mezza. Mi lavo il viso, mi faccio la doccia, mi faccio la barba, mi pettino e per ultimo mi vesto e vado in cucina. Faccio colazione da solo. Mangio latte e cereali, del pane tostato con marmellata e bevo caffè con latte. Dopo, mi lavo i denti, e mi preparo per andare a scuola, e verso le sette esco di casa. **(Mario, 16)**

5. Find in Mario's text the Italian for:

a. I get up

b. I wash my face

c. I comb my hair

d. I brush my teeth

e. I get ready

f. I shave

g. I shower

h. I drink

i. I leave the house

6. Complete

a. Mi facci__ la doccia   *[I shower]*

b. Si prepar__   *[She prepares herself]*

c. Ci facci__ __ __ la doccia   *[We shower]*

d. Vi lav__ __ __   *[You guys wash]*

e. Mi prepar__   *[I prepare myself]*

f. Si pettina__ __   *[They comb their hair]*

g. Mi lav__ i denti   *[I brush my teeth]*

h. Si fan__ __ il bagno   *[They bathe]*

8. Translate

a. Normally, I shower at seven o'clock

b. He never brushes his teeth

c. We shave three times a week

d. They get up early

e. He never combs his hair

f. I put make up on

g. We get ready for school

h. They relax in the living room

4. Find in Chiara's text below the Italian for:

a. They wake up

b. My father gets up

c. He showers

d. She gets ready

e. My mother gets up

f. He leaves the house

g. He shaves

h. He combs his hair

I miei genitori si svegliano molto presto. Mia madre si alza verso le cinque e mezza, per preparare la colazione a me e a mio padre. Prima di preparare la colazione, si veste, si prepara e prende un caffé guardando la televisione. Mio padre si alza mezz'ora piú tardi. Si fa la doccia, si fa la barba, si pettina, e dopo fa colazione con mia madre in cucina. Lui esce di casa alle sette. **(Chiara, 12)**

7. Complete

a. _____ _______________ alle sei
[They get up at six]

b. _____ ___________la barba alle sette
[They shave at seven]

c. _____ _______________ presto
[I get up early]

d. Non _____ _______________ la barba
[He doesn't shave]

e. _____ _______________ i denti dopo aver mangiato
[We brush our teeth after eating]

f. _____ __________ sempre
[She always puts make up on]

Revision Quickie 5: Clothes/ Food / Free Time /Jobs

1. Clothes – Match up

Una sciarpa (1)	A hat
Un completo	A skirt
Un cappello	A dress
Una cravatta	A shirt
Una gonna	A t-shirt
Un vestito	boots
Una maglietta	A suit
Una camicia	Socks
Stivali	Trousers
Calzini	A scarf (1)
Pantaloni	A tie

2. Food – Provide a word for each of the cues below

A fruit starting with **M**	la mela
A vegetable starting with **P**	
A dairy product starting with **F**	
A meat starting with **P**	
A drink starting with **S**	
A drink made using lemons **L**	
A sweet dessert starting with **G**	
A fruit starting with **A**	

3. Complete the translations below

a. Shoes : sca_______________

b. Hat: cap_______________

c. Hair: cape_______________

d. Curly: ric_______________

e. Grey: gri_______________

f. Milk: la_______________

g. Water: ac_______________

h. Drink: bib_______________

i. Job: lav_______________

j. Clothes: ves_______________

4. Classify the words into the correct columns.

Vestiti	Colori	Lavori	Cibo

camicia	azzurro	professoressa	operaio
carne	marrone	avvocato	pollo
gonna	cuoco	formaggio	cravatta
arancia	cappello	riso	rosso

5. Match questions and answers

Che lavoro fa tuo padre?	Indosso una tuta
Quale colore ti piace?	Alle otto e mezza
Quale tipo di carne non ti piace?	È avvocato
Di solito, cosa indossi per andare in palestra?	Gioco a scacchi
A che ora vai a scuola?	Il blu
Qual è la tua bibita preferita?	Non mi piace l'agnello.
Cosa fai nel tempo libero?	Il succo di frutta

6. (Free time) Complete with *faccio*, *vado* or *gioco* as appropriate

a. Non ___________ sport

b. Non ___________ mai a pallacanestro

c. Spesso ___________ in palestra

d. ___________ ginnastica tutti i giorni

e. ___________ sempre alla PlayStation

f. Oggi non ___________ in piscina

7. Complete with the missing verb, choosing from the list below

a. _____________ tanto succo di frutta.

b. ____________ le fragole perché sono buone.

c. Nel pomeriggio, _______ al centro sportivo o __________ ai videogiochi.

d. ____________ molto sport perché è salutare.

e. La mattina non _____________ molto a colazione. Solo dei cereali.

f. Mio padre ___________ come ingegnere. Io non ___________ perché ________ studente.

g. Non mi _________ giocare sul telefonino. ___________ guardare una serie su Netflix.

h. La mattina, mi ________ verso le sei.

alzo	gioco	adoro	lavoro
vado	faccio	preferisco	sono
lavora	bevo	piace	mangio

8. Time markers – Translate

a. Mai:

b. A volte:

c. Sempre:

d. Tutti i giorni:

e. Raramente:

f. Una volta alla settimana:

g. Due volte al mese:

9. Split sentences

Mi piace giocare	piace nuotare
Non mi	videogiochi
I miei genitori	a pallavolo
A colazione	libero leggo un libro
Mia sorella indossa	sono severi
Il mio professore	bevo un caffè
A scuola porto	sempre i leggings
A cena mangio	è simpatico
Nel mio tempo	la divisa blu
Lui gioca spesso ai	tanta verdura

11. Translate into Italian

a. I play tennis every day

____

b. I wear a jacket sometimes

____

c. I go to the gym often

____

d. I don't watch cartoons

____

e. I get up at around six a.m.

____

f. I shower twice a day

____

g. I prefer fruit and vegetables

____

h. I drink coffee every day

____

10. Complete the translation

a. Mio fratello _______________ pane tostato a colazione *[My brother eats toast for breakfast]*

b. Non ___________. Sono _______________
[I don't work. I am a student]

c. A volte ________ al cinema con mio padre
[From time to time I go to the cinema with my father]

d. Non _________ mai la televisione
[I never watch tv]

e. ______ i miei professori *[I love my teachers]*

f. I miei genitori sono _______________
[My parents are strict]

g. Non ______ mai corsa *[I never go jogging]*

UNIT 17
Describing my house, where it is located and saying what I like/dislike about it

In this unit you will learn how to say in Italian

- Where your house/apartment is located
- What your favourite room is
- What you like to do in each room
- The present indicative of key reflexive verbs in -ARE

You will revisit:
- Adjectives to describe places
- Frequency markers
- Countries

Vivo in una casa *I live in a house*	**bella** *pretty* **brutta** *ugly* **grande** *big* **nuova** *new* **piccola** *small* **vecchia** *old*	**che si trova** *which is located* **in campagna** *in the countryside* **in montagna** *in the mountains* **in periferia** *on the outskirts* **in una zona residenziale** *in a residential area*	**Nella mia casa ci sono due/tre/quattro stanze** *in my house there are 2/3/4 rooms*	
Vivo in un appartamento *I live in a flat*	**bello** *pretty* **brutto** *ugly* **grande** *big* **nuovo** *new* **piccolo** *small* **vecchio** *old*	**nel centro della città** *in the city centre* **sulla costa** *on the coast*	**La mia stanza preferita è** *my favourite room is*	**il bagno** *the bathroom* **il giardino** *the garden* **il salotto** *the living room* **la cucina** *the kitchen* **la mia camera da letto** *my bedroom* **la sala da pranzo** *the dining room* **la terrazza** *the terrace*

Unit 17. Describing my house: VOCABULARY BUILDING PART 1

1. Match up

vivo in	*a flat*
una casa	*new*
un appartamento	*residential*
grande	*area*
nuovo	*I live in*
la campagna	*a house*
zona	*big*
residenziale	*the countryside*

2. Translate into English

a. Vivo in una casa piccola e vecchia.

b. Vivo in un appartamento grande e nuovo.

c. Il mio appartamento si trova in periferia.

d. La mia casa si trova in campagna.

e. La mia stanza preferita è la mia camera da letto.

f. Mi piace la cucina.

g. Mi piace mangiare in cucina.

h. Mi riposo sempre in salotto

3. Complete with the missing words

a. Vivo _____ costa *[I live on the coast]*

b. Mi _____la mia casa *[I like my house]*

c. _______in una casa vecchia ma _______
[I live in an old but pretty house]

d. Mi piace il mio ____________
[I like my living room]

e. La mia _______ si trova in _________
[My house is on the outskirts]

f. Non mangio mai nella mia _________ da
_______ *[I never eat in the bedroom]*

4. Complete the words (about 'una casa')

a. una s_____ *[a room]*   g. la c_______ *[the coast]*

b. b_______ *[ugly]*   h. la p________ *[the outskirts]*

c. n_______ *[new]*   i. il c__________ *[the centre]*

d. v_______ *[old]*   j. il g__________ *[the garden]*

e. g_______ *[big]*   k. la t________ *[the terrace]*

f. la mia c________da______ *[my bedroom]*

5. Classify the words/phrases below in the table below

a. sempre	i. grande
b. mangiare	j. a volte
c. mai	k. camera da letto
d. bello	l. campagna
e. nuovo	m. piccolo
f. montagna	n. cucina
g. si trova	o. costa
h. cucina	p. vivo

Time phrases	Nouns	Verbs	Adjectives
a.			

6. Translate into Italian

a. I live in an old flat

b. I live in a new house

c. In the town centre

d. I like my garden

e. In the living room

f. I live in a residential area

g. My favourite room is the kitchen

h. My house is located in a residential area

Unit 17. Describing my house: VOCABULARY BUILDING PART 2

1. Match up

Si trova	costa
una casa sulla	residenziale
vivo in	la mia casa
un appartamento	in centro
Nel	moderno
una zona	una casa grande
Mi piace	centro

2. Complete with the missing word

a. Non mi piace la mia ____________ [I don't like my kitchen]

b. È piccolo ma _________ [It is small but pretty]

c. Si trova nel ________ della città [It is in the town centre]

d. Si trova nella _____________ [It is on the outskirts]

e. Vivo in una __________ grande [I live in a big house]

f. In una _________ residenziale [In a residential area]

g. La mia _____________ preferita è... [My favourite room is...]

h. Mi rilasso nel ______________ [I relax in the garden]

i. Studio nel _____________ [I study in the living room]

j. Ci ________ quattro stanze [There are four rooms]

zona	cucina	sono	centro	giardino
casa	salotto	bello	stanza	periferia

3. Translate into English

a. Vivo in una casa piccola

b. Si trova sulla costa

c. Un appartamento grande ma brutto

d. Si trova in una zona residenziale

e. Nella mia casa ci sono tre stanze

f. Mi piace studiare in salotto

g. Mi piace mangiare in cucina

h. Vivo in una villa sulla costa

i. Vivo nella periferia della città

4. Broken words

a. Mi piace il mio g_____________ [I like my garden]

b. Vivo in m______________ [I live in the mountains]

c. Nel centro della c__________ [In the city centre]

d. Studio nella mia s__________ [I study in my room]

e. Una zona re______________ [A residential area]

f. La mia stanza pr____________ è... [My favourite room is...]

5. Il or 'La'

a. ____La____ costa

b. _________ campagna

c. __________ sala da pranzo

d. _________ salotto

e. ________ città

f. _________ giardino

g. _________ bagno

h. _________ stanza

i. ________ periferia

j. ________ zona

6. Bad translation – spot any translation errors and fix them

a. Vivo in una casa alla costa [I live in a house on the coast]

b. La mia stanza preferita è la cucina
[My favourite room is the dining room]

c. Mi piace mangiare nella sala da pranzo
[I like eating in my bedroom]

d. Vivo in un appartamento in una zona residenziale
[I live in a house in a residential area]

e. Mi piace la mia casa perché è grande e bella
[I don't like my house because it is big and ugly]

f. Mi piace mangiare in cucina [I like to work in a canteen]

Unit 17. Describing my house: READING

Mi chiamo Dante. Sono italiano, di Verona. Vivo in una casa grande e bella sulla costa. Mi piace molto. Nella mia casa ci sono dieci stanze e la mia stanza preferita è la cucina. Mi piace **cucinare** *[to cook]* in cucina con mia madre. Mi sveglio e mi lavo la faccia, dopo mi vesto nella mia stanza da letto.
Il mio amico Paolo vive in una casa piccola in montagna. Paolo è molto simpatico e diligente. Non gli piace la sua casa perché è piccola.

Mi chiamo Giovanna e sono di Bolzano, però vivo a Roma, nel Lazio. La mia casa si trova nel centro della città, vivo in un appartamento. In casa parlo italiano e tedesco. Il tedesco è una lingua molto bella ma difficile. Vivo in una casa piccola, nuova e molto bella. Ci sono sei stanze e anche un giardino grande. Il mio cane vive nel giardino e si chiama Bruno, è molto affettuoso. La mia stanza preferita è la sala da pranzo perché mi piace molto mangiare. Mi piace rilassarmi e non fare niente. Guardo sempre i cartoni animati e una serie su Netflix. Mi piace anche ascoltare musica e passare il mio tempo libero nella mia camera da letto.

Mi chiamo Lenny. Sono francese e vivo in una casa molto vecchia ma bella, nella campagna, in Italia. Adoro la mia casa. Nella mia casa ci sono cinque stanze però la mia preferita è la mia stanza da letto. Tutti i giorni, dopo la scuola mi piace rilassarmi in salotto e guardo la televisione con mia sorella. Non mi piace il bagno perché è piccolo e sempre sporco.

Mi chiamo Ariella. Sono di Milano. Mi sveglio sempre alle cinque di mattina perché vivo **lontano** *[far]* dalla scuola, nella periferia della città. Vivo in un appartamento in un edificio molto antico. L'appartamento è molto vecchio e un po' brutto, però mi piace. Mi piace riposarmi nella mia stanza da letto. A volte leggo libri oppure ascolto musica su Spotify. La camera da letto è la mia stanza preferita.

1. Answer the following questions about Dante

a. Where is he from?

b. What is his house like?

c. How many rooms are there in his house?

d. Which is his favourite room?

e. Where does he get dressed?

f. Where does Paolo live?

g. Does he like his house? Why?

2. Find the Italian or the phrases below in Giovanna's text

a. My house is in the centre

b. I live in a flat

c. I speak Italian and German

d. And also a big garden

e. I really like to eat

f. He lives in the garden

g. I like to relax

h. I like to spend my time

3. Find Someone Who – which person...

a. Lives far from school

b. Speaks two languages

c. Has a really big house

d. He lives in an old building

e. Has a pet that lives outside the house

f. Has a dirty bathroom

g. Is a foodie (loves food)

h. Listens to music on a streaming platform

i. Watches TV with their sister

4. Find the Italian for the following phrases/sentences in Ariella's text

a. I am from Milan

b. I always wake up at 5

c. I live far from school

d. The flat is very old

e. And a bit ugly

f. But I like it

g. Sometimes I read books

Unit 17. Describing my house: TRANSLATION

1. Gapped translation

a. Vivo in periferia *[I live on the _______________]*

b. La mia casa è molto grande però un po' brutta
[My house is _______ big but ___ ______ ugly]

c. Si ____________ nella... *[It is located in the ...]*

d. Vivo nel centro _________ __________
[I live in the city centre]

e. Nella mia casa ___ _______ cinque stanze
[In my house there are five rooms]

f. Non mi piace molto la ________ perché è _____________
[I don't really like the kitchen because it's ugly]

2. Translate into English

a. la costa

b. un appartamento

c. vivo in

d. il centro

e. della città

f. la mia stanza preferita

g. mi piace cucinare

h. la mia camera da letto

i. il salotto

3. Translate into English

a. Vivo in un appartamento piccolo e brutto.

b. La casa è moderna ma abbastanza piccola.

c. Il mio appartamento è vecchio però mi piace molto.

d. Vivo in una casa sulla costa.

e. Nella mia casa ci sono cinque stanze.

f. La mia stanza preferita è la camera da letto.

4. Translate into Italian

a. Big: G___________________

b. Small: P___________________

c. Outskirts: P________________

d. Coast: C__________________

e. Area: Z__________________

f. Residential: R______________

g. Ugly (m): B________________

h. Room: S__________________

i. There are: C____ s__________

j. Old (f): V_________________

5. Translate into Italian

a. I live in a small house

b. in the city centre

c. in my house there are...

d. seven rooms

e. my favourite room is...

f. the living room

g. I like to relax in my bedroom

h. and I like to work in the living room

i. I live in a small and old flat

j. in a residential area

Grammar Time 15: VIVERE– to live

				MASC
(Io) vivo *I live* **(Tu) vivi** *You live* **(Lui) vive** *He lives* **(Lei) vive** *She lives* **(Noi) viviamo** *We live* **(Voi) vivete** *You all live* **(Loro) vivono** *They live*	**in un apartamento** *in a flat*	**in campagna** *in the countryside* **in periferia** *on the outskirts* **in una zona residenziale** *in a residential area*	**Mi piace perché è** *I like it because it is* **Mi piace molto perché è** *I really like it because it is*	**accogliente** *cosy* **bello** *pretty* **brutto** *ugly* **grande** *big* **nuovo** *new* **piccolo** *small* **spazioso** *spacious* **vecchio** *old*
	in una casa *in a house* **in una villa** *in a villa*	**nel centro della città** *in the city centre* **in montagna** *in the mountains* **sulla costa** *on the coast*	**Non mi piace perché è** *I don't like it because it is* **Non mi piace per nulla perché è** *I dont' like it at all because it is*	**FEM** **accogliente** *cosy* **bella** *pretty* **brutta** *ugly* **grande** *big* **nuova** *new* **piccola** *small* **spaziosa** *spacious* **vecchia** *old*

1. Match

vivono	*I live*
viviamo	*You live*
vive	*She lives*
vivo	*We live*
vivete	*You guys live*
vivi	*They live*

2. Complete with the correct form of 'vivere'

a.__________ in una casa bella
[I live in a beautiful house]

b. Dove __________ ? *[Where do you live?]*

c. ____________ a Londra da tre anni
[We have been living in London for three years]

d. ____________ in una casa sulla costa
[She lives in a house on the coast]

e. __________ in una casa o in un appartamento?
[Do you live in a house or in a flat?]

f. ____________ in un appartamento vecchio
[They live in an old flat]

g. __________ in periferia

[We live on the outskirts]

h. Mio padre __________ in una fattoria
[My father lives on a farm]

3. Complete with the correct form of 'vivere'

a. Mia madre ed io ______________ a

Barcellona. Mio padre __________ a

 Madrid.

b. (voi) Dove ____________?

c. Io ________ a Londra. Mio fratello

__________ a Roma.

d. I miei zii ____________ in America.

e. Mia sorella non __________ qui.

f. (Io) ___________ in una casa molto grande

in periferia

g. (tu) __________ in una casa enorme!

4. Spot and correct the errors

a. (Io) Non vivi nel centro della città

b. I miei genitori viviamo qui

c. Mia sorella vivono in una casa nella costa

d. Mia madre ed io vivete in una zona residenziale

e. I miei fratelli non vive a Roma.

f. Mio nonno vivi a Milano.

5. Complete the translation

a. My siblings live in the countryside

= *I miei fratelli ________in __________*

b. I live in a flat = *________ in un ________*

c. My mother doesn't live with my father

= *Mia madre non ______ _____ mi padre*

d. We live on the outskirts

= *__________ nella __________*

e. Where do you live? = *Dove ________?*

f. They live in a small house

= *________ in una ________ _____________.*

6. Translate into Italian

a. My parents and I live in a cosy house

b. My mother lives in a small house on the coast

c. My cousins live in a beautiful house in the countryside

d. My girlfriend lives in a modern flat in the centre

e. My sisters live in an old flat on the outskirts

f. My best friend Paolo lives in a spacious flat near the town centre

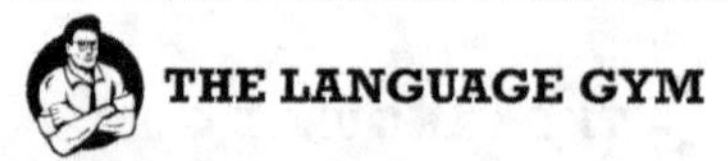

UNIT 18
Saying what I do at home in my spare time, how often and where

In this unit you will learn how to provide a more detailed account of your daily activities.

You will revisit:
- Time markers
- Reflexive verbs
- Parts of the house
- Description of people and places
- Telling the time
- Nationalities
- The verbs 'fare', 'giocare' and 'andare'

A volte *Sometimes*	**ascolto musica**	*I listen to music*	**in cucina** *in the kitchen*
	carico foto su Instagram	*I upload pics on Instagram*	
Di solito *Usually*	**faccio i compiti**	*I do my homework*	**in sala da pranzo** *in the dining room*
	gioco alla playstation	*I play PlayStation*	
Due volte alla settimana *Twice a week*	**guardo una serie su Netflix**	*I watch series on Netflix*	
	guardo Youtube	*I watch Youtube*	**nella mia camera** *in my bedroom*
	leggo un libro/fumetti	*I read a book/comics*	
Il fine settimana *At the weekend*	**parlo al telefono**	*I talk on the phone*	**nella camera di mio fratello** *in my brother's bedroom*
	preparo la cena	*I prepare dinner*	
Quando ho tempo *When I have time*	**mi rilasso**	*I relax*	
	mi riposo	*I rest*	
	scarico canzoni	*I download songs*	**in giardino** *in the garden*
	suono la chitarra	*I play the guitar*	
Sempre *Always*	**mi piace** *I like*	**ascoltare musica** *listening to music*	**nella sala giochi** *in the games room*
Tutti i giorni *Every day*	**non mi piace** *I don't like*	**caricare foto** *uploading photos*	**in salotto** *in the living room*
	mi piace molto *I really like*	**parlare al telefono** *talking on the phone*	
		leggere un libro *reading a book*	**in terrazza** *in the terrace*
	amo *I love*	**scaricare canzoni** *downloading songs*	**nel garage** *in the garage*
	preferisco *I prefer*	**guardare YouTube** *watching YouTube*	

Unit 18. Saying what I do at home: VOCABULARY BUILDING PART 1

1. Match up

1. Leggo fumetti	a. I talk
2. Guardo un film	b. I wash my hands
3. Preparo la cena	c. I watch a movie
4. Leggo un libro	d. I prepare dinner
5. Mi vesto	e. I read a book
6. Parlo	f. I shower
7. Mi lavo le mani	g. I get dressed
8. Faccio la doccia	h. I read comics

2. Complete with the missing words

a. Mi ___________ [I get dressed]

b. Leggo ___________ [I read comics]

c. ___________ al telefono [I talk on the phone]

d. Mi lavo i ________ [I wash my teeth]

e. Faccio una ________ [I shower]

f. ___________ la cena [I prepare dinner]

g. ________ su Internet [I go on the Net]

h. Ascolto ___________ [I listen to music]

i. ___________ foto su Instagram
[I upload photos on Instagram]

3. Translate into English

a. Di solito faccio la doccia verso le sei del mattino

b. Il venerdì sera guardo sempre un film

c. Normalmente leggo fumetti in salotto

d. Faccio colazione verso le sette nella sala da pranzo

e. Di tanto in tanto parlo con mia madre in cucina

f. A volte faccio colazione in cucina

g. Raramente gioco alla playstation con mio fratello

h. Esco sempre di casa verso le otto del mattino

i. Mi lavo sempre le mani **prima di** [before]
preparare la cena

4. Complete the words

a. A ___________ [I listen] g. Mi ve_____ [I get dressed]

b. L___________ [I read] h. G___________ [I play]

c. P___________ [I talk] i. E___________ [I leave]

d. P________ [I prepare] j. F___________ [I do]

e. C________ [I upload] k. M__ r___________ [I rest]

f. Mi l______ [I wash] l. G___________ [I watch, see]

5. Classify the words/phrases below in the table below

a. verso le sei
b. sempre
c. mai
d. camera da letto
e. guardo la tele
f. gioco alla Play
g. preparo la cena
h. carico foto su Instagram
i. faccio colazione
j. a volte
k. tutti i giorni
l. ascolto musica
m. leggo fumetti
n. vado in bici
o. due volte alla settimana
p. chatto su Skype

Time phrases	Rooms in the house	Things you do in the kitchen	Free-time activities
a.			

6. Fill in the table with what activities you do in which room

Gioco con la Xbox	camera da letto
Guardo la tele	
Faccio la doccia	
Faccio i compiti	
Mi lavo i denti	
Mi riposo	
Preparo la cena	

Unit 18. Saying what I do at home: VOCABULARY BUILDING PART 2

7. Complete the table

English	Italiano
I get dressed	
I shower	
	Faccio i compiti
I upload photos	
	Esco di casa
	Parlo al telefono
I rest	

8. Multiple choice quiz

	Option a	Option b	Option c
Mai	always	never	sometimes
A volte	sometimes	always	every day
Sempre	never	often	always
Mi lavo	I shave	I wash	I go out
La mattina	morning	afternoon	evening
Mi rilasso	I go out	I watch	I relax
Giardino	garden	garage	kitchen
Cucina	bedroom	lounge	kitchen
Gioco	I rest	I play	I prepare
Leggo	I watch	I read	I play
Esco	I go out	I rest	I read
Camera da letto	bathroom	bedroom	dining room

9. Anagrams: Italian-English

1. aMi = *mai = never*

2. ciCuna =

3. sEco =

4. oeLgg =

5. emSpre =

6. aricoC=

7. voste iM =

10. Broken words

a. La cu_______________   [The kitchen]

b. M__________________   [Never]

c. A vo_______________   [Sometimes]

d. Se_______________   [Always]

e. Sp_______________   [Often]

f. I fum_______________   [Comics]

g. La mia cam__________   [My bedroom]

h. Es_______________   [I go out]

i. Ch__________________   [I chat]

11. Complete based on the translation in brackets

a. V______ l__ s______ e mezza, m__ l_______ i
d___________ *[Around seven thirty, I brush my teeth]*

b. F______ c___________ a______ o_______ e un q_________
[I have breakfast at quarter past eight]

c. A v______ p___________ l___ c___________
[Sometimes I prepare the dinner]

d. G______ s______ l__ t________ n___ s___________
[I always watch television in the living room]

e. D__ s________ e_______ d__ c______ a____ o______ e
mezza *[I usually leave the house at eight thirty]*

f. L______ f__________ r___________ *[I read comics rarely]*

g. F______ i c___________ v________ l______ c_________
[I do my homework at around five]

12. Gap-fill from memory

a. A volte _________ fumetti

b. Mi _________ sempre i denti

c. Spesso _________ una serie su Netflix

d. Non _______ mai libri sul tablet

e. Il pomeriggio __________ i compiti

f. _________ foto su Instagram tutti i giorni

g. Il fine settimana _________ in bici

h. _________ di casa verso le otto

i. Spesso _____________ musica rock perché mi piace.

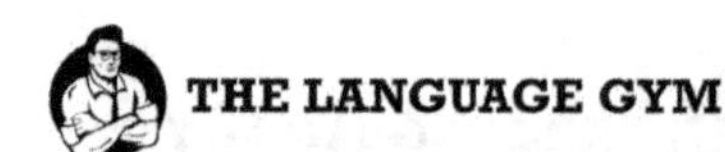

Unit 18. Saying what I do at home in my free time: READING

Mi chiamo Fabio. Sono di Gibilterra e ho un cane nero. Mi sveglio sempre presto, verso le cinque e un quarto. Dopo, vado un'ora in palestra e poi faccio una doccia. Mio fratello Joe, invece, è molto pigro e inattivo. Lui non gioca mai a calcio, né fa altri sport. Per questo motivo è un po' grasso. Nel pomeriggio di solito leggo fumetti o ascolto musica nella mia camera. In settimana, quando torno a casa dopo scuola, faccio i compiti con mia madre nel salotto. Lei mi piace perché è intelligente e mi aiuta sempre. La sera vado a letto in camera verso le nove.

Salve, mi chiamo Ilaria e vivo in Danimarca. Tutti i giorni mi alzo alle cinque. Poi mi lavo e faccio colazione in giardino. Esco di casa alla sette e vado a scuola a cavallo. Quando torno a casa chatto sempre su Skype con la mia famiglia in Inghilterra e vado su Internet nella mia camera. Poi vado in bici o gioco in giardino con il cane. A volte vado su internet o carico foto su Instagram. Mio fratello Samuel carica video su TikTok di nuovi balli. Vado d'accordo con mio fratello perché è divertente e dinamico. Balla molto bene! Parliamo sempre o giochiamo a carte. Samuel è il mio migliore amico.

Ciao, sono Valentino e sono italiano. Mi sveglio sempre presto, verso le sei e mezza. Poi faccio la doccia e mi lavo i denti in bagno. Non faccio mai colazione, invece mia sorella Valeria mangia cereali in sala da pranzo. Vado a scuola a piedi. Torno a casa verso le tre e mezza e mi rilasso un po'. Di solito guardo la televisione in salotto. Navigo su internet, guardo una serie su Netflix o video su TikTok nella mia camera. Poi, verso le otto, preparo la cena in cucina con mia madre. Amo preparare insalate perché, a mio parere, sono deliziose e sane. Normalmente vado a letto alle dieci.

1. Answer the following questions about Fabio

a. Where is he from?

b. What animal does he have?

c. What time does he wake up? What does he do after?

d. Why is Joe a bit fat?

e. Where does he do his homework on weekdays?

f. Who helps him with his homework?

g. When does he go to bed?

2. Find the Italian for the phrases below in Ilaria's text

a. I get up

b. Then I get washed

c. I go to school

d. By horse

e. I always chat

f. I go on the internet

g. Uploads videos to TikTok

h. New dances

3. Find Someone Who – which person…

a. Wakes up earliest

b. Has a family member that likes to dance

c. Likes to watch videos of people dancing

d. Has nothing for breakfast

e. Has a really lazy brother

f. Likes to prepare healthy food

g. Has a family member that is their best friend

h. Goes to school in the most exciting way

4. Find the Italian for the following phrases/sentences in Valentino's text

a. I am Italian

b. I wake up early

c. I have nothing for breakfast

d. Valeria eats cereals

e. In the dining room

f. In the living room

g. I watch TikTok videos

Unit 18. Saying what I do at home in my free time: WRITING

1. Split sentences

1. Parlo	a. cena
2. Mi rilasso nella	b. presto
3. Preparo la	c. con mia madre
4. Carico foto	d. mia camera
5. Faccio i	e. videogiochi
6. Mi sveglio	f. su Instagram
7. Gioco ai	g. i denti
8. Mi lavo	h. compiti

2. Complete with the correct option

a. Mi alzo alle sei del ___________

b. Gioco a pallone in ____________

c. Vedo la televisione in _____________

d. Ascolto musica nella mia ___________

e. Preparo la __________ con mio padre

f. Mi ___________ i denti

g. ________ una serie su Netflix

h. ________a scuola in autobus

salotto	mattino	lavo	camera
vado	cena	guardo	giardino

3. Spot and correct the grammar and spelling mistakes [note: in several cases a word is missing]

a. facio la doccia verso sette

b. faccio colazione in coocina

c. nel mia camera da letto

d. gioco al viodegiochi

e. esco di cassa

f. lego un libro

g. veddo una serie a Netflix

h. vado a schuola in autobus

i. la camera di mio fratella

4. Complete the words

a. Faccio co____________ *[I have breakfast]*

b. La cu________ *[The kitchen]*

c. La mia ___________da ________ *[My bedroom]*

d. Il ________ *[The garage]*

e. E_______ di c___________ *[I leave the house]*

f. Nel __________________ *[In the living room]*

g. Nella _______ da ________ *[In the dining room]*

h. Nel ________________ *[In the bathroom]*

i. G_________f______ n______ c________d__ m__
   f___________
[I watch films in my brother's bedroom]

5. Guided writing –write 3 short paragraphs in the <u>first person [I]</u> using the details below

Person	When	Gets up	Has breakfast	Goes to school	Evening activity 1	Evening activity 2
Elaine	every day	6.15	kitchen	with sister	read a book	prepare dinner
Mauro	usually	7.30	living room	with brother	go to the gym	talk to family on Skype
Claire	sometimes	6.45	dining room	with mother	listen to music in garden	talk to my sister on the phone

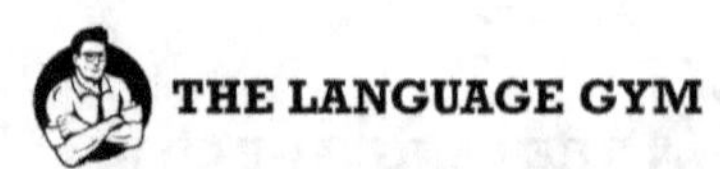

Grammar Time 16: GIOCARE, (Part 3) FARE (Part 3) ANDARE (Part 2)

1. Complete with 'Faccio', 'Gioco' or 'Vado'

a. ___________ la doccia

b. ___________ a scacchi

c. ___________ in Spagna

d. ___________ in piscina

e. ___________ ai videogiochi

f. ___________ nuoto

g. ___________ a rugby

h. Non _________ niente

2. Complete with the missing forms of the present indicative of the verbs below

	Fare	Andare	Giocare
io **[I]**		vado	gioco
tu **[you]**	fai		
lui/lei **[he/she]**			
noi **[we]**			
voi **[you all]**	fate		giocate
loro **[they]**		vanno	

3. Complete with the appropriate verb

a. Mia madre ____ in chiesa la domenica

b. Mia sorella non ______ mai i compiti

c. (noi) __________ a pallacanestro tutti i giorni

d. I miei genitori non _________molto sport

e. I miei amici spesso_________ a pallone

f. La mia ragazza ed io __________ al cinema

g. Cosa ____________ tu?

h. (voi) Dove __________?

i. Che lavoro _________ tu?

j. Mio zio ________ il professore.

k. I miei cugini _______ allo stadio il fine settimana

l. Mio padre __________ a tennis due volte a settimana

m. In estate noi___________ in spiaggia

n. Il fine settimana io e mio fratello non __________ niente

o. A che ora voi _________ a scuola?

4. Complete with the 'noi' form of giocare/fare/andare

a. ___________ a rugby

b. ___________ a scuola

c. ___________ a calcio

d. ___________ in chiesa

e. ___________ a hockey

f. ___________ al parco

g. ___________ a cricket

h. ___________ in piscina

i. ___________ sport

j. ___________ ciclismo

k. ___________ footing

l. ___________ a scacchi

5. Complete with the 'loro' form of the verbs

a. ________ a tennis

b. ________ allo stadio

c. ________ arrampicata

d. ________ i compiti

e. ________ nuoto

f. ________ in spiaggia

g. ________ a casa

h. ________ a pallavolo

i. ________ a golf

j. ________ footing

k. ________ la spesa

l. ________ in montagna

UNIT 19
My holiday plans
(Talking about future plans for holidays)

In this unit you will learn how to talk about:

- What you intend to do in future holidays
- Where you are going to go
- Where you are going to stay
- Who you are going to travel with
- How it will be
- Means of transport

You will revisit:
- The verb 'andare'
- Free-time activities
- Previously seen adjectives

UNIT 19
My holiday plans
'Dove andrai in vacanza?'
Where are you going on holiday?

***Quest'estate** *This summer* **Quest'inverno** *This winter* **Il prossimo anno** *Next year* **A Natale** *This Christmas* **Tra due settimane** *In two weeks*	**andrò in vacanza in** *I am going to go on holiday to* **andremo in** *we're going to go to*	Australia Francia Italia Grecia Spagna Liguria Puglia Toscana	**in aereo** *by plane* **in autobus** *by coach* **in camper** *by campervan* **in macchina** *by car* **in nave** *by boat* **in treno** *by train*	**ballerò** *I will dance* **dormirò** *I will sleep* **farò immersioni** *I will go diving* **farò compere** *I will go shopping*
	passerò *I will spend* **passeremo** *we will spend*	**una settimana** *1 week* **due settimane** *2 weeks*	**lì** *there* **con la mia famiglia** *with my family*	**mangerò** *I am going to eat* **non vedo l'ora!** *I can't wait!*
	starò *I am going to stay* **staremo** *we are going to stay*	**nella casa di famiglia** *in the family home* **in un campeggio** *in a campsite* **in un hotel economico** *a cheap hotel* **in un hotel di lusso** *a luxury hotel*		**mi riposerò** *I am going to rest* **sarà divertente** *it will be fun*
	mi piacerebbe... *I would like to...* **ci piacerebbe...** *we would like to...*	**ballare** — *dance* **fare compere** — *do shopping* **fare immersioni** — *go diving* **fare un giro turistico** — *go sightseeing* **mangiare e dormire** — *eat and sleep* **prendere il sole** — *sunbathe* **riposare** — *rest* **suonare l'ukulele** — *play the ukulele* **viaggiare** — *travel* **uscire in centro** — *go out into town*		**sarà fantastico** *it will be fantastic* **sarà noioso** *it will be boring*

Author's notes: a. **Questo/questa** *means 'this'. When it is followed by a word starting with a vowel it becomes* **quest'** *like in* **quest'estate**. *Elision is very common in Italian : l'acqua/ un'insalata...*
 b. *Have you noticed the verbs: andrò/ mangerò/ riposerò. What does this ending suggest to you? These verbs in the future can be translated both as 'I will...' or 'I am going to...'*

Unit 19. My holiday plans: VOCABULARY BUILDING

1. Match up

1. andrò	a. I will eat
2. mangerò	b. a campsite
3. starò	c. I'm going to go
4. un hotel economico	d. it will be fun
5. un campeggio	e. I'm going to stay
6. mi piacerebbe	f. to rest
7. riposare	g. a cheap hotel
8. sarà divertente	h. I would like to

2. Complete with the missing word

a. Mangiare e ____________ *[To eat and sleep]*

b. _____________ tanto *[I will rest a lot]*

c. Mi ____________ andare a… *[I would like to go to…]*

d. _____ _______ l'ukulele *[I want to play the ukulele]*

e. Prenderò ___ _________ *[I will sunbathe]*

f. _________ noioso *[It will be boring]*

g. Passeremo ____ ______________ in Italia
[We are going to spend 2 weeks in Italy]

h. Viaggerò in _________ *[I'm going to travel by plane]*

i. Staremo in un hotel ___ __________
[We are going to stay in a luxury hotel]

3. Translate into English

a. Quest'estate andrò in Grecia

b. Viaggerò in nave

c. Andrò a Cuba in aereo

d. Farò compere

e. Mi piacerebbe fare un giro turistico

f. Mi riposerò tutti i giorni

g. Ci piacerebbe mangiare e dormire

h. A volte farò immersioni

i. Andremo in vacanza in Spagna

4. Complete with the missing words

a. M____________ e dormire *[To eat and sleep]*

b. ________________ in un campeggio
[We will stay in a campsite]

c. _________una settimana
[I am going to spend 1 week]

d. Mi_____________ andare *[I would like to go to]*

e. Andare in_____________ *[To go to the beach]*

f. Fare un giro_______________ *[To go sightseeing]*

g. ________ il sole *[To sunbathe]*

h. Non vedo l'________ *[I can't wait]*

5. Broken words

a. Andr___________ *[I will go]*

b. Andre_______ *[We will to go]*

c. Vacan__________ *[Holiday]*

d. Camp__________ *[Campsite]*

e. Immers_________ *[Diving]*

f. In a____________ *[By plane]*

g. I__ n___________ *[By boat]*

h. Ball___________ *[To dance]*

i. Mang___________ *[To eat]*

j. Ripos___________ *[To rest]*

6. Bad translation – spot any translation errors and fix them

a. Il prossimo anno andrò: *Next summer I will go*

b. Andrò in Argentina in aereo: *I am going to go to Argentina by boat*

c. Mangerò e dormirò: *I am going to drink and sleep*

d. Mi piacerebbe riposarmi tanto: *I would like to rest a bit*

e. Staremo in un hotel: *I am going to stay in a hotel*

f. Passerò due settimane lì: *I am going to spend one week here*

g. Viaggeremo in autobus: *I am going to travel by train*

h. Staremo a casa della mia famiglia: *We stay in my family's house*

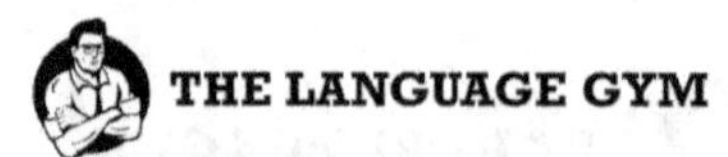

Unit 19. My holiday plans: READING (Part 1)

Mi chiamo Hugo. Sono di Oviedo ma vivo a Madrid. Quest'estate andrò in vacanza nel sud della Spagna, in Andalusia. Viaggerò in macchina con il mio ragazzo Alejandro. Passeremo quattro settimane lì. Andremo in spiaggia tutti i giorni e mangeremo cibi deliziosi. Non farò un giro turistico, a mio parere è faticoso. Preferisco prendere il sole e ballare!

Mi chiamo Deryk e vivo in Canada. Nella mia famiglia siamo in quattro. Quest'estate andremo in Inghilterra e poi in Quebec, in Canada. Durante le vacanze riposerò e leggerò un libro. Penso che andrò anche a sciare con i miei amici in Canada. Mi piacerebbe mangiare cibi deliziosi, come 'poutine' (simile a patate fritte con formaggio). Sarà fantastico!

Mi chiamo Dino. Sono italiano ma vivo in Cina. Tra due settimane andrò in Svizzera in aereo. Passerò quindici giorni lì, da solo, e starò in un camper in montagna. Mi piacerebbe vedere il lago di Ginevra. Penso che visiterò anche musei. Non mi piace molto lo sport, preferisco **scoprire** [discover] la cultura del posto. Sarà interessante!

Mi chiamo Diana, sono polacca ma vivo in Germania. Il prossimo anno andrò a Roma con la mia amica, Natasha. Viaggerò in aereo e poi in macchina, perché ho molto tempo. Passerò cinque settimane lì e starò in una casa di famiglia, in campagna. Non vedo l'ora di andare in centro di mattina e visitare il Vaticano. Non mi piace fare compere, secondo me è noioso. Preferisco andare a cena fuori, in un ristorante o in una pizzeria.

1. Find the Italian for the following in Hugo's text

a. I am from

b. but I live in

c. I am going to travel by

d. with my boyfriend

e. four weeks

f. we will go

g. in my opinion

h. I prefer to sunbathe

2. Find the Italian for the following in Diana's text

a. next year

b. by car

c. I have a lot of time

d. I don't like to do shopping

e. in the family home

f. in the morning

g. according to me

3. Complete the following statements about Deryk

a. He is from ________________

b. There are _______ people in his family

c. They will travel to ______________ and ______________

d. Deryk is going to ________________ and ______________

e. He thinks that he is going to ___________ with his friends

f. "Poutine" is made up of ______________and ______________

4. List any 8 details about Dino (in 3rd person) in English

1.

2.

3.

4.

5.

6.

7.

8.

5. Find Someone Who...

a. ...is going to England this summer

b. ...loves learning about culture

c. ...prefers the sun to sightseeing

d. ...is going on holiday to Europe

e. ...is going to travel by car

Unit 19. My holiday plans: READING (Part 2)

Mi chiamo Berta. Sono tedesca. Ho una tartaruga in casa. È grossa e molto buffa ed è la mia migliore amica. Quest'estate andrò in vacanza in Italia, con la mia famiglia. Viaggerò in aereo e poi in macchina. Passerò due settimane sul Lago di Garda e starò in un hotel di lusso. Non vedo l'ora! Poi andremo tre giorni a Verona. Penso che vedremo monumenti famosi, come l'Arena di Verona (un antico anfiteatro romano), dove fanno opera e concerti di musica. Tutti i giorni mangerò tanti cibi deliziosi e gelati. Mi piacerebbe fare compere e comprare vestiti italiani firmati, se avrò **soldi!** [money]

Mi chiamo Oliver. Sono di Sidney, in Australia . Il prossimo anno andrò in vacanza in Toscana con mio fratello. Viaggeremo in aereo e passeremo tre settimane lì. In Toscana visiteremo tanti posti. Non vedo l'ora di andare a Firenze, famosa per i suoi musei e monumenti, e visitare il Duomo. Poi andremo a Siena per vedere il *Palio* (antico festival dei cavalli), penso che sarà emozionante. Infine, riposerò qualche giorno in campagna, in una villa con piscina e un grande giardino. Sicuramente mangerò tanti cibi locali come la *ribollita* (zuppa di pane, fagioli e verdure) e tanti salumi.

Mi chiamo Catrina, ho dodici anni e vivo a Genova. Quest'estate andrò in vacanza ad Amalfi, nel sud dell'Italia per dieci giorni. Viaggerò in macchina con mio padre e mia nonna. Staremo in un hotel economico, **a pochi metri** [a few metres away] dalla spiaggia. Andrò al mare tutti i giorni e prenderò il sole. La costa lì è spettacolare! Farò lunghe passeggiate e mangerò tanti gelati. Faremo anche un giro turistico a Napoli e andremo a vedere Pompei, famosa per il sito archeologico. Ho un'amica che vive a Sorrento, vicino Amalfi, si chiama Anna. Mi piacerebbe giocare con lei e fare immersioni. Sarà divertente, non vedo l'ora!

1. Answer the following questions about Berta

a. Where is she from?

b. What does she say about her pet?

c. Who will she go on holiday with? How will they travel?

d. Where will they stay?

e. What are they going to visit?

f. What is the "Arena" in Verona?

g. What will she do every day?

h. What would she like to buy?

2. Find the Italian in Catrina's text

a. this summer

b. for 10 days

c. the coast

d. long walks

e. famous for

f. I have a friend

g. to go diving

h. sunbathe

i. I can't wait

3. Find the Italian for the following phrases/sentences in Oliver's text

a. Next year

b. Famous for its museums

c. Old horse festival

d. It will be exciting

e. Finally

f. A few days in the countryside

g. With a swimming pool

h. Local food

4. Find Someone Who...

a. ...is going to travel south

b. ...would like to buy Italian clothes

c. ...has a funny pet

d. ...is going to be staying in a villa with pool

e. ...is going to see a spectacular coast

f. ...is travelling from Australia

g. ...is going to visit an archeological site

h. ...is planning to eat ice-cream every day

Unit 19. My holiday plans: TRANSLATION/WRITING

1. Gapped translation

a. *I am going to go on holiday:* Andrò in _______________

b. *I am going to travel by car:* Viaggerò in _______________

c. *We are going to spend one week there:*
_______________ una settimana _______________

d. *I am going to stay in a cheap hotel:*
Starò in un hotel _______________

e. *We are going to eat and sleep every day:*
Mangeremo e _______________ tutti i giorni

f. *When the weather is nice I am going to go to the beach:*
Quando farà bel tempo _______________ _______________ spiaggia

g. *I am going to go shopping:* Farò _______________

2. Translate to English

a. Mangiare

b. Comprare

c. Riposare

d. Fare un giro turistico

e. Andare in spiaggia

f. Tutti i giorni

g. In aereo

h. Fare immersioni

i. Andare in centro

j. Fare compere

3. Spot and correct the grammar and spelling mistakes [note: in several cases a word is missing]

a. Faro imersioni

b. Passerò una setimana li

c. Starò in hotel lusso

d. Staremo in un hotel a centro

e. Mi piacerebbe farò compere

f. Viaggerò con aereo e machina

g. Andrò vacanza per due settimana

h. Suonerò l'ukulele e sara divartento

i. Mangerro cibi delizioso

4. Categories: Positive or Negative? Write P or N

a. Sarà divertente: **P**

b. Sarà noioso:

c. Sarà piacevole:

d. Sarà rilassante:

e. Sarà interessante:

f. Sarà terribile:

g. Sarà spettacolare:

h. Sarà faticoso:

i. Sarà affascinante:

j. Sarà impressionante:

5. Translate into Italian

a. I am going to rest

b. I will go diving

c. We will go to the beach

d. I will sunbathe

e. I would like to go sightseeing

f. I will stay in…

g. a cheap hotel

h. We are going to spend 2 weeks

i. I will go by plane

j. It will be fun

Revision Quickie 6: Daily Routine/House/Home life/Holidays

1. Match-up

1. In periferia	a. In the garden
2. In bagno	b. In the living room
3. In cucina	c. In my bedroom
4. A casa	d. In my house
5. In giardino	e. In the shower
6. Nella mia camera	f. In the dining room
7. In sala da pranzo	g. In the bathroom
8. Nella doccia	h. In the kitchen
9. In salotto	i. On the outskirts

2. Complete with the missing letters

a. Faccio la ___________ *[I shower]*

b. Mi sve__________ *[I wake up]*

c. Gu__________ la televisione *[I watch tv]*

d. Le_________ fumetti *[I read comics]*

e. E________ di casa *[I leave home]*

f. V________ a scuola *[I go at school]*

g. Pre_______ l'autobus *[I catch the bus]*

h. Mi ve__________ *[I get dressed]*

3. Spot and correct any of the sentences below which do not make sense

a. Faccio la doccia in cucina

b. Pranzo in bagno

c. Preparo il pranzo nella camera da letto

d. Mi lavo i capelli in salone

e. Vado nella mia camera in autobus

f. Gioco a ping-pong col mio cane

g. Mi lavo le mani in salotto

h. Guardo la televisione in giardino

i. Dormo nell'armadio

j. Faccio colazione in bagno

4. Split sentences

1. Guardo	a. l'autobus
2. Ascolto	b. colazione
3. Leggo	c. la televisione
4. Prendo	d. un caffè
5. Faccio	e. musica
6. Vado in Giappone	f. fumetti
7. Bevo	g. compiti
8. Carico foto	h. in aereo
9. Faccio i miei	i. su Instagram
10. Dormo	j. a carte
11. Lavoro con	k. nella mia stanza da letto
12. Gioco	l. il computer

5. Match the opposites

1. buono	a. malsano
2. simpatico	b. cattivo
3. facile	c. bello
4. divertente	d. antipatico
5. sano	e. difficile
6. brutto	f. noioso
7. caro	g. rapido
8. lento	h. alto
9. spesso	i. economico
10. mai	j. raramente
11. basso	k. sempre

6. Complete with the missing words

a. Andrò in Giappone _______ aereo.

b. Andrò in Italia ______ i miei genitori.

c. Non gioco mai ______ calcio.

d. Odio ____ nuoto.

e. Alloggio in un hotel ____ lusso

f. Vado al parco una volta ____ settimana

g. Guardo una serie ____ Netflix

h. Carico foto _____ Instagram

7. Draw a line in between each word

a. Mipiacemoltogiocareapallacanestro

b. Guardolatelevisioneeascoltomusica

c. Nelmiotempoliberogiococonivideogiochi

d. Andròingermaniainmacchina

e. Staròinunalbergodilusso

f. Lamattinaandròinspiaggia

g. Questestateandròinvacanza

h. Avoltevadoinpalestra

8. Spot the translation mistakes and correct them

a. Mi alzo presto: *I go to bed early*

b. Odio la pallacanestro: *I hate volleyball*

c. Andrò in piscina: *I will go to the beach*

d. Mangeremo e dormiremo: *We will rest and dance*

e. Nuoterò tutti i giorni: *I am going to run every day*

f. Viaggerò in macchina: *I will travel by plane*

g. Alloggerò in un caravan: *I will stay in a cheap hotel*

h. Prenderò il sole in spiaggia: *I will sunbathe in the pool*

i. A volte faccio una passeggiata: *Sometimes I go to the gym*

9. Translate into English

a. Prendo l'aereo

b. Andrò

c. Starò

d. Mi lavo

e. Suono il violino

f. Preparo la cena

g. Mangio verdure

h. Vado a scuola

i. Non faccio niente

j. Faccio i compiti sul tablet

10. Translate into Italian

a. I have dinner: C_ _ _

b. I watch: G_ _ _ _ _

c. I do: F_ _ _ _ _

d. I get washed: M_ l_ _ _

e. I read: L_ _ _ _

f. I work: L_ _ _ _ _

g. I rest: M_ r_ _ _ _ _

h. I play (sport): G_ _ _ _

i. I play (instrument): S_ _ _ _

j. I upload: C_ _ _ _ _

k. I eat: M _ _ _ _ _

11. Translate into Italian

a. I shower then I have breakfast

b. Tomorrow I am going to go to Japan

c. I brush my teeth every day

d. I never play basketball

e. I get up early

f. I have dinner at six

g. I am going to go to Italy by car

h. In my free time I play chess and read books

i. I spend many hours on the Internet

Question Skills 4: Daily routine/House/Home life/Holidays

1. Complete the questions with the correct option

Dove	A che	Quante	Cosa
Perché	Qual	Quando	Con chi

a. __ _____ ora ti alzi?

b. _________ fai nel tuo tempo libero?

c. _________ è il tuo compleanno?

d. _________ ore passi davanti al computer?

e. _____ ___ giochi alla playstation?

f. _________ non fai mai sport?

g. _________ vai il venerdì sera?

h. _________ è la tua stanza preferita?

2. Split questions

A che ora	non giochi a pallone con noi?
Cosa mangi	starai in Italia?
Cosa fai	esci di casa?
Con	sei?
Perché	a colazione?
Quante settimane	chi giochi a scacchi?
Di dove	nel tuo tempo libero?
Ti piace	in vacanza?
Dove andrai	suonare la chitarra?

3. Match each statement below to one of the questions included in activity 1 above

a. Due o tre

b. Gioco a tennis o suono la chitarra

c. Con mio fratello minore

d. Verso le sei

e. Vado al cinema con un amico

f. Il dodici aprile

g. Perché sono pigro e non ho tempo

h. La mia camera da letto, ovvio!

4. Translate into Italian

a. Who?

b. When?

c. Who with?

d. Why?

e. How many?

f. How much?

g. Which ones?

h. Where to?

i. Do you like...?

j. Can you...?

k. Where is...?

l. How many hours?

m. How many people?

n. What is your favourite...?

5. Translate into Italian

a. Where is your room?

b. Where do you go after school?

c. What do you do in your free time?

d. Until what time do you study?

e. How long do you spend on the Internet?

f. What is your favourite pastime?

g. What do you do to help in the house?

h. Do you like doing sport?

VOCABULARY TESTS

On the following pages you will find one vocabulary test for every unit in the book. You could set them as class assessments or as homeworks at the end of a unit. Students could also use them to practice independently.

1a. Translate the following sentences (worth one point each) into Italian

Hello, I am well	
Hello, I am very well because I am happy	
How old are you?	
I am five years old	
I am seven years old	
I am nine years old	
Good morning, I am feeling great.	
What is your name?	
My name is Paolo	
Good morning, I feel bad because I am sad	
Score	**/10**

1b. Translate the following sentences (worth two points each) into Italian

What is your brother called?	
What is your sister called?	
My brother is called Mario	
My sister is fourteen years old	
My brother is fifteen years old	
I don't have any siblings	
My name is Jean and I am French	
I have a brother who is called Alfie	
I live in the capital of Japan	
I live in the capital of Italy	
Score	**/20**

UNIT 2: "Saying when my birthday is" TOTAL SCORE: /30

1a. Translate the following sentences (worth one point each) into Italian

My name is Sergio	
I am eleven years old	
I am fifteen years old	
Where are you from?	
I am English. I speak a little Italian	
I am Scottish. I speak Spanish quite well.	
My friend is Polish. He speaks German fluently.	
The 6th September	
The 10th October	
The 8th July	
Score	**/10**

1b. Translate the following sentences (worth two points each) into Italian

I am 17. My birthday is on 21st June	
My brother is called Joe. He is 19	
My sister is called Maria. She is 22	
My brother's birthday is on 23rd March	
My name is Felipe. I am 15. My birthday is on 27th July	
I live in Venice.	
We live in Rome	
I do not like my town because it is rather noisy	
I love my city because it is very pretty	
Is your birthday in May or June?	
Score	**/20**

1a. Translate the following sentences (worth one point each) into Italian

Black hair	
Brown eyes	
Blond hair	
Blue eyes	
My name is Gabriella	
I am 12 years old	
I have long hair	
I have short hair	
I have green eyes	
I have brown eyes	
Score	**/10**

1b. Translate the following sentences (worth two points each) into Italian

I have grey hair and grey eyes	
I have red straight hair	
I have curly white hair	
I have brown hair and brown eyes	
I wear glasses and have spiky hair	
I don't wear glasses and I have a beard	
My brother has blond hair and has a moustache	
My brother is 22 years old and has a crew cut	
Do you wear glasses?	
My sister has blue eyes and wavy black hair	
Score	**/20**

1a. Translate the following sentences (worth one point each) into Italian

My name is	
I am from	
I live in	
In a house	
In a modern building	
In an old building	
On the outskirts	
In the centre	
On the coast	
In Rome	
Score	**/10**

1b. Translate the following sentences (worth two points each) into Italian

My brother is called Marco	
My sister is called Anna	
I live in an old building	
I live in a modern building	
I live in a beautiful house on the coast	
I live in an ugly house in the centre	
I am from Milan but I live in an apartment in the centre of Glasgow	
I am 15 years old and I am Italian	
I am Spanish, from Madrid but I live in Florence, in Tuscany	
I live in Switzerland in a small villa in the countryside	
Score	**/20**

1a. Translate the following sentences (worth one point each) into Italian

My younger brother	
My older brother	
My older sister	
My younger sister	
My father	
My mother	
My uncle	
My auntie	
My male cousin	
My female cousin	
Score	**/10**

1b. Translate the following sentences (worth two points each) into Italian

In my family there are four people	
My father, my mother and two brothers	
I don't get along with my older brother	
My older sister is 15	
My younger sister is 8	
My grandfather is 78	
My grandmother is 67	
My uncle is 54	
My auntie is 44	
My female cousin is 17	
Score	**/20**

1a. Translate the following sentences (worth one point each) into Italian

Tall (masculine)	
Short (feminine)	
Ugly (masculine)	
Good-looking (masculine)	
Generous (masculine)	
Boring (feminine)	
Intelligent (masculine)	
Sporty (masculine)	
Good (feminine)	
Slim (feminine)	
Score	**/10**

1b. Translate the following sentences (worth two points each) into Italian

My mother is strict and boring	
My father is stubborn and unfriendly	
My older sister is intelligent and hard-working	
My younger sister is sporty	
In my family I have five people	
I get along with my older sister because she is nice	
I don't get along with my younger sister because she is annoying	
I love my grandparents because they are funny and generous	
What are your parents like?	
My uncle and auntie are fifty and I don't get along with them	
Score	**/20**

1a. Translate the following sentences (worth one point each) into Italian

A horse	
A rabbit	
A dog	
A turtle	
A bird	
A parrot	
A duck	
A guinea pig	
A cat	
A mouse	
Score	**/10**

1b. Translate the following sentences (worth three points each) into Italian

I have a white horse	
I have a green turtle	
At home we have two fish	
My sister has a spider	
I don't have pets	
My friend Pedro has a blue bird	
My cat is very fat	
I have a snake that is called Adam	
My duck is funny and noisy	
How many pets do you have at home?	
Score	**/30**

1a. Translate the following sentences (worth one point each) into Italian

He is a male chef	
He is a journalist	
She is a waitress	
She is a nurse	
He is a househusband	
She is a doctor	
He is a teacher	
She is a businesswoman	
He is a hairdresser	
She is an engineer	
Score	**/10**

1b. Translate the following sentences (worth three points each) into Italian

My uncle is a chef	
My mother is a nurse	
My grandparents don't work	
My sister works as a teacher	
My auntie is an actress	
My (male) cousin is a student	
My cousins are lawyers	
He doesn't like it because it is hard	
He likes it because it is gratifying	
He hates it because it is stressful	
Score	**/30**

1a. Translate the following sentences (worth two points each) into Italian

He is taller than me	
He is more generous than her	
She is less intelligent than him	
He is more friendly than her	
She is better looking than him	
She is more talkative than me	
I am more funny than him	
My dog is less noisy	
My rabbit is more fun	
She is as talkative as me	
Score	**/20**

1b. Translate the following sentences (worth 3 points each) into Italian

My brother is stronger than me	
My mother is shorter than my father	
My uncle is better looking than my father	
My older sister is more talkative than my younger sister	
My sister and I are taller than my cousins	
My grandfather is less strict than my grandmother	
Paolo is more generous than Fabio	
My rabbit is quieter than my duck	
My cat is fatter than my dog	
My mouse is faster than my turtle	
Score	**/30**

THE LANGUAGE GYM

1a. Translate the following sentences (worth one point each) into Italian

I have a pen	
I have a ruler	
I have a rubber	
In my bag	
In my pencil case	
My friend Luigi	
Pietro has	
I don't have	
A purple exercise book	
A yellow pencil sharpener	
Score	/10

1b. Translate the following sentences (worth three points each) into Italian

In my schoolbag I have four books	
I have a yellow pencil case	
I have a red schoolbag	
I don't have black markers	
There are two blue pens	
Lucia has a pencil sharpener	
Do you guys have a rubber?	
Do you have a red pen?	
Is there a ruler in your pencil case?	
What is there in your schoolbag?	
Score	/30

1a. Translate the following sentences (worth three points each) into Italian

I don't like milk	
I love meat	
I don't like fish much	
I hate chicken	
Fruit is good	
Honey is healthy	
I prefer mineral water	
Milk is disgusting	
Chocolate is delicious	
Cheese is unhealthy	
Score	**/30**

1b. Translate the following sentences (worth five points each) into Italian

I love chocolate because it is delicious	
I like apples a lot because they are healthy	
I don't like red meat because it is unhealthy	
I don't like sausages because they are unhealthy	
I love fish with potatoes	
I hate seafood because it is disgusting	
I like fruit because it is light and delicious	
I like spicy chicken with vegetables	
I like eggs because they are rich in protein	
Roast chicken is tastier than fried fish	
Score	**/50**

1a. Translate the following sentences (worth one point each) into Italian

I have breakfast	
I have lunch	
I have 'snack'	
I have dinner	
Delicious	
Light	
Disgusting	
Refreshing	
Hard	
Sweet	
Score	**/10**

1b. Translate the following sentences (worth three points each) into Italian

I eat eggs and coffee for breakfast	
I have seafood for lunch	
I never have dinner	
For snack I have two toasts	
In the morning I usually eat fruit	
I love meat because it is tasty	
From time to time I eat cheese	
In the evening I eat little	
We eat a lot of meat and fish	
I don't eat sweets often	
Score	**/30**

1a. Translate the following sentences (worth two points each) into Italian

A red skirt	
A blue suit	
A green scarf	
Black trousers	
A white shirt	
A brown hat	
A yellow T-shirt	
Blue jeans	
A purple tie	
Grey shoes	
Score	/20

1b. Translate the following sentences (worth three points each) into Italian

I often wear a black baseball cap	
At home I wear a blue track suit	
At school we wear a green uniform	
At the beach I wear a red bathing suit	
My sister always wears jeans	
My brother never wears a watch	
My mother wears branded clothes	
I very rarely wear suits	
My girlfriend wears a pretty dress	
My brothers always wears trainers	
Score	/30

1a. Translate the following sentences (worth two points each) into Italian

I do my homework	
I play football	
I go rock climbing	
I go cycling	
I do weights	
I go to the swimming pool	
I do sport	
I go horse riding	
I play tennis	
I go to the beach	
Score	**/20**

1b. Translate the following sentences (worth five points each) into Italian

I never play basketball because it is boring	
I play PlayStation with my friends	
My father and I go fishing from time to time	
My brother and I go to the gym every day	
I do weights and go jogging every day	
When the weather is nice, we go hiking	
When the weather is bad, I play chess	
My father goes swimming at the weekend	
My younger brothers go to the park after school	
In my free time, I go rock climbing or to my friend's house	
Score	**/50**

1a. Translate the following sentences (worth two points each) into Italian

In my free time	
Every day	
On Sunday	
During my holidays	
In the summer	
I go swimming	
I play with my friends	
I go to the stadium	
I go to the gym	
I go on a bike ride	
Score	**/20**

1b. Translate the following sentences (worth four points each) into Italian

At the weekend I go cycling	
According to me it is exciting	
I do skiing, I think that it is fun	
I do rock climbing. In my opinion it is dangerous	
I often go jogging. I like it because it is relaxing	
In the winter we stay at home and play cards	
Every day I play videogames even if it is tiring	
I play football with my friends because it is dynamic	
We never do sport. We play on the computer or on PlayStation	
In my free time I go on a bike ride because it is thrilling	
Score	**/40**

UNIT 16 "Talking about my daily routine" TOTAL SCORE: /40

1a. Translate the following sentences (worth one point each) into Italian

I get up	
I have breakfast	
I eat	
I drink	
I go to bed	
Around six o' clock	
I rest	
At noon	
At midnight	
I do my homework	
Score	**/10**

1b. Translate the following sentences (worth three points each) into Italian

Around 7.00 in the morning I have breakfast	
I shower then I get dressed	
I eat then I brush my teeth	
Around 8 o'clock in the evening I have dinner	
I go to school by bus	
I watch television in my room	
I go back home at 4.30	
From 6 to 7 I play on the computer	
Afterwards, around 11.30, I go to bed	
My daily routine is simple	
Score	**/30**

1a. Translate the following sentences (worth one point each) into Italian

I live	
In a new house	
In an old house	
In a small house	
In a big house	
On the coast	
In the mountains	
In an ugly apartment	
On the outskirts	
In the centre of town	
Score	**/10**

1b. Translate the following sentences (worth three points each) into Italian

In my house there are four rooms	
My favourite room is the kitchen	
I enjoy relaxing in the living room	
In my apartment there are seven rooms	
My parents live in a big house	
My uncle lives in a small house	
We live near the coast	
My friend Martina lives on a farm	
My cousins live in Barcelona	
My parents and I live in a cosy house	
Score	**/30**

1a. Translate the following sentences (worth one point each) into Italian

I chat with my mother	
I play on the PlayStation	
I read magazines	
I read comics	
I watch films	
I listen to music	
I rest	
I do my homework	
I go on a bike ride	
I leave the house	
Score	**/10**

1b. Translate the following sentences (worth three points each) into Italian

Usually I read a book in my room	
Twice a week I play the guitar	
I like downloading songs	
I upload many photos onto Instagram	
Every day I watch series on Netflix	
I always watch videos on YouTube	
After school I rest in the garden	
When I have time, I play with my brother	
I don't like talking on the phone	
I prefer uploading photos on Facebook.	
Score	**/30**

1a. Translate the following sentences (worth two points each) into Italian

I am going to go	
I am going to stay	
I am going to play	
I am going to eat	
I am going to drink	
I am going to rest	
I am going to go sightseeing	
I am going to go to the beach	
I am going to do sport	
I am going to dance	
Score	**/20**

1b. Translate the following sentences (worth five points each) into Italian

We are going to buy souvenirs and clothes	
I am going to stay in a cheap hotel near the beach	
We are going to stay there for three weeks	
I am going to spend two weeks there with my family	
We are going to go on holiday to Argentina tomorrow	
We are going to Spain for two weeks and we are going to travel by plane	
I would like to do sport, go to the beach and dance	
We are going to spend three weeks in Italy, we will stay in a caravan	
We are going to go stay in a luxury hotel near the beach	
We are going to go sightseeing and shopping every day	
Score	**/50**

The End

We hope you have enjoyed using this workbook and found it useful!

As many of you will appreciate, the penguin is a fantastic animal. At Language Gym, we hold it as a symbol of resilience, bravery and good humour; able to thrive in the harshest possible environments, and with, arguably the best gait in the animal kingdom (black panther or penguin, you choose). There are several hidden penguins (pictures)in this book, did you spot them all?